The Letter of James

The Letter of James

Worship to Live By

JOHN PAUL HEIL

 CASCADE *Books* • Eugene, Oregon

THE LETTER OF JAMES
Worship to Live By

Copyright © 2012 John Paul Heil. All rights reserved. Except for brief quotations in critical publications or reviews, no part of this book may be reproduced in any manner without prior written permission from the publisher. Write: Permissions, Wipf and Stock Publishers, 199 W. 8th Ave., Suite 3, Eugene, OR 97401.

Cascade Books
An Imprint of Wipf and Stock Publishers
199 W. 8th Ave., Suite 3
Eugene, OR 97401

www.wipfandstock.com

ISBN 13: 978-1-61097-601-5

Cataloging-in-Publication data:

Heil, John Paul

    The Letter of James : worship to live by / John Paul Heil

    viii + 228 p. ; 23 cm. Includes bibliographical references and indexes.

    ISBN 13: 978-1-61097-601-5

    1. Bible. N.T. James—Criticism, interpretation, etc. 2. Worship—Biblical teaching. I. Title.

BS2785.3 H35 2012

Manufactured in the U.S.A.

Contents

Abbreviations · vii

Introduction · 1
James 1:1–16 · 29
James 1:17–27 · 51
James 2:1–13 · 65
James 2:14–26 · 78
James 3:1–10 · 92
James 3:11–18 · 108
James 4:1–10 · 122
James 4:11–17 · 143
James 5:1–6 · 157
James 5:7–11 · 171
James 5:12–20 · 186
Summary and Conclusion · 207

Bibliography · 215
Scripture Index · 219
Author Index · 226

Abbreviations

AB	Anchor Bible
BECNT	Baker Exegetical Commentary on the New Testament
Bib	*Biblica*
BSac	*Bibliotheca Sacra*
BT	*The Bible Translator*
BTB	*Biblical Theology Bulletin*
BZ	*Biblische Zeitschrift*
CBQ	*Catholic Biblical Quarterly*
CBQMS	Catholic Biblical Quarterly Monograph Series
CTR	*Criswell Theological Review*
EDNT	*Exegetical Dictionary of the New Testament*, ed. H. Balz, G. Schneider (Grand Rapids, 1990–1993)
EvQ	*Evangelical Quarterly*
ExpTim	*Expository Times*
GTJ	*Grace Theological Journal*
HTR	*Harvard Theological Review*
HvTSt	*Hervormde teologiese studies*
JBL	*Journal of Biblical Literature*
JOTT	*Journal of Translation and Textlinguistics*
JSNT	*Journal for the Study of the New Testament*
JSNTSup	Journal for the Study of the New Testament: Supplement Series
LNTS	Library of New Testament Studies
NCBC	New Cambridge Bible Commentary
NICNT	New International Commentary on the New Testament
NIGTC	New International Greek Testament Commentary
NovT	*Novum Testamentum*
NTS	*New Testament Studies*
RevExp	*Review and Expositor*

Abbreviations

SP	Sacra pagina
SBLDS	Society of Biblical Literature Dissertation Series
SBLECL	Society of Biblical Literature: Early Christianity and Its Literature
SBLSCS	Society of Biblical Literature Septuagint and Cognate Studies
STDJ	Studies on the Texts of the Desert of Judah
TGl	*Theologie und Glaube*
TJ	*Trinity Journal*
TynBul	*Tyndale Bulletin*
WBC	Word Biblical Commentary
WTJ	*Westminster Theological Journal*
WUNT	Wissenschaftliche Untersuchungen zum Neuen Testament
ZKT	*Zeitschrift für katholische Theologie*
ZNW	*Zeitschrift für die neutestamentliche Wissenschaft und die Kunde der älteren Kirche*

Introduction

Two closely related aims motivate my writing of this book. First, I intend to demonstrate a completely new structure for the New Testament document commonly known as the letter of James.[1] The discovery of this structure stems from a consideration of James as an epistolary homily or sermon composed of rhetorical strategies meant for an oral performance to be heard by its audience gathered together as a worshiping assembly.[2] This structure consists of a series of eleven microchiastic units arranged in a cohesive and coherent macrochiastic framework embracing the entire letter.[3] These chiastic structures are linguistically rather than conceptually or thematically determined.[4]

The chiastic phenomenon seems to have been a very common way in antiquity of organizing material to be delivered orally. I have demonstrated similar chiastic structures for other NT letters.[5] Although the ancient authors and audiences may and need not necessarily have consciously identified these chiastic structures as they composed and listened to them, the identification of them provides a visual aid to

---

1. This document is often referred to simply as "James."

2. On the importance of recognizing the oral and rhetorical culture of NT writings, see Witherington, *New Testament Rhetoric*, 1–9; idem, *What's in the Word*, 7–17.

3. The steady trend in recent scholarship has been away from the view that James is an incoherent paraenesis, as influentially advocated many years ago by Dibelius, *James*.

4. For the state of the research regarding the structure of James, see Taylor, *Discourse Structure*, 8–34. His own proposal includes a chiastic structure that is conceptually or thematically rather than linguistically based. See also Taylor and Guthrie, "Structure of James," 681–705; McKnight, *James*, 47–55.

5. Heil, "Philemon"; idem, *Ephesians*; idem, *Philippians*; idem, *Colossians*; idem, *Hebrews*.

guide the interpretation of modern audiences. Based on my identification of the chiastic structures comprising the letter of James, I will provide an interpretation focused on how the implied audience are to respond to the rhetorical strategies presented by the dynamics of these chiastic structures as they hear them.[6]

Secondly, I will present a new proposal for the unifying or organizing theme of the letter of James in accord with the comprehensive chiastic structure that is a key to its interpretation. "Worship to live by" best expresses what the whole of James, as an epistolary homily or sermon, is exhorting and persuading its audience to adopt.[7] The word "worship" is to be understood comprehensively as including not only liturgical or cultic worship but also the ethical or moral behavior that complements it, so that the result is a holistic way of worshiping God. And the words "to live by" embrace the worshipful conduct by which to live out presently one's birth to a new life as a believer before the final coming of the Lord Jesus Christ, with a view to the future eschatological or eternal life to be granted at the last judgment as the outcome of such worship. In other words, the letter of James urges its audience to practice the worship to live by now in order to live eternally.[8]

---

6. The collective noun "audience" will be used as a plural noun, so that it conforms to the Greek text of James, which employs plural terms in reference to its audience, who are conceived of as a group composed of individual members with responsibilities toward one another.

7. On James as a hortatory sermon employing rhetorical strategies, see Witherington, *Jewish Christians*, 388–93. According to Moo (*James*, 8–9), we should "think of James as a sermon or homily. The author, separated from his readers by distance, cannot exhort them in person or at length. So he must put his preaching in written form, using a letter to cover briefly the main points that he wants them to understand." See also Johnson, *James*, 17–24; Cheung, *Genre*.

8. There have been a number of other proposals for the main theme of James. Its central theme is "a 'deep structure' of polar opposition between 'friendship with the world' and 'friendship with God,'" according to Johnson (*James*, 14). The concept of "perfection" is what "gives meaning to the entire letter," according to Hartin (*Spirituality of Perfection*, 39). Spiritual "wholeness" is "the central concern of the letter," according to Moo (*James*, 46). "The fundamental motif that runs straight through James is his concern with genuine faith," according to McCartney (*James*, 63). See also Ong, *Strategy*, 66–71. In my view all of these worthy proposals for the central theme of James can be subsumed within the much more fundamental concern for eschatological life rather than death, expressed by "the worship to live by" as the

Introduction

In the rest of this chapter I will introduce and explain the text-centered, linguistically based chiastic structures of the letter of James, and then I will provide a preliminary indication from these structures of its unifying main theme. In the remaining chapters of this book I will present a comprehensive interpretation in accord with the chiastic structures, which illustrate and confirm that the letter of James is exhorting its implied audience to adopt the worship to live by now and for eternity.

Chiastic Structures and the Letter of James

My investigation of the chiastic structures of the letter of James will be guided by the following list of criteria for detecting an extended chiasm:

1. There must be a problem in perceiving the structure of the text in question, which more conventional outlines fail to resolve.

2. There must be clear examples of parallelism between the two "halves" of the hypothesized chiasm, to which commentators call attention even when they propose quite different outlines for the text overall.

3. Linguistic (or grammatical) parallelism as well as conceptual (or structural) parallelism should characterize most if not all of the corresponding pairs of subdivisions.

4. The linguistic parallelism should involve central or dominant imagery or terminology important to the rhetorical strategy of the text.

5. Both linguistic and conceptual parallelism should involve words and ideas not regularly found elsewhere within the proposed chiasm.

6. Multiple sets of correspondences between passages opposite each other in the chiasm as well as multiple members of the chiasm itself are desirable.

---

main theme of the letter of James.

7. The outline should divide the text at natural breaks, which would be agreed upon even by those proposing very different structures to account for the whole.

8. The central or pivotal as well as the final or climactic elements normally play key roles in the rhetorical strategy of the chiasm.

9. Ruptures in the outline should be avoided.[9]

An important and distinctive feature of this investigation is that all of the proposed chiasms are determined mainly by precise linguistic parallels with an objective basis in the text, rather than on thematic or conceptual parallels, which can often be subjective. Indeed, the main criterion for the establishment of chiasms in this investigation is the demonstration of these linguistic parallels. I will seek to determine how the subsequent occurrence(s) of a paralleled word or phrase develops the first occurrence after a central unparalleled element or central parallel elements serve as a pivot from the first to the second half of the chiasm.

Since they are based strictly on linguistic parallels, some of the proposed chiasms may or may not exhibit a balance in the length of the various parallel elements or units—one parallel element or unit may be much longer or much shorter than its corresponding parallel. This may seem odd to a modern audience, but an ancient audience would presumably be attuned to the key linguistic parallels that are heard rather than the balance of length between the elements or units of a given chiasm. The main presupposition of this investigation is that if there are demonstrable linguistic parallels with a pivotal section between them, then a chiasm is operative regardless of a certain lack of balance between various elements or units.

Furthermore, some of the linguistic parallels involve what might be considered by a modern audience as rather ordinary or trivial words,

---

9. For a slightly different and more detailed version of this list, as well as an example of an extended biblical chiasm, see Blomberg, "Structure of 2 Cor 1–7," 4–8. And for more discussion of criteria and more biblical examples of extended chiasms, see Brouwer, *Literary Development*. See also Welch, "Chiasmus"; idem, "Criteria"; Thomson, *Chiasmus in the Pauline Letters*, 13–45; Wilson, *Victor Sayings*, 3–8; deSilva, "Chiasmus in Revelation."

unlikely to be key words in chiastic parallels. But it should be kept in mind that what may seem to be insignificant words or phrases on the surface to a modern audience may have been very significant indeed to the particular rhetorical strategy of the author and the particular situation of the original audience as they listened to the entire oral performance of the letter of James. In some cases the parallels may be between cognates or between synonyms, antonyms, and/or alliterative terms. And in some cases an identical grammatical form of a word determines the chiastic parallel.

Not all of the proposed chiasms have the same number of elements or units. Some chiasms may exhibit a single unparalleled central element, e.g., A-B-C-B´-A´, while others may exhibit dual, parallel central or pivotal elements, e.g., A-B-C-C´-B´-A´. Nevertheless, both of these types operate as chiasms in the ears of the implied audience, since they both involve a pivot from the first to the second half of the chiasm. In one type a central unparalleled element serves as the pivot, whereas in the other type two parallel elements together serve as the pivot to the second half of parallel elements. In addition it may often be more accurate to speak of the central element or elements as the pivotal point of the chiasm and the final A´ element as the climax. This is important to keep in mind, lest one think that chiastic patterns are a type of circular or merely repetitive argument, rather than exhibiting an ongoing, dynamic development.

Chiastic patterns serve to organize the content to be heard and not only aid the memory of the one delivering or performing a document, but also make it easier for the implied audience to follow and remember the content. A chiasm works by leading its audience through introductory elements to a central, pivotal point or points, and then reaching its conclusion by recalling and developing, via the chiastic parallels, aspects of the initial elements that led to the central, pivotal point or points. Since chiasms were apparently very common in ancient oral-auricular and rhetorical cultures,[10] the original ancient audience may and need not necessarily have been consciously identifying or reflecting upon any of these chiastic structures in themselves as they heard them. They unconsciously experienced the chiastic phenomenon

10. For some of the evidence of this see Brouwer, *Literary Development*, 23–27.

The Letter of James

as an organizing dynamic that had a subtle but purposeful effect on how they received and perceived the content.[11] But a discovery, delineation, and bringing to consciousness of the underlying chiastic structures of ancient documents can greatly aid the modern audience to a more accurate interpretation of them.

In what follows, then, I will first demonstrate how the text of the letter of James naturally divides itself into eleven distinct literary units based upon their microchiastic structures as determined by very precise linguistic parallels found objectively in the text. Where applicable I will point out how other lexical and grammatical features often confirm the integrity of these units. Secondly, I will demonstrate how these eleven units form a macrochiastic pattern based upon very precise linguistic parallels found objectively in the text between the chiastically paired units.[12] Thirdly, I will point out the various transitional words that connect a unit to the unit that immediately precedes it. These various transitional words, which occur at the conclusion of one unit and at the beginning of the following unit, indicate that the chiastic units are heard as a cohesive sequence. These various transitional words are italicized in the translations of the units below.

The Eleven Microchiastic Units of James

1. *Do Not Be Led Astray by Sin That Brings Forth Death (1:1–16)*

Blessed is a man who endures temptation for the crown of life[13]

A ¹:¹ James, of God [θεοῦ] and of the Lord Jesus Christ a servant, to the twelve tribes, the ones in the diaspora, "Joyful greetings!"

---

11. On chiasms as an aid to both listener and performer, see Dewey, "Mark as Aural Narrative," 50–52.

12. On the interpretive significance of chiastic structures, see Man, "Value of Chiasm"; Stock, "Chiastic Awareness," 23–27; Breck, "Biblical Chiasmus," 70–74. For a discussion of chiasm in relation to chain-link interlock, see Longenecker, *Rhetoric at the Boundaries*, 16–17, 22–23.

13. The main heading of each unit is intended to summarize the unit as it relates to its parallel unit within the overall macrochiastic structure of the letter, while the subheading of each unit is intended to summarize or characterize the microchiastic dimension of each unit.

² Consider it all joy, my brothers [ἀδελφοί μου], whenever you tumble into teeming temptations [πειρασμοῖς], ³ knowing that the testing [δοκίμιον] of your faith produces endurance [ὑπομονήν]. ⁴ And let endurance [ὑπομονή] have its perfect work, so that you may be perfect and complete, lacking in nothing. ⁵ But if anyone of you is lacking wisdom, let him ask from the God [θεοῦ] who gives to all unreservedly, indeed not reproaching, and it will be given to him. ⁶ But let him ask in faith, disputing nothing, for the one who disputes is like a wave of the sea blown and driven about by the wind. ⁷ For that person must not suppose that he will receive [λήμψεταί] anything from the Lord, ⁸ a double-minded man [ἀνήρ], unstable in all the ways of him.

B ⁹ Let the humble brother boast in his exaltedness, ¹⁰ᵃ but the rich one [πλούσιος] in his lowliness,

    C ¹⁰ᵇ for like a flower [ἄνθος]

        D ¹⁰ᶜ of grass [χόρτου] he will pass away.

            E ¹¹ᵃ For the sun rises with its heat

        D′ ¹¹ᵇ and dries up the grass [χόρτον]

    C′ ¹¹ᶜ and its flower [ἄνθος] falls away and the beauty of its appearance is destroyed.

B′ ¹¹ᵈ So also the rich one [πλούσιος] in his pursuits will die out.

A′ ¹² Blessed is a man [ἀνήρ] who endures [ὑπομένει] temptation [πειρασμόν], for having become tested [δόκιμος], he will receive [λήμψεταί] the crown of life that he [the Lord] promised to those who love him. ¹³ Let no one being tempted [πειραζόμενος] say, "I am being tempted [πειράζομαι] by God [θεοῦ]," for God [θεός] is untempted [ἀπείραστός] of evil things, and he himself tempts [πειράζει] no one. ¹⁴ But each one is tempted [πειράζεται] by his own desire, being dragged away and enticed. ¹⁵ When the desire conceives, it gives birth to sin, and the sin having been brought to completion, *brings birth to* death. ¹⁶ Do not be led astray, my brothers [ἀδελφοί μου] beloved.[14]

---

14. The translation of this and all subsequent units is my own, presenting what

An A-B-C-D-E-D'-C'-B'-A' chiastic pattern secures the integrity and distinctness of this first unit (1:1-16). The following linguistic occurrences constitute the parallelism between the A (1:1-8) and A' (1:12-16) elements of this chiasm: the only occurrences in this unit of the word for "God" (θεοῦ in 1:1, 5, 13 and θεός in 1:13); the only occurrences in this unit of the address "my brothers" (ἀδελφοί μου in 1:2, 16); the only occurrences in James of terms expressing "temptation" or "being tempted" (πειρασμοῖς in 1:2, πειρασμόν in 1:12, πειραζόμενος in 1:13, πειράζομαι in 1:13, ἀπείραστός in 1:13, πειράζει in 1:13, and πειράζεται in 1:14); the only occurrences in James of the cognates "testing" (δοκίμιον in 1:3) and "tested" (δόκιμος in 1:12); the only occurrences in this unit of the cognates "endurance" (ὑπομονήν in 1:3), "endurance" (ὑπομονή in 1:4), and "endures" (ὑπομένει in 1:12); the only occurrences in James of the verbal form "will receive" (λήμψεταί in 1:7, 12); and the only occurrences in this unit of the word "man" (ἀνήρ in 1:8, 12).[15]

The only occurrences in James of the singular form of the adjective for "rich" ("rich one," πλούσιος, in 1:10a, 11d) determine the parallelism between the B (1:9-10a) and B' (1:11d) elements. The only occurrences in James of the word for "flower" (ἄνθος) establish the parallelism between the C (1:10b) and C' (1:11c) elements. The only occurrences in James of the word for "grass" (χόρτου in 1:10c and χόρτον in 1:11b) form the parallelism between the D (1:10c) and D' (1:11b) elements. Finally, the unparalleled central and pivotal E (1:11a) element contains the only occurrence in James of the expression "for the sun rises with its heat" (ἀνέτειλεν γὰρ ὁ ἥλιος σὺν τῷ καύσωνι).

I call an "exegetical" translation. The aim is to present a strictly literal translation that attempts, as far as possible, to follow the Greek word order and to render the same Greek words with the same English equivalents. Where possible, I have also tried to represent some of the noteworthy alliteration in the Greek text, e.g., "tumble into teeming temptations" for the impressive alliteration of πειρασμοῖς περιπέσητε ποικίλοις in Jas 1:2.

15. Some of these chiastic elements, especially the longer ones, form chiastic subunits in themselves, which will be illustrated in the subsequent exegetical chapters.

Introduction

2. Be Slow to Speak Not Deceiving the Heart for Useless Worship (1:17–27)

Worship to save your souls is to care for orphans and widows in their affliction

> **A** ¹⁷ Every good giving and every perfect gift from above is descending from the Father [πατρός] of lights, within whom there is no variation or shadow of turning.
>
>> **B** ¹⁸ Having decided, he *brought birth to* us by a word [λόγῳ] of truth that we may be a kind of firstfruits of his creatures. ¹⁹ Know, my brothers beloved, let every person be quick to hear, slow to speak, slow to anger, ²⁰ for the anger of a man does not work the righteousness of God. ²¹ Therefore, putting away all filthiness and excess of evil, in humility welcome the implanted word [λόγον] that is able to save your souls. ²²ᵃ Become [Γίνεσθε] doers [ποιηταί] of the word [λόγου] and not only hearers [ἀκροαταί],
>>
>>> **C** ²²ᵇ deluding yourselves.
>>
>> **B′** ²³ For if anyone is a hearer [ἀκροατής] of the word [λόγου] but not a doer [ποιητής], this one is like a man observing the appearance of his birth in a mirror. ²⁴ For he observes himself and goes away and immediately forgets what sort he was. ²⁵ But one peering into the perfect law, the one of freedom, and persevering, having become [γενόμενος] not a hearer [ἀκροατής] of forgetfulness but a doer [ποιητής] of work, this one will be blessed in his doing [ποιήσει].
>
> **A′** ²⁶ If anyone thinks he is religious, not bridling his tongue but deceiving his heart, the religion of this one is useless. ²⁷ Religion pure and undefiled before the God and Father [πατρί] is this: to *care for* orphans and widows in their affliction, to keep oneself spotless from the world.

The expression that "he [God] brought birth to [ἀπεκύησεν] us" toward the beginning of this unit in 1:18 recalls the contrasting statement that "having been brought to completion, it [sin] brings birth to [ἀποκύει] death" toward the conclusion of the preceding unit in 1:15. These expressions for "bringing birth to," which occur only here in James, serve as the transitional words linking the first unit (1:1–16) to the second unit (1:17–27).

An A-B-C-B'-A' chiastic pattern secures the integrity and distinctness of this second unit (1:17–27). The only occurrences in this unit of the term "Father" for God (πατρός in 1:17 and πατρί in 1:27) constitute the parallelism between the A (1:17) and A' (1:26–27) elements of this chiasm. The following linguistic occurrences determine the parallelism between the B (1:18–22a) and B' (1:23–25) elements: the only occurrences in this unit of the term for "word" (λόγῳ in 1:18, λόγον in 1:21, and λόγου in 1:22, 23); the only occurrences in this unit of expressions for "become" (γίνεσθε in 1:22a and γενόμενος in 1:25); the only occurrences in this unit of the term "doer(s)" and its cognate verb "doing" (ποιηταί in 1:22a, ποιητής in 1:23, 25, and ποιήσει in 1:25); and the only occurrences in James of the term "hearer(s)" (ἀκροαταί in 1:22a and ἀκροατής in 1:23, 25). Finally, the unparalleled central and pivotal C (1:22b) element contains the only occurrence in James of the expression "deluding yourselves" (παραλογιζόμενοι ἑαυτούς).

3. A Rich One Enters for Worship but the Poor Who Enters Is Rich in Faith (2:1–13)

The doing of mercy results in life

A ^{2:1} My brothers, do not with partiality have the faith in our Lord Jesus Christ of glory. ² For if a man with a gold ring and in fine clothing enters into your assembly, and a poor one enters in filthy clothing, ³ and you *pay attention to* the one wearing the fine clothing and say, "you rightly sit here," and to the poor one say, "you stand there or sit at my footstool," ⁴ have you not been divided among yourselves and become judges [κριταί] with evil designs? ⁵ Hear this, my brothers beloved, did not God choose the poor in this world to be rich in faith and heirs of the kingdom that he promised to those who love him? ⁶ But you have dishonored the poor one. Are not the rich oppressing you and they themselves dragging you into courts [κριτήρια]? ⁷ Do they not blaspheme the praiseworthy name that was invoked over you?

B ⁸ If however you complete the royal law according to the scripture, "You shall love your neighbor as yourself" (Lev 19:18), you are doing rightly. ⁹ But if you show partiality, you are working sin, convicted by the law as transgressors [παραβάται]. ¹⁰ For whoever keeps the whole law, but stumbles in one point, has become [γέγονεν] guilty of all of it.

C ¹¹ᵃ For the one who said, "Do not commit adultery [μοιχεύσῃς]" (Exod 20:14; Deut 5:18), said also, "Do not murder [φονεύσῃς]" (Exod 20:13; Deut 5:17).

C′ ¹¹ᵇ If then you do not commit adultery [μοιχεύεις] but you murder [φονεύεις],

B′ ¹¹ᶜ you have become [γέγονας] a transgressor [παραβάτης] of the law.

A′ ¹² So speak and so do as those about to be judged [κρίνεσθαι] through a law of freedom. ¹³ For the judgment [κρίσις] is merciless for the one not doing mercy; *mercy* boasts over judgment [κρίσεως].

The statement that "you pay attention to [ἐπιβλέψητε] the one wearing the fine clothing" toward the beginning of this unit in 2:3 recalls the exhortation "to care for [ἐπισκέπτεσθαι] orphans and widows in their affliction" at the conclusion of the preceding unit in 1:27, which contains the last word the audience have heard beginning with the prefix ἐπι-, and carries a similar conceptual connotation. These similar verbs serve as the transitional words linking the second unit (1:17–27) to the third unit (2:1–13).

An A-B-C-C′-B′-A′ chiastic pattern secures the integrity and distinctness of this third unit (2:1–13). The only occurrences in this unit of expressions for "judge," "courts," "judging," and "judgment" (κριταί in 2:4, κριτήρια in 2:6, κρίνεσθαι in 2:12, κρίσις in 2:13, and κρίσεως in 2:13) constitute the parallelism between the A (2:1–7) and the A′ (2:12–13) elements of this chiasm. The only occurrences in James of the term "transgressor(s)" (παραβάται in 2:9 and παραβάτης in 2:11c) as well as the only occurrences in this unit of the verb "become" (γέγονεν in 2:10 and γέγονας in 2:11c) determine the parallelism between the B (2:8–10) and the B′ (2:11c) elements. And the only occurrences in James of "commit adultery" (μοιχεύσῃς in 2:11a and μοιχεύεις in 2:11b) as well as the only occurrences in this unit of the verb "to murder" (φονεύσῃς in 2:11a and φονεύεις in 2:11b) establish the parallelism between the central and pivotal C (2:11a) and C′ (2:11b) elements of this chiasm.

4. You Want To Know That Faith without Works Is Useless for Life (2:14–26)

Faith without works is dead

> A [14] What is the *benefit*, my brothers, if someone says he has faith but does not have works? That faith is not able to save him, is it? [15] If a brother or sister is without clothing and lacking daily food, [16] and one of you says to them, "Go in peace, keep warm and be well fed," but you do not give them what is necessary for the body [σώματος], what is the benefit? [17] So also faith, if it does not have works, is dead [νεκρά] by itself.
>
> B [18] But someone will say, "You have faith and I have works." Show me your faith without works, and I will show you, from my works, faith. [19a] You believe [πιστεύεις] that God [θεός] is one. You are doing rightly. Even the demons are believing [πιστεύουσιν]
>
> C [19b] but shuddering.
>
> B′ [20] Do you want to know, O senseless person, that faith without works is useless? [21] Was not Abraham our father justified from works, having offered Isaac his son on the altar? [22] You notice that faith was working together with his works and from the works the faith was perfected, [23] and the scripture was fulfilled that says, "Abraham believed [ἐπίστευσεν] God [θεῷ], and it was reckoned to him as righteousness" (Gen 15:6) and friend of God [θεοῦ] he was called. [24] See that from works a person is justified and not from faith alone. [25] And likewise was not also Rahab the prostitute justified from

Introduction

works, having welcomed the messengers and sent them out by a different way?

A' ²⁶ For just as the *body* [σῶμα] without a spirit is dead [νεκρόν], so also faith without works is dead [νεκρά].

The statement that "mercy [ἔλεος] boasts over judgment" concludes the preceding unit in 2:13, while a question containing a similar-sounding word, "what is the benefit [ὄφελος]?," introduces this next unit in 2:14. These alliterative terms serve as the transitional words linking the third unit (2:1–13) to the fourth unit (2:14–26).

An A-B-C-B'-A' chiastic pattern secures the integrity and distinctness of this fourth unit (2:14–26). The only occurrences in this unit of the term "body" (σώματος in 2:16 and σῶμα in 2:26) as well as the only occurrences in James of the adjective "dead" (νεκρά in 2:17, 26 and νεκρόν in 2:26) constitute the parallelism between the A (2:14–17) and the A' (2:26) elements of this chiasm. The only occurrences in James of the verb "believe" (πιστεύεις and πιστεύουσιν in 2:19a and ἐπίστευσεν in 2:23) as well as the only occurrences in this unit of "God" (θεός in 2:19a, θεῷ and θεοῦ in 2:23) determine the parallelism between the B (2:18–19a) and the B' (2:20–25) elements. Finally, the unparalleled central and pivotal C (2:19b) element contains the only occurrence in James of the expression "but shuddering" (καὶ φρίσσουσιν).

5. *The Tongue Is Constituted a World of Unrighteousness within Our Members (3:1–10)*

The tongue is full of death-bringing poison

A ³:¹ Not many of you should become [γίνεσθε] teachers, my brothers [ἀδελφοί μου], knowing that we will receive a greater judgment.

    B ²ᵃ For [γάρ] we all stumble in many ways. If anyone does not stumble in word, this one is a perfect man able [δυνατός] to bridle

        C ²ᵇ even the whole *body* [ὅλον τὸ σῶμα]. ³ If we place bits into the mouths of horses to persuade them toward us, even their whole body [ὅλον τὸ σῶμα] we guide. ⁴ Behold also ships, being so large and driven by rough winds, are guided by a tiny rudder wherever the inclination of the pilot decides.

D ⁵ᵃ So also the tongue is a small member [μέλος], but boasts of great things.

E ⁵ᵇ Behold how small a fire [πῦρ] so great a forest kindles.

E' ⁶ᵃ And the tongue is a fire [πῦρ].

D' ⁶ᵇ The tongue is constituted as the world of unrighteousness within our members [μέλεσιν],

C' ⁶ᶜ defiling the whole body [ὅλον τὸ σῶμα] and setting fire to the course of the birth and being set on fire by Gehenna.

B' ⁷ For [γάρ] every species of animals and also of birds, of reptiles and also of sea creatures is tamed and has been tamed by the human species. ⁸ But the tongue no one among human beings is able [δύναται] to tame, an unstable evil, full of death-bringing poison.

A' ⁹ With it we bless the Lord and Father and with it we curse human beings who have become [γεγονότας] in accord with the likeness of God. ¹⁰ *From the same* mouth come out blessing and cursing. It is not necessary, my brothers [ἀδελφοί μου], that these things become [γίνεσθαι] so.

The term "body" (σῶμα) occurs toward the conclusion of the preceding unit in 2:26 and near the beginning of this next unit in 3:2. These occurrences serve as the transitional words linking the fourth unit (2:14–26) to the fifth unit (3:1–10).

An A-B-C-D-E-E'-D'-C'-B'-A' chiastic pattern secures the integrity and distinctness of this fifth unit (3:1–10). The only occurrences in this unit of the verb "become" (γίνεσθε in 3:1, γεγονότας in 3:9, γίνεσθαι in 3:10) and of the address "my brothers" (ἀδελφοί μου in 3:1, 10) constitute the parallelism between the A (3:1) and A' (3:9–10) elements of this chiasm. The only occurrences in this unit of the conjunction "for" (γάρ in 3:2a, 7) and of expressions for being "able" (δυνατός in 3:2b and δύναται in 3:8) determine the parallelism between the B (3:2a) and the B' (3:7-8) elements. The only occurrences in James of the expression "whole body" (ὅλον τὸ σῶμα in 3:2b, 3, 6c) establish the parallelism between the C (3:2b-4) and the C' (3:6c) elements. The only occurrences in this unit of the term "member" (μέλος in 3:5a and μέλεσιν in 3:6b) form the parallelism between the D (3:5a) and D' (3:6b) elements. Finally, the central and pivotal E (3:5b) and E' (3:6a) elements contain the only occurrences in this unit of the term "fire" (πῦρ).

6. Worship in the Humility of Wisdom That Is from Above (3:11–18)

A fruit of righteousness in peace is sown among those who make peace to live by

- **A** ¹¹ A spring *from the same* opening does not pour forth the sweet and the bitter, does it? ¹² My brothers, a fig tree is not able to make [ποιῆσαι] olives or a vine figs, is it? Neither is salty able to make [ποιῆσαι] sweet water.

    - **B** ¹³ Who is wise [σοφός] and understanding among you? Let him show from praiseworthy conduct his works in humility of wisdom [σοφίας]. ¹⁴ But if you have bitter envy [ζῆλον] and selfishness [ἐριθείαν] in your heart, do not boast against and lie against the truth. ¹⁵ᵃ This is not the wisdom from above [σοφία ἄνωθεν] coming down

        - **C** ¹⁵ᵇ but earthly, this-worldly, demonic.

    - **B'** ¹⁶ For where there is envy [ζῆλος] and selfishness [ἐριθεία], there is disorder and every foul practice. ¹⁷ᵃ But the *from above* wisdom [ἄνωθεν σοφία] is first of all pure,

- **A'** ¹⁷ᵇ then peaceable, gentle, compliant, full of mercy and good fruits, nondisputive, nonpretentious. ¹⁸ And a fruit of righteousness in peace is sown among those who make [ποιοῦσιν] peace.

The phrase "from the same" (ἐκ τοῦ αὐτοῦ) referring to "mouth" occurs at the conclusion of the preceding unit in 3:10 and the phrase "from the same" (ἐκ τῆς αὐτῆς) referring to "opening" occurs again at the beginning of this next unit in 3:11. These successive occurrences of this phrase serve as the transitional words linking the fifth unit (3:1–10) to the sixth unit (3:11–18).

An A-B-C-B'-A' chiastic pattern secures the integrity and distinctness of this sixth unit (3:11–18). The only occurrences in this unit of the verb "make" (ποιῆσαι twice in 3:12 and ποιοῦσιν in 3:18) constitute the parallelism between the A (3:11–12) and A' (3:17b–18) elements of this chiasm. The following linguistic occurrences determine the parallelism between the B (3:13–15a) and B' (3:16–17a) elements: the only occurrences in this unit of the terms "wise" or "wisdom," and in James of "wisdom from above" (σοφός in 3:13, σοφίας in 3:13, σοφία ἄνωθεν in 3:15a, and ἄνωθεν σοφία in 3:17a); the only occurrences in James of the term "envy" (ζῆλον in 3:14 and ζῆλος in 3:16); and the only occurrences in James of the term "selfishness" (ἐριθείαν in 3:14 and ἐριθεία in 3:16). Finally, the unparalleled central and pivotal C (3:15b) element contains the only occurrence in James of the expression "but earthly, this-worldly, demonic" (ἀλλὰ ἐπίγειος, ψυχική, δαιμονιώδης).

7. Passions Battle within Your Members and an Enemy with God Is Constituted (4:1–10)

Be humbled before the Lord and he will exalt you with life

A ^{4:1} *Whence* are the wars and whence are the fights among you [ὑμῖν]? Is it not from this, from your [ὑμῶν] passions battling within your [ὑμῶν] members? ² You desire but you do not have; you murder and envy but you are not able to obtain; you fight and wage war; you do not have because you [ὑμᾶς] do not ask; ³ you ask but you do not receive because you ask wrongly, so that you may spend on your [ὑμῶν] passions.

    B ⁴ Adulteresses! Do you not know that friendship with the world is enmity with God? Whoever then [οὖν] decides to be a friend with the world, an enemy with God is constituted.

> C ⁵ Or do you think in vain the scripture says [λέγει], "Toward envy longs the spirit that he caused to dwell in us"? ⁶ᵃ But he gives [δίδωσιν] greater grace [χάριν].
>
> C′ ⁶ᵇ Therefore it says [λέγει], "God opposes the haughty, but to the humble he gives [δίδωσιν] grace [χάριν]" (Prov 3:34).
>
> B′ ⁷ᵃ Submit then [οὖν] to God, but resist the devil
>
> A′ ⁷ᵇ and he will flee from you [ὑμῶν]. ⁸ Draw near to God and he will draw near to you [ὑμῖν]. Cleanse hands, sinful ones, and purify hearts, double-minded ones. ⁹ Be miserable and mourn and weep. Let your [ὑμῶν] laughter to mourning be turned and the joy to *dejection*. ¹⁰ Be humbled before the Lord and he will exalt you [ὑμᾶς].

The adverb "above" (ἄνωθεν) occurs near the conclusion of the preceding unit in 3:17 and the adverb "whence" (πόθεν), which contains the next instance of the syllable -θεν, occurs twice at the beginning of this next unit in 4:1. The successive occurrences of these adverbs serve as the transitional words linking the sixth unit (3:11–18) to the seventh unit (4:1–10).

An A-B-C-C′-B′-A′ chiastic pattern secures the integrity and distinctness of this seventh unit (4:1–10). The only occurrences in this unit of the second-person plural pronoun (ὑμῖν 4:1, 8, ὑμῶν in 4:1 [*bis*], 3, 7b, 9, and ὑμᾶς in 4:2, 10) constitute the parallelism between the A (4:1–3) and the A′ (4:7b–10) elements of this chiasm. The only occurrences in this unit of the coordinating conjunction "then" (οὖν in 4:4, 7a) determine the parallelism between the B (4:4) and the B′ (4:7a) elements. The only occurrences in James of the third-person singular present active indicative verb "says" (λέγει in 4:5, 6b); the only occurrences in James of the third-person singular present active indicative verb "gives" (δίδωσιν in 3:6a, 6b); and the only occurrences in James of the term "grace" (χάριν in 3:6a, 6b) establish the parallelism between the central and pivotal C (4:5–6a) and C′ (4:6b) elements.

8. If the Lord Wants It Then We Will Live to Do What Is Praiseworthy (4:11–17)

You do not know what your life will be like tomorrow

A ¹¹ᵃ Do not *speak against* one another, brothers. He who speaks against a brother or judges his brother speaks against the law and judges the law. But if you judge the law, you are not a doer [ποιητής] of the law

   B ¹¹ᵇ but a judge [κριτής].

      C ¹²ᵃ One is the lawgiver

   B' ¹²ᵇ and judge [κριτής] who is able to save and to destroy. But who are you who judges the neighbor?

A' ¹³ *Come now* those saying, "Today or tomorrow we will go to this or that city and do [ποιήσομεν] business there a year and buy and sell and make a profit."¹⁶ ¹⁴ You do not know what your life will be like tomorrow. For you are a vapor that for a short time appears, and then disappears. ¹⁵ Instead of you saying, "If the Lord wants it, then we will live and do [ποιήσομεν] this or that," ¹⁶ now you are boasting in your arrogances.¹⁷ All such boasting is evil. ¹⁷ To one knowing then the praiseworthy thing to do [ποιεῖν] and not doing [ποιοῦντι] it, to him it is sin.

The word "dejection" (κατήφειαν) occurs near the conclusion of the preceding unit in 4:9, while the word "speak against" (καταλαλεῖτε) introduces this next unit in 4:11. These successive occurrences of terms beginning with κατα- serve as the transitional words linking the seventh unit (4:1–10) to the eighth unit (4:11–17).

An A-B-C-B'-A' chiastic pattern secures the integrity and distinctness of this eighth unit (4:11–17). The only occurrences in this unit of expressions for "doing" (ποιητής in 4:11a, ποιήσομεν in 4:13, 15, ποιεῖν

---

16. Literally, the Greek reads simply "let us do there a year." I have added "business" to the verb "do" to make better sense of the expression in accord with the context. The rest of the verse, "buy and sell and make a profit," thus elaborates the "doing [of business]."

17. For this construal of 4:15–16, see McKnight, *James*, 374–75.

in 4:17, and ποιοῦντι in 4:17) constitute the parallelism between the A (4:11a) and A' (4:13–17) elements of this chiasm. The only occurrences in this unit of the noun "judge" (κριτής) in 4:11b, 12b determine the parallelism between the B (4:11b) and B' (4:12b) elements. Finally, the unparalleled central and pivotal C (4:12a) element contains the only occurrence in James of the statement "one is the lawgiver" (εἷς ἐστιν [ὁ] νομοθέτης).

9. The Cries Caused by the Rich Have Entered into the Ears of the Lord of Hosts (5:1–6)

The rich who have murdered the righteous one have fattened their hearts for slaughter

A **5:1** *Come now* you rich, weep, wailing over the miseries that are coming upon you. **2** Your wealth has rotted and your clothes have become moth-eaten, **3a** your gold and silver have corroded and their corrosion will be a testimony against you [ὑμῖν] and it will devour your flesh like fire.

> B **3b** You have stored up treasure in the last days [ἡμέραις].

>> C **4a** Behold the wages of the [τῶν] workers who [τῶν] mowed your fields,

>>> D **4b** which have been withheld by you,

>> C' **4c** are crying out, and the cries of the [τῶν] harvesters have entered into the ears of the *Lord* of hosts.

> B' **5** You have reveled on the earth and lived luxuriously. You have fattened your hearts in a day [ἡμέρᾳ] of slaughter!

A' **6** You have condemned, you have murdered the righteous one; he does not oppose you [ὑμῖν].

The directive "come now" (ἄγε νῦν) opening this unit in 5:1 repeats the identical directive that occurs near the conclusion of the preceding unit in 4:13. These are the only occurrences in James of this directive, which provides the transitional words linking the eighth unit (4:11–17) to the ninth unit (5:1–6).

The Letter of James

An A-B-C-D-C'-B'-A' chiastic pattern secures the integrity and distinctness of this ninth unit (5:1-6). The only occurrences in this unit of the dative second person plural pronoun "you" (ὑμῖν in 5:3a, 6) constitute the parallelism between the A (5:1-3a) and the A' (5:6) elements of this chiasm. The only occurrences in James of the term "day" (ἡμέραις in 5:3b and ἡμέρᾳ in 5:5) determine the parallelism between the B (5:3b) and B' (5:5) elements. The only occurrences in this unit of the genitive masculine plural of the definite article "the" (τῶν in 5:4a [*bis*], 4c) establish the parallelism between the C (5:4a) and the C' (5:4c) elements. Finally, the unparalleled central and pivotal D (5:4b) element contains the only occurrence in James of the expression "which have been withheld by you" (ὁ ἀπεστερημένος ἀφ' ὑμῶν).

10. Strengthen Your Hearts Like Prophets Who Spoke in the Name of the Lord (5:7-11)

Be patient and endure until the coming of the Lord who gives life

A ⁷ Be patient [μακροθυμήσατε] then, brothers [ἀδελφοί], until the coming of the *Lord* [κυρίου]. Behold the farmer awaits the precious fruit of the earth, being patient [μακροθυμῶν] for it until it receives [λάβῃ] the early rain and the late rain. ⁸ Be patient [μακροθυμήσατε] you also. Strengthen your hearts, for the coming of the Lord [κυρίου] is near. ⁹ᵃ Do not complain, brothers [ἀδελφοί], against one another,

B ⁹ᵇ so that you may not be judged [κριθῆτε].

B' ⁹ᶜ Behold the judge [κριτής] is standing before the gates.

A' ¹⁰ As an example of suffering and patience [μακροθυμίας] receive [λάβετε], *brothers* [ἀδελφοί], the prophets who spoke in the name of the Lord [κυρίου]. ¹¹ Behold we call blessed those who have endured. Of the endurance of Job you have heard and the outcome of the Lord [κυρίου] you have seen, for very sympathetic is the Lord [κύριος] and compassionate.

Introduction

The term "Lord" (κυρίου) occurs near the conclusion of the preceding unit in 5:4. Its next occurrence is near the beginning of this unit in 5:7. These successive occurrences serve as the transitional words linking the ninth unit (5:1–6) to the tenth unit (5:7–11).

An A-B-B'-A' chiastic pattern secures the integrity and distinctness of this tenth unit (5:7–11). The following linguistic occurrences constitute the parallelism between the A (5:7–9a) and A' (5:10–11) elements of this chiasm: the only occurrences in James of expressions for "being patient" and "patience" (μακροθυμήσατε in 5:7, 8, μακροθυμῶν in 5:7, and μακροθυμίας in 5:10); the only occurrences in this unit of the address "brothers" (ἀδελφοί in 5:7, 9a, 10); the only occurrences in this unit of "Lord" (κυρίου in 5:7, 8, 10, 11 and κύριος in 5:11); and the only occurrences in this unit of the verb "receive" (λάβῃ in 5:7 and λάβετε in 5:10). Finally, the only occurrences in this unit of the verb "being judged" and the noun "judge" (κριθῆτε in 5:9b and κριτής in 5:9c) determine the parallelism between the B (5:9b) and B' (5:9c) elements.

11. *Whoever Brings Back One Led Astray Will Save Him from Death (5:12–20)*

Pray for one another that you may be healed and raised up to life

- **A** ^{12} Before all, my *brothers* [ἀδελφοί μου], do not swear by heaven [οὐρανόν] or by earth or by any other oath. But let your "Yes" be yes and your "No" be no, so that you may not fall under judgment.

  - **B** ^{13} If anyone is suffering among you, let him pray [προσευχέσθω]. If anyone is cheerful, let him sing praise. ^{14} If anyone is sick among you, let him summon the elders of the church and let them pray [προσευξάσθωσαν] over him, anointing him with oil in the name of the Lord.

    - **C** ^{15a} And the prayer [εὐχή] of faith will save the one who is ill and the Lord will raise him up.

      - **D** ^{15b} And if he has done sins [ἁμαρτίας],

        - **E** ^{15c} they will be forgiven him.

> **D′** [16a] Confess then to one another the sins [ἁμαρτίας]
>
> **C′** [16b] and pray [εὔχεσθε] for one another that you may be healed. A request of a righteous one is very powerful in its working.
>
> **B′** [17] Elijah was a person similar in nature to us, and with prayer he prayed [προσευχῇ προσηύξατο] for it not to rain, and it did not rain on the earth for three years and six months. [18a] And again he prayed [προσηύξατο],
>
> **A′** [18b] and the heaven [οὐρανός] gave rain and the earth sprouted its fruit. [19] My brothers [ἀδελφοί μου], if anyone among you should be led astray from the truth and someone brings him back, [20] let him know that whoever brings back a sinful one from the straying of his way will save his soul from death and will cover a multitude of sins.

The address "brothers" (ἀδελφοί) occurs toward the conclusion of the preceding unit in 5:10. Its next occurrence introduces this unit in 5:12. These successive occurrences serve as the transitional words linking the tenth unit (5:7–11) to the eleventh unit (5:12–20).

An A-B-C-D-E-D′-C′-B′-A′ chiastic pattern secures the integrity and distinctness of this final eleventh unit (5:12–20). The only occurrences in this unit of the address "my brothers" (ἀδελφοί μου in 5:12, 19) as well as the only occurrences in James of the term "heaven" (οὐρανόν in 5:12 and οὐρανός in 5:18b) constitute the parallelism between the A (5:12) and A′ (5:19–20) elements of this chiasm. The only occurrences in James of the verb "pray" and the noun "prayer" as forms of προσεύχομαι and προσευχή (προσευχέσθω in 5:13, προσευξάσθωσαν in 5:14, προσευχῇ in 5:17, and προσηύξατο in 5:17, 18) determine the parallelism between the B (5:13–14) and B′ (5:17–18) elements.

The only occurrences in James of the noun "prayer" and the verb "pray" as forms of εὐχή and εὔχομαι (εὐχή in 5:15a and εὔχεσθε in 5:16b) establish the parallelism between the C (5:15a) and C′ (5:16b) elements. The only occurrences in James of the accusative plural form of "sins" (ἁμαρτίας in 5:15b, 16a) form the parallelism between the D (5:15b) and D′ (5:16a) elements. And finally, the unparalleled central and pivotal E (5:15c) element contains the only occurrence in James of the statement "they will be forgiven him" (ἀφεθήσεται αὐτῷ).

The Macrochiastic Structure of James

Having illustrated the sequence of the various microchiastic structures operative in the eleven distinct units of the letter of James, I will now demonstrate how these eleven main units form an A-B-C-D-E-F-E'-D'-C'-B'-A' macrochiastic structure organizing the entire letter.

> A Do Not Be *Led Astray* by Sin That Brings Forth *Death* (1:1–16)
>
> A' Whoever Brings Back One *Led Astray* Will Save Him from *Death* (5:12–20)

Repetitions of terms significant for the letter's overall rhetorical strategy indicate the parallelism between the opening A unit (1:1–16) and the closing A' unit (5:12–20) within the macrochiastic structure of James. The A' unit concludes with a climactic exhortation that if anyone among the audience should be "led astray" (πλανηθῇ) from the truth, and someone brings him back, let him know that whoever brings back a sinful one from the "straying" (πλάνης) of his way will save his soul from "death" (θανάτου) and will cover a multitude of sins (5:19–20). This recalls and resonates with the climactic conclusion of the A unit, which explains that each one is tempted by his own desire, being dragged away and enticed (1:14). When the desire conceives, it gives birth to sin, and the sin having been brought to completion, brings birth to "death [θάνατον]" (1:15). The audience of brothers beloved are then exhorted: do not be "led astray [πλανᾶσθε]" (1:16). That these are the only occurrences in James of expressions for "being led astray" or "straying," as well as of the term "death," enhances the distinctiveness of this chiastic parallelism.

> B Be Slow to *Speak* Not Deceiving the *Heart* for Useless Worship (1:17–27)
>
> B' Strengthen Your *Hearts* Like Prophets Who *Spoke* in the Name of the Lord (5:7–11)

The exhortation for the audience to strengthen their "hearts" (καρδίας), for the coming of the Lord is near, in 5:8 of the B' unit recalls and resonates with the admonition that if anyone thinks he is religious, not bridling his tongue but deceiving his "heart" (καρδίαν), the religion of this one is useless, in 1:26 of the B unit. That these are the first and last occurrences of the term "heart" in James enhances the distinctiveness of this chiastic parallelism.[18]

The exhortation for the audience to receive, as an example of suffering and patience, the prophets who "spoke" (ἐλάλησαν) in the name of the Lord, in 5:10 of the B' unit reinforces the exhortation for every person to be quick to hear, slow to "speak" (λαλῆσαι), and slow to anger in 1:19 of the B unit. That these are the first and last occurrences of the verb "speak" in James enhances the distinctiveness of this chiastic parallelism.[19]

> C A *Rich* One *Enters* for Worship but the Poor Who *Enters* Is *Rich* in Faith (2:1–13)
>
> C' The Cries Caused by the *Rich* Have *Entered* into the Ears of the Lord of Hosts (5:1–6)

The warning for the "rich" (πλούσιοι) to weep and wail over the miseries that are coming upon them in 5:1 of the C' unit recalls and resonates with the charge that the "rich" (πλούσιοι) are oppressing the audience in 2:6, as well as with the assertion that God chose the poor of this world to be "rich" (πλουσίους) in faith in 2:5 of the C unit. That these are the only occurrences of the term "rich" in the plural in James enhances the distinctiveness of this chiastic parallelism.[20]

The statement that the cries of the harvesters have "entered" (εἰσεληλύθασιν), as prayers in worship, into the ears of the Lord of hosts in 5:4 of the C' unit recalls and resonates with the contrast between a man with a gold ring and fine clothing who "enters" (εἰσέλθῃ) into the worshiping assembly of the audience and a poor one who "enters" (εἰσέλθῃ) in filthy clothing in 2:2 of the C unit. That these are the only

---

18. The other occurrences of the term "heart" (καρδία) in James are in 3:14; 4:8; 5:5.

19. The only other occurrence of the verb "speak" (λαλέω) in James is in 2:12.

20. The term "rich" (πλούσιος) occurs in the singular in 1:10, 11.

occurrences in James of the verb "enter," and that both are related to a context of worship, enhances the distinctiveness of this chiastic parallelism.

> D You *Want* to Know That Faith without Works Is Useless for Life (2:14–26)
>
> D' If the Lord *Wants* It Then We Will Live to Do What Is Praiseworthy (4:11–17)

The advice for the audience to say that if the Lord "wants" (θελήσῃ) it, then we will live to do this or that, in 4:15 of the D' unit recalls and resonates with the question of whether a senseless person "wants" (θέλεις) to know that faith without works is useless for one's life in 2:20 of the D unit. These are the only occurrences in James of the verb "want" and they both occur in a context regarding issues important for life. This enhances the distinctiveness of this chiastic parallelism.

> E The Tongue *Is Constituted* a World of Unrighteousness *within Our Members* (3:1–10)
>
> E' 4:1–10: Passions Battle *within Your Members* and an Enemy with God *Is Constituted* (4:1–10)

The question about the wars and fights among the audience that originate from their passions battling "within your members" (ἐν τοῖς μέλεσιν ὑμῶν) in 4:1 of the E' unit recalls and resonates with the assertion that the tongue is constituted as a world of unrighteousness "within our members" (ἐν τοῖς μέλεσιν ἡμῶν) in 3:6 of the E unit. That these are the only occurrences in James of the phrase "in your/our members" enhances the distinctiveness of this chiastic parallelism.[21]

The warning that whoever decides to be a friend with the world, an enemy with God "is constituted" (καθίσταται) in 4:4 of the E' unit parallels the assertion that the tongue "is constituted" (καθίσταται) as a world of unrighteousness within our members in 3:6 of the E unit. That these are the only occurrences in James of the verbal form "is constituted" enhances the distinctiveness of this chiastic parallelism.

---

21. The only other occurrence of the term "member" (μέλος) is in 3:5 of the E unit.

F Worship in the Humility of Wisdom That Is from Above (3:11–18)

The F unit functions as the unparalleled central and pivotal unit within the macrochiastic structure of James. The pivotal parallels within this unit itself involve the only occurrences in James of the terms "envy" and "selfishness" in 3:14, 16. This unit exhibits most of the letter's vocabulary involving wisdom, including the unique occurrence in James of the chiastically parallel progression from the phrase "the wisdom from above" (ἡ σοφία ἄνωθεν) in 3:15 to the phrase "the from above wisdom" (ἡ δὲ ἄνωθεν σοφία) in 3:17.[22]

Outline of the Macrochiastic Structure of James

A 1:1–16: Do Not Be *Led Astray* by Sin That Brings Forth *Death*

  B 1:17–27: Be Slow to *Speak* Not Deceiving the *Heart* for Useless Worship

    C 2:1–13: A *Rich* One *Enters* for Worship but the Poor Who *Enters* Is *Rich* in Faith

      D 2:14–26: You *Want* to Know That Faith without Works Is Useless for Life

        E 3:1–10: The Tongue *Is Constituted* a World of Unrighteousness *within Our Members*

          F 3:11–18: Worship in the Humility of Wisdom That Is from Above

        E' 4:1–10: Passions Battle *within Your Members* and an Enemy of God *Is Constituted*

      D' 4:11–17: If the Lord *Wants* It Then We Will Live to Do What Is Praiseworthy

    C' 5:1–6: The Cries Caused by the *Rich* Have *Entered* into the Ears of the Lord of Hosts

---

22. This central F unit contains three of the four occurrences in James of the noun "wisdom" (σοφία in 1:5; 3:13, 15, 17) and the only occurrence of the adjective "wise [σοφός]" (3:13).

> B' 5:7-11: Strengthen Your *Hearts* Like Prophets Who *Spoke* in the Name of the Lord
>
> A' 5:12-20: Whoever Brings Back One *Led Astray* Will Save Him from Death

Preliminary Indication of the Main Theme of James

The literary inclusion formed by the climactic conclusion of the first A unit (1:1-16) with the climactic conclusion of the final A' unit (5:12-20) of James provides a preliminary indication of its main theme. That James is concerned, first of all, with matters of worship begins to become explicitly evident with an introductory instruction about prayer in the A unit at the beginning of the letter. James advises that "if anyone is lacking in wisdom, let him ask from the God who gives to all unreservedly, indeed not reproaching, and it will be given to him" (1:5).

This introductory instruction regarding prayer forms an inclusion with the final instructions regarding prayer in the A' unit at the end of the letter. There James instructs that "if anyone is suffering among you, let him pray" (5:13). "If anyone is sick among you, let him summon the elders of the church and let them pray for him" (5:14). "The prayer of faith will save the one who is ill and the Lord will raise him up (to eternal life)" (5:15). The audience are "to pray for one another that you may be healed" (5:16). And Elijah is presented as an example to the audience of one who prayed effectively (5:17-18). This provides us with a preliminary indication that an overall theme of worship oriented to avoiding eternal death and to being granted eternal life embraces the entire letter of James.

In the A unit, after warning that the rich one in his pursuits "will die out [μαρανθήσεται]" (1:11), James declares blessed by God a man who endures temptation, for having become tested, he will receive the crown of "life" (ζωῆς), that is, of eschatological or eternal life, that the Lord promised to those who love him (1:12). The A unit concludes with the warning that "each one is tempted by his own desire, being dragged away and enticed. When the desire conceives, it gives birth to sin, and the sin having been brought to completion, brings birth to death [θάνατον]" (1:14–15), that is, to eschatological or eternal death. Consequently, the audience are exhorted not to be "led astray" (1:16) by the desires that lead to eternal death rather than to eternal life.

This concern for the eternal life rather than the eternal death of the audience as a worshiping assembly in the A unit forms an inclusion with a development of the same concern in the final and climactic exhortation in the A' unit. There James urges his audience that if anyone among them should be "led astray" from the truth and someone brings him back (5:19), let him know that whoever brings back to the worshiping assembly a sinful one from the "straying" of his way will save his soul from "death" (θανάτου), that is, from eschatological or eternal death, and will cover a multitude of sins (5:20). This preliminary indication that "the worship to live by," that is, the worship to live by now and for eternity, expresses the main theme embracing the whole of the letter of James will be confirmed by the remainder of my investigation into its chiastic structures in the chapters to follow.

Summary

1. There are eleven distinct units in the letter of James with each exhibiting its own microchiastic structure.

2. The eleven units comprising James operate as a macrochiastic structure with five pairs of parallel units and with the pivot of the entire macrochiastic structure occurring as the unparalleled central F unit in 3:11–18.

3. The literary inclusion between the first A chiastic unit (1:1–16) and the final A' chiastic unit (5:12–20) provides a preliminary indication of the main theme embracing the letter of James, namely, a concern for the eternal life rather than the eternal death of the audience as a worshiping community. Thus, James presents us with the "the worship to live by" now and for eternity.

James 1:1–16

Do Not Be Led Astray by Sin That Brings Forth Death (A)

Blessed is a man who endures temptation for the crown of life

A ¹:¹ James, of *God* and of the Lord Jesus Christ a servant, to the twelve tribes, the ones in the diaspora, joyful greetings! ² Consider it all joy, *my brothers*, whenever you tumble into teeming *temptations*, ³ knowing that the *testing* of your faith produces *endurance*. ⁴ And let *endurance* have its perfect work, so that you may be perfect and complete, lacking in nothing. ⁵ But if anyone of you is lacking wisdom, let him ask from the *God* who gives to all unreservedly, indeed not reproaching, and it will be given to him. ⁶ But let him ask in faith, disputing nothing, for the one who disputes is like a wave of the sea blown and driven about by the wind. ⁷ For that person must not suppose that he *will receive* anything from the Lord, ⁸ a double-minded *man*, unstable in all the ways of him.

    B ⁹ Let the humble brother boast in his exaltedness, ¹⁰ᵃ but the *rich one* in his lowliness,

        C ¹⁰ᵇ for like a *flower*

            D ¹⁰ᶜ of *grass* he will pass away.

                E ¹¹ᵃ For the sun rises with its heat

            D′ ¹¹ᵇ and dries up the *grass*

> **C′** ¹¹ᶜ and its *flower* falls away and the beauty of its appearance is destroyed.
>
> > **B′** ¹¹ᵈ So also the *rich one* in his pursuits will die out.
>
> **A′** ¹² Blessed is a *man* who *endures temptation*, for having become *tested*, he *will receive* the crown of life that he (the Lord) promised to those who love him. ¹³ Let no one being *tempted* say, "I am being *tempted* by *God*," for *God* is *untempted* of evil things, and he himself *tempts* no one. ¹⁴ But each one is *tempted* by his own desire, being dragged away and enticed. ¹⁵ When the desire conceives, it gives birth to sin, and the sin having been brought to completion, brings birth to death. ¹⁶ Do not be led astray, *my brothers* beloved.[1]

Audience Response to 1:1–16

1:1–8 (A): A Faithless Unstable Man Will Not Receive Anything from the Lord

The audience hear the A element (1:1–8) of this chiastic unit as a chiastic pattern in itself:[2]

a) James, of God and of the *Lord* Jesus Christ a servant, to *the* twelve tribes, *the* ones in the diaspora, joyful greetings! Consider it all joy, my brothers, whenever you tumble into teeming temptations (1:1–2),

> **b)** knowing that the testing of your *faith* produces endurance. And let endurance have its perfect work, so that you may be perfect and complete, lacking in *nothing* (1:3–4).
>
> > **c)** But if anyone of you is lacking wisdom, let him ask from the God who gives to all unreservedly, indeed not reproaching, and it will be given to him (1:5).

---

1. For the establishment of Jas 1:1–16 as a chiasm, see the Introduction.
2. The term "audience" will be used throughout the work as a collective plural noun, since in the Greek text plural terms are used in reference to the audience, who are conceived of as a group composed of individual members with responsibilities toward one another.

b′) But let him ask in *faith*, disputing *nothing*, for the one who disputes is like a wave of the sea blown and driven about by the wind (1:6).

a′) For that person must not suppose that he will receive anything from the *Lord*, a double-minded man, unstable in all *the* ways of him (1:7–8).[3]

The audience hear the exhortation, "but if anyone of you is lacking wisdom, let him ask from the God who gives to all unreservedly, indeed not reproaching, and it will be given to him" (1:5), as the unparalleled central and pivotal sub-element in this chiastic sub-unit. They then experience a pivot of parallels involving the only occurrences in this sub-unit of the terms "faith" and "nothing." They hear a progression of parallels from "the testing of your faith [πίστεως]" and "lacking in nothing [μηδενί]" in the b) sub-element (1:3–4) to "let him ask in faith [πίστει], disputing nothing [μηδέν]" in the b′) sub-element (1:6). Finally, they experience another progression via the chiastic parallels determined by the only occurrences in this sub-unit of the term "Lord" and the definite article "the" in the dative feminine plural. "The Lord [κυρίου] Jesus Christ" and "to the [ταῖς] twelve tribes, the [ταῖς] ones in the diaspora" in the a) sub-element (1:1–2) progress to "anything from the Lord [κυρίου]" and "unstable in all the [ταῖς] ways of him" in the a′) sub-element (1:7–8).

This letter, a hortatory homily to be read publicly to a worshiping assembly, presents itself as sent by someone named "James," describing himself as "a servant of God and of the Lord Jesus Christ" (1:1). In all probability this refers to the James who was a brother of Jesus (Matt 13:55; Mark 6:3) and became the leader of the Christian community at Jerusalem (1 Cor 15:7; Gal 1:19; 2:9, 12; Acts 12:17; 15:13; 21:18). Whether or not he was the actual author, his authority and status stand behind the letter.[4]

---

3. I translate ἐν πάσαις ταῖς ὁδοῖς αὐτοῦ literally as "in all the ways of him" rather than "in all his ways" in order to better illustrate the chiastic parallelism with 1:1, based on the only occurrences in this sub-unit of the article in the dative feminine plural.

4. For discussions of the letter's authorship, see Johnson, *James*, 89–121; Moo, *James*, 9–22; Hartin, *James*, 16–25; Witherington, *Jewish Christians*, 385–401; Batten,

As a "servant" (1:1), James humbly submits himself in obedience to both God and to the Lord Jesus Christ as one who "serves" them within a context of worship.[5] As a "servant" who has been divinely authorized by both God and the Lord Jesus Christ, James addresses and thus also "serves" his audience, gathered together as a worshiping assembly to hear his epistolary homily. Implicitly, with James, the audience are to consider themselves fellow servants of God and of the Lord Jesus Christ.[6] They are likewise to humbly submit themselves in obedience to both God and to the Jesus God sent as "Christ," God's chosen messianic agent, who became "Lord" as God exalted him from death to eternal life

---

James, 34–43; McCartney, *James*, 8–32; McKnight, *James*, 13–34. I concur with the following conclusions. "[T]he arguments do tend strongly toward the conclusion that James is a very early writing from a Palestinian Jewish Christian source. And James the Brother of the Lord is a reasonable candidate. A letter from *this* James to 'the twelve tribes in the dispersion' accords well with the fairest reading of our earliest sources and the self-presentation of the composition itself" (Johnson, *James*, 121). "[T]here are no serious arguments to weigh against the plausibility of the epistolary situation indicated by James 1:1. The letter can be read as what it purports to be: an encyclical from James of Jerusalem to the Diaspora" (Bauckham, *James*, 25). "When all the data are considered, the simplest solution is to accept the verdict of early Christians: the letter was written by James of Jerusalem, 'the Lord's brother.' Nothing in the letter is inconsistent with this conclusion, and several, albeit minor and indecisive, points favor it" (Moo, *James*, 22). "I thus conclude that this document was written at least by the 50s, by someone we know as James brother of the Lord, as a hortatory sermon" (Witherington, *Jewish Christians*, 401). "[T]he connection of James to the letter from the Jerusalem Council in Acts 15 and a parallel connection to the Jesus traditions make the authorship by James the brother of Jesus credible and even make him the James most likely in mind in the letter's salutation" (McKnight, *James*, 28).

5. According to Dibelius (*James*, 65) the term "servant" or "slave" (δοῦλος) "expresses a definite relationship to the God to whose cult a person is committed."

6. "What qualified James to write such a letter was not his physical relationship to Jesus but his spiritual relationship" (Moo, *James*, 48). "James identifies himself not as Jesus's brother but as Jesus's servant, thus classifying himself along with all his readers" (McCartney, *James*, 79). "If James is *doulos* of 'God and of the Lord Jesus Christ,' then he is certified to readers as one who is himself defined by the measure he applies to them. His life is one of service to God and to Jesus as Lord . . . he is a reliable spokesperson for God and the Lord Jesus Christ, since he lives out what he preaches. The term *doulos* also has the (paradoxical) connotation of religious leader . . . the term designates the prophetic spokepersons for the Lord: the one who best serves is the one who best represents. Thus the designation supports both the implied author's genuine personal commitment and his authoritative role" (Johnson, *James*, 171).

with God (Phil 2:6–11; Rom 10:9; Acts 2:36).[7] Along with all believers, the audience expected Jesus to come again to complete God's plan of salvation from death to eternal life for all of God's people.[8]

The letter is sent to an audience characterized as "the twelve tribes, the ones in the diaspora" (1:1). God's chosen people Israel were originally constituted and unified as "twelve tribes," but later scattered among the Gentiles "in the diaspora" outside of their divinely inherited land of Israel. The hope arose for their restoration in the end time when God would complete his plan of salvation. As addressed by James, a servant of God and of the Lord Jesus Christ, "the twelve tribes" refer to Christian believers as the beginning of the fulfillment of this hoped for restoration. The letter possesses the character of an encyclical addressed to several similar audiences of such believers. The address thus situates each such audience within a context of looking forward in hope, as a worshiping assembly, to the final completion of this restoration, which would include their participation in the eternal life of the risen Lord Jesus Christ.[9]

---

7. "'Christ' could designate Jesus as a special authority figure, who proclaimed and instigated restoration of the people of God, by the righteous doing of God's will. It is highly unlikely that anyone associated with the movement around Jesus could have been unaware of his crucifixion. Thus, the honorific titles given to Jesus must be understood in relation to this, although the events themselves are not explicitly referred to in the Epistle of James. Thus, 'Lord' (κύριος), and even more so, 'Christ' (Χριστός), must demonstrate the conviction of God's ultimate vindication of Jesus, which is, of course, explicitly recounted elsewhere with reference to the resurrection" (Hutchinson Edgar, *Has God Not Chosen*, 49–50).

8. "In calling Jesus 'Lord' James reflects a practice found in very early Christian liturgical texts: 'Come, Lord Jesus!' (Rev 22:20) and 'Our Lord, come!' (1 Cor 16:22)" (Hartin, *James*, 50).

9. This resonates with what Paul says about the role of worship in the Jewish hope for resurrection in his speech to King Agrippa: "But now I stand being judged because of hope in the promise made by God to our ancestors, to which our twelve tribes, worshiping in earnestness night and day, hope to attain. Concerning this hope I am being accused by Jews, O king. Why is it judged unbelievable among you if God raises the dead?" (Acts 26:6–8). "The 'hope' of which Paul speaks is hope in the resurrection of the dead, as 24:15 and 26:8 make clear . . . Paul appeals to the daily cult of Yahweh in the Jerusalem Temple and argues that it makes no sense unless it is related to the hope of resurrection" (Fitzmyer, *Acts*, 756–57). "The tribes give constant worship to God for the hope of resurrection . . . Central to the hope is that God gives life to the

The designation "the twelve tribes" has both a literal and figurative dimension. Literally, it refers primarily to Jewish Christians, but not exclusive of Gentile believers, living geographically "in the diaspora" outside of Israel and among non-believers. Figuratively, it refers to all Christians, as the restored people of Israel living spiritually in a this-worldly, earthly "diaspora" characterized by mortality, who in hope are awaiting their final other-worldly, heavenly restoration with its promise of resurrection to eternal life. That "the twelve tribes" are immediately specified as "the ones in the diaspora" recognizes the difficulties of an audience who find themselves in a position in which they have not yet been fully restored to their promised homeland as "the twelve tribes" of God's chosen people.[10] It thus underscores their situation of waiting in hope for the final coming of the Lord Jesus Christ.[11]

---

dead. Central to the resurrection is the raising of Jesus. This act showed that God can perform resurrection. Through this resurrection Jesus was elevated to a position of authority at God's side. From this position Jesus offers salvation or judgment, with all people accountable to him (Acts 2:30–36; 10:40–43)" (Bock, *Acts*, 714). See also Peterson, *Acts*, 662–63.

10. "Whether intended literally or figuratively, the 'twelve tribes in the dispersion' is a designation that makes sense only within the framework of one specific set of texts and one shared story in the Mediterranean world. Readers who accept their status as recipients of this letter--in whatever age they are readers, it should be noted--accept also this designation and a place within that symbolic world: they *become*, for the purposes of this composition, the hoped-for restored Israel among the nations. Whoever receives the author's 'greetings' welcomes as well a self-definition as part of a spiritual Israel normed by the texts of Torah and living in service to God and the Lord Jesus Christ" (Johnson, *James*, 171–72). See also Jackson-McCabe, "Messiah Jesus," 726; Penner, *James and Eschatology*, 181–83. "The most important insight is to understand James as addressing several audiences existing in a similar social and religious setting of the Jewish diaspora. The difficult social and religious context which was the Jewish diaspora called forth the need for encouragement of social and religious solidarity" (Lockett, *Purity*, 75–76).

11. "'The twelve tribes in the Diaspora' implies the chosenness and unity of God's people and, in the link with the author as 'slave of God and of the Lord Jesus Christ' in the first part of 1.1, probably should also be seen as asserting the decisive importance of Jesus and the movement associated with him in this context of the special status of God's people. The use of this appellation is also very likely to have been influenced by the sense of eschatological restoration and the fulfilment of God's promises to Israel in the early Christian movement" (Hutchinson Edgar, *Has God Not Chosen*, 104). "[C]ountless first-century Jews were desperately looking for the full return from exile, the restoration of the tribes, and—the point of it all—the establishment of proper

The audience are to hear the declaration of "joyful greetings" that introduces this epistolary homily as coming not from James alone but from James as the servant authorized to speak on behalf of God and of the Lord Jesus Christ (1:1). As a worshiping assembly gathered together to hear this epistolary homily, the audience are to begin to experience the joy of a greeting that ultimately comes from a divine source. The Greek term χαίρειν, normally translated as simply "greetings" but literally meaning "to rejoice," is here translated as "joyful greetings," making explicit the greeting's connotation of "joy" in order to facilitate an appreciation for the wordplay with the directive for the audience to "consider it all joy [χαράν]" (1:2), which immediately follows the greeting.[12]

Affectionately addressed by James as "my brothers" (1:2), the audience are to regard themselves as fellow "servants" fraternally linked to James, a "servant" of God and of the Lord Jesus Christ.[13] The brotherly status the audience share with James facilitates their reception from him of instructions regarding their "service," as a worshiping fraternal community, of God and of the Lord Jesus Christ. As members of "the twelve tribes, the ones in the diaspora" (1:1), the audience are to "consider it all joy" whenever they "tumble into teeming temptations" (1:2). The striking alliteration of "tumble into teeming temptations" (πειρασμοῖς περιπέσητε ποικίλοις) provokes their attention with a perplexing paradox that begs for further explanation, even as it acknowledges the difficulties they face living "in the diaspora" among non-believers.[14]

James then begins to give the explanation for the joy of the audience whenever they fall into numerous temptations. The audience may be joyful "knowing," not just intellectually but experientially, that this

---

worship" (Perrin, *Jesus the Temple*, 184).

12. "The infinitive χαίρειν ('to rejoice') is a conventional epistolary greeting" (Johnson, *James*, 168). "James deliberately employs this brief greeting to create a connection with χαράν (joy) in the following verse. This literary device of catchphrases occurs frequently and develops the flow of the letter. It is a clear illustration of the writer's literary ability" (Hartin, *James*, 51).

13. As McCartney (*James*, 85) points out, in NT letters the term "brothers" (ἀδελφοί) is used generally to mean "fellow Christians," both male and female.

14. "[T]he word 'Diaspora' calls attention to the suffering of a people cut off from social and religious support systems. The LXX uses the word to locate God's people in a world of conflict for their spiritual testing and refinement" (Wall, *Community*, 42).

testing of their faith, that is, their trust in and fidelity toward God and the Lord Jesus Christ (1:1), produces "endurance [ὑπομονήν]" (1:3). Such "endurance" refers to not just their passive patience but their active resistance to temptations.[15]

The audience are to allow the endurance that the testing of their faith "produces" or "works [κατεργάζεται]" (1:3) to have or to yield its perfect "work" (ἔργον), with the wordplay underlining the connection between faith and the "work" that faith "works" or produces (1:4a).[16] In a continuation of the chain-like repetition of key terms, the audience are to let endurance, the endurance that the testing of their faith produces or works (1:3), have its "perfect" work, that is, work its perfection, so that they may be "perfect" and complete, lacking in nothing (1:4).

The word "perfect" (τέλειος) carries connotations not only of maturity through growth but of completeness or wholeness within a context of both cultic and moral or ethical worship acceptable to God. In the biblical tradition a sacrifice to be worthily used in worship had to be "perfect" in the sense of being whole and integral, without any defects.[17] This notion of being "perfect" for worship acceptable to God was also applied to the character of human beings in their relationship to God. The ethical perfection or integrity of their moral behavior could be considered as worship pleasing to God.[18] And being "perfect" or

---

15. On "endurance," McCartney (*James*, 87) notes, "The Greek term thus has a more active character than the English word 'patience,' which connotes passivity." "ὑπομονή is more than patience, though it does contain that element of passive staying power... The component of steadfastness under trial and a persistent determination to win through to the end is marked as believers yield their lives to God and remain faithful in anticipation of their reward" (Martin, *James*, 15–16).

16. "The term [κατεργάζεται] sets up the use of ἔργον in the next line. More significantly, the construction shows from the start of the composition how James characteristically connects 'faith' and its 'work/deed/product,' namely as the effective development and expression of faith itself" (Johnson, *James*, 178).

17. E.g., the Passover sacrifice had to be a "perfect" (τέλειον) sheep (LXX Exod 12:5; on this as a sacrifice, see Wis 18:9). See also Judg 20:26; 21:4. "Only what was whole or complete could be offered to God. Here appears the essence of the concept of perfection: a being that conforms to its original makeup; its wholeness or completeness" (Hartin, *James*, 72).

18. E.g., "Noah was a just man; being perfect (τέλειος) in his generation, Noah pleased God" (LXX Gen 6:9; cf. Sir 44:17). "One who is τέλειος is one who is whole,

complete for proper ethical worship often included the originally cultic notion of being pure, that is, without any defect, defilement, or contamination from things profane or unholy.[19] In order for the audience to be "perfect" for worship pleasing to God (1:4), then, they must not allow themselves to be defiled or contaminated by the unholy "diaspora" in which they find themselves (1:1).

That the audience may be "perfect" is further elaborated and reinforced by their being "complete" and "lacking in nothing" (1:4) that they need to offer worship pleasing to God.[20] As fellow servants, along with James, of God and of the Lord Jesus Christ (1:1a), the audience, as a worshiping assembly, may rejoice in knowing that the many temptations they must endure ultimately render them "perfect" for worship pleasing to God (1:2-4). Being "perfect and complete, lacking in nothing" will thus place them in a position of being worshipers pleasing to God, properly prepared for the fulfillment of their restoration as "the twelve tribes" at the final coming of the Lord Jesus Christ (1:1).

The focus on the audience as a whole shifts to a focus on each individual within the audience as a worshiping assembly. With a continuation of the chain-like repetition of key terms, James moves from the need for the audience to be "lacking" (λειπόμενοι) in nothing (1:4b) to the possibility of anyone of them "lacking" (λείπεται) in wisdom (1:5a).

---

complete, perfect and so without blame" (Wevers, *Genesis*, 81). See also Deut 18:13; 2 Sam 22:26. According to Bauckham (*James*, 146), τέλειος "can mean both moral integrity and the unblemished wholeness of a sacrifice offered in the Temple."

19. "For him [James] the concept of τέλειος embraces a search for *wholeness* as an individual and as a community *in relationship to the one God* who *guides them through the Torah*. The cultic origin of τέλειος remains essential to this understanding of perfection. In expressing his understanding of τέλειος James relies heavily on the fundamental notions of purity and holiness within his own society, notions he owes to his Jewish heritage . . . Purity rules are designed to indicate how to have and maintain access to God. They set the individual and the community off from the wider society (emphases original)" (Hartin, *James*, 73). "[O]ne cannot properly understand James's concern for perfection without first understanding James's concern for purity from the world" (Lockett, *Purity*, 25). See also Elliott, "Holiness-Wholeness," 71-81.

20. "The combination of 'perfect' with the word for 'complete' (ὁλόκληρος) suggests another dimension to the imagery: sacrifice. Offerings that in the OT were acceptable to God had to be perfect and whole, that is, without defect" (McCartney, *James*, 88).

A lack of the moral attribute of wisdom would be a defect preventing one from being "perfect and complete" (1:4b) for the ethical worship that is pleasing to God. And so James, a "servant" (1:1) within a context of worship, serves his audience as a worshiping assembly by instructing them with regard to prayer: If anyone is lacking wisdom, he should perform a prayer of petition and "ask" (αἰτείτω) from the God who gives to all unreservedly, indeed not reproaching for such asking, and it will be given to him (1:5). This implies that every member of the audience needs wisdom from God in order to be perfect for ethical worship (cf. Wis 9:6; Prov 2:6). But what, more precisely, such wisdom entails for the audience remains to be heard.[21]

The exhortation for a prayer of petition—an instruction regarding worship—in which the individual is to "ask" (αἰτείτω) for wisdom from God (1:5) progresses to the exhortation to "ask" (αἰτείτω) in "faith [πίστει]" (1:6a), as the testing of "faith" (πίστεως) through temptations (1:3) renders the audience "perfect and complete" for such worship (1:4). The one who asks in faith, lacking in "nothing" (μηδενί) as one fit for proper worship (1:4b), should ask, correspondingly, disputing "nothing" (μηδέν) regarding the wise ways of God, for the one who disputes with God detracts from the undivided focus of proper worship, becoming "like a wave of the sea blown and driven about by the wind" (1:6b).[22]

Such a person who prays without a singularly focused and wholehearted faith (1:6) must not expect to receive anything from the Lord (1:7). At this point the term "Lord," as shared by God and Jesus Christ, begins to function with a double meaning for the audience. It refers, first of all, to the "Lord" God who unreservedly gives to all who pray for wisdom (1:5). But it also refers to the "Lord" Jesus Christ (1:1a), the only previous explicit occurrence of the term in the letter. Thus, the one

---

21. According to Hartin (*James*, 59) wisdom is "knowing how to conduct life in conformity with God's Law. Wisdom is practical, not theoretical." See also Verseput, "Wisdom," 691–707.

22. For the meaning of "dispute" rather than "doubt" for διακρινόμενος in 1:6, see Spitaler, "Dispute with God," 560–79, who concludes that "at the beginning of his letter, James portrays a 'disputer' quarreling with God. This particular conflict anticipates and complements accounts of interpersonal, social controversies that James addresses later in the letter" (579).

who prays without proper faith will receive nothing from the Lord God presently and nothing from the Lord Jesus Christ at his final coming.[23]

That such a person is "double-minded" and "unstable in all the ways of him" (1:8) elaborates and reinforces the thoroughly divided and misguided focus of his being "like a wave of the sea blown and driven about by the wind" (1:6).[24] And that such a person is unstable in all "the" (ταῖς) ways of him contradicts his being a fellow servant of God and of the Lord Jesus Christ as a member of the audience, the worshiping assembly, designated as "the" (ταῖς) twelve tribes, "the" (ταῖς) ones in the diaspora (1:1).[25]

1:9–10a (B): Let the Rich One Boast in His Lowliness

The audience continue to be exhorted as a worshiping assembly: "Let the humble brother boast in his exaltedness, but the rich one in his lowliness" (1:9–10a). The double exhortation with a third-person singular imperative regarding worship, "let him ask" (αἰτείτω) from God (1:5, 6), continues with the next exhortation in the third person singular imperative, "let him boast [καυχάσθω]" (1:9). The dependency upon God of anyone in the audience who lacks wisdom to ask God for it in prayer (1:5) progresses quite naturally to the dependency upon God of a "humble" or "lowly" (ταπεινός) brother (1:9) in the audience.[26]

---

23. On this "dynamic oneness" regarding the divine lordship shared by the Lord Jesus and the Lord God in the letters of Paul, see Nicholson, *Dynamic Oneness*.

24. Wypadlo, "Von Gott," 74–92. "James 1:6–8 is not describing someone whose faith is in doubt, so much as a fair weather friend, who will distance himself from or object to God, ultimately indicating how unstable (1:8) and unreliable he truly is" (Batten, *Friendship*, 114).

25. That these are the only occurrences of ταῖς in this sub-unit (1:1–8) enhances this connection.

26. "The principal meaning of ταπείνωσις is not socio-economically poor; rather the word means humble, of lowly standing, in a servile or subservient position. In general, a humble or servile position would imply a lack of material resources on the part of such a person, but lack of possessions is not the decisive feature of the term as an indicator of social standing. This sense of humble status predominates in the LXX use of the term, where it is also used of submission to God" (Hutchinson Edgar, *Has God Not Chosen*, 147).

The term "boast" or "glory" refers to proudly and joyfully celebrating now what one can confidently expect to receive from God in the future when God completes his plan of salvation. Such a celebratory declaration may appropriately take place as part of the liturgical worship of the assembly. The joy in such "boasting" continues and develops the joy the audience are to experience when falling into the temptations that test their faith (1:2–3), one of the causes for their humble or lowly condition. The exhortation thus invites each member of the audience to become a brother with a humble attitude who may "boast" or "glory" in the worshiping assembly presently in view of the future reversal of his lowliness into his "exaltedness" (ὕψει) from God (1:9).[27]

In ironic contrast to the boasting of a humble brother in his exaltedness (1:9), a "rich one" (πλούσιος), whether a brother in the assembly or not,[28] may boast not, surprisingly, in his wealth but only in his "lowliness" or "humbleness" (1:10a). In other words, a rich person, despite his present socioeconomic wealth, may only boast or glory in his present

---

27. With regard to "boasting" in the NT, as Spicq ("καυχάομαι," 2.298–99) states, "The religious meaning is predominant. It originates with the OT theology and expresses a fundamental conviction of the new faith: all exaltation of the creature by virtue of its qualities, advantages, or spiritual or temporal successes, partakes of the character of a lie. Everything has been given by God, so to God alone belong the praise and the glory. The emphasis is on this exclusivity of καυχάομαι . . . So one 'glories' not only at being destined for a blessed eternity but also in all that leads to it and allows it to be obtained: tribulation, weakness, infirmities." "Sometimes rendered 'boast,' it [καυχάομαι] signifies either the feelings or the declarations of pride and joy that result when someone or something that is dear to one is recognized and honored by others (see BDAG 536). The term therefore can be used in either a good sense ('delight in, be proud of, rejoice over') or a bad sense ('brag about'). The determining factor is whether the cause of the delight is appropriate" (McCartney, *James* 96). "Our author is looking at the situation with the thought that eschatological blessings await (and are presently the possession of) God's humble servants. The readers of James can enjoy their present 'exalted' status as well as anticipate their future glorious inheritance" (Martin, *James*, 25). According to Martin (26), here "the verb καυχᾶσθαι is used with an eschatological overtone to sound a warning of impending judgment."

28. That the word "brother" (ἀδελφός) in 1:9 is not explicitly repeated, but could be implied in 1:10a, just as "let him boast" in 1:9 is implied in 1:10a, facilitates the ambiguity at this point. But the contrast strongly suggests to the audience the inappropriateness and undesirability for a brother to be a "rich one." See Stulac, "Who Are 'the Rich'?," 89–102; Williams, "Of Rags and Riches," 273–82; Penner, *James and Eschatology*, 208n3.

lowliness before God in view of God's future reversal of the lofty status of his richness into his ultimate lowliness. Ironically, the "humble" (ταπεινός) brother will be exalted by God, but the elevated status of a rich person will be lowered by God to a condition of "humbleness" (ταπεινώσει).

1:10b (C): For Like a Flower

The reason the rich one is to boast in his lowliness (1:10a) begins to be explained with the words, "for like a flower" (1:10b). The audience are to appreciate how a rich person can be compared to a wild "flower" or "blossom" (ἄνθος). Just as such a flower, with its beautiful color and fragrance, stands out from the vegetation surrounding it, so a rich person, with his or her attractive material wealth, stands out from the rest of the population.

1:10c (D): Of Grass He Will Pass Away

The comparison regarding a rich person continues with the assertion that like a flower (1:10b) "of grass he will pass away" (1:10c). With the phrase, "like a flower of grass" (ὡς ἄνθος χόρτου), the implied audience, an ideal audience presupposed to be familiar with the Greek scriptures of Israel, are to recognize the allusion to the only OT occurrence of this phrase in LXX Isa 40:6: "all flesh is grass (χόρτος) and all glory of mankind like a flower of grass [ὡς ἄνθος χόρτου]." The allusion enables the audience to appreciate how a rich person, corresponding to "all glory of mankind," can often stand out from other people, the "grass" which is "all flesh," "like a flower of grass."

But that the rich person "will pass away" (παρελεύσεται) like a flower of grass further explains why the rich person can boast only in his lowliness (1:10a). His future destiny is the lowliness of "passing away." In the eschatological context in which James and his audience are looking forward to participation in their full and final restoration to life with God as "the twelve tribes" (1:1), that the rich person "will pass

The Letter of James

away" refers not just to his inevitable physical mortality but to his "passing away" from eschatological life with God at the final judgment.[29]

1:11a (E): For the Sun Rises with Its Heat

The future passing away of the rich person like a flower of grass continues to be explained with the clause, "for the sun rises with its heat" (1:11a). Following upon the eschatological overtone of the assertion that the rich person "will pass away" (1:10c), that the sun rises with its "heat" (καύσωνι) adds to the eschatological context here. This heat has its ultimate source in the God who created the sun to rise with its heat, and the audience are undoubtedly familiar with the traditional biblical associations of heat, fire, and burning with God's eternal condemnation in the final judgment.[30]

1:11b (D'): And Dries Up the Grass

What the sun that rises with its heat (1:11a) effects begins to be described: "and dries up the grass" (1:11b). At this point, after the unparalleled central E element of this chiastic unit (1:11a), the audience experience a pivot of parallels from "of grass" (χόρτου) in the D element (1:10c) to the "grass" (χόρτον) in the D' element (1:11b). In accord with the allusion to LXX Isa 40:7, in which the "grass" (χόρτος) correspond-

---

29. On how the allusion to Isaiah 40 contributes to the eschatological horizon here, see Penner, *James and Eschatology*, 204–10. He states that "this oft-cited Old Testament text is almost always understood in an eschatological sense, particularly pertaining to the judgment of God and his reversal of the present status of his people" (204). "The verb παρέρχομαι (pass away) is used by Jesus to refer to the passing away of heaven and earth (Matt. 5:18 [=Luke 16:17]; Matt. 24:34–35 and pars.) and thus is associated with judgment (cf. 2 Pet. 3:10) and the change of the ages (2 Cor. 5:17)" (McCartney, *James*, 97n8). See also Sand, "παρέρχομαι," 3:38–39.

30. In Heb 6:8 earth that bears forth thorns and thistles is rejected and near a curse, so that its end or destiny is a "burning" (καῦσιν), an image of divine judgment (see Heil, *Hebrews*, 149). In 2 Pet 3:10 on the Day of the Lord the heavens "will pass away" (παρελεύσονται; cf. Jas 1:10c) with a roar and the elements will be dissolved by "burning" (καυσούμενα; see also 2 Pet 3:12). Green (*Jude and 2 Peter*, 330) refers to "repeated affirmations in the biblical literature regarding the final destruction of the earth by fire."

ing to people (40:6) "is dried up" (ἐξηράνθη), that the sun "dries up" (ἐξήρανεν) the "grass" (1:11b) explains why the rich person, who often stands out from the rest of people like a flower, nevertheless "will pass away" (1:10c).

1:11c (C'): Its Flower Falls Away and the Beauty of Its Appearance Is Destroyed

The sun that rises with its heat (1:11a) dries up the grass (1:11b) "and its flower falls away and the beauty of its appearance is destroyed" (1:11c). At this point the audience hear a progression, via the chiastic parallels, from "like a flower [ἄνθος]" in the C element (1:10b) to "its flower [ἄνθος] falls away" in the C' element (1:11c). In accord with the allusion to LXX Isa 40:7, in which "the flower [ἄνθος] falls away [ἐξέπεσεν]," that the "flower" of the grass "falls away" (ἐξέπεσεν) here (1:11c) further explains why the rich person, who is like a "flower" (1:10b), will pass away (1:10c). And a consequence of the grass's flower falling away is that the beauty that the flower lends to the grass's appearance is destroyed (1:11c). So also the beauty that a rich person, who is like a flower, exhibits for people is destined to be destroyed. Since the verb "destroyed" (ἀπώλετο) often has an eschatological sense, the implication for the audience is that the rich person is destined for the final destruction of eternal death at God's last judgment.[31]

1:11d (B'): So Also the Rich One in His Pursuits Will Die Out

The comparison of a rich person with a flower of grass that will pass away (1:10) is completed: "so also the rich one in his pursuits will die out" (1:11d). At this point the audience experience a progression, via the chiastic parallels, from the "rich one" (πλούσιος) who is to boast in his lowliness in the B element (1:9-10a) to the "rich one" (πλούσιος) who will die out in his pursuits in the B' element (1:11d). That a rich person

---

31. As noted by Penner (*James and Eschatology*, 148n39), "the verb ἀπόλλυμι, used in 1.11, occurs again in 4.12 in a strongly eschatological context, and is frequently used with this eschatological sense in the synoptic gospels, e.g. Mk 8.35; Mt. 10.28, 39; also Jude 5."

"in his pursuits" (ἐν ταῖς πορείαις αὐτοῦ) will die out associates him with a double-minded man, unstable "in all his ways [ἐν πάσαις ταῖς ὁδοῖς αὐτοῦ]" (1:8), who may not suppose that he will receive anything from the Lord (1:7), either in prayer (1:5-6) or at the last judgment.[32] And that the rich person in his pursuits with regard to wealth "will die out" (μαρανθήσεται) makes explicit the implications of the series of preceding verbs—"will pass away" (1:10c), "dries up" (1:11b), "falls away" (1:11c), and "is destroyed" (1:11c)—reinforcing the audience's realization that a rich person is destined for eternal death rather than eternal life.[33]

1:12-16 (A'): A Man Who Endures Temptation Will Receive the Crown of Life

The audience hear the A' element (1:12-16) of this chiastic unit as a chiastic pattern in itself:

a) Blessed is a man who endures temptation, for having become tested, he will receive the crown of life that he (the Lord) promised to those who *love* him (1:12).

b) Let no one being *tempted* say, "I am being *tempted* by God" (1:13a),

---

32. "The occurrence of ὁδός at the end of 1.5-8 and πορεία at the end of 1.9-11 may be a conscious linking device on the part of the writer. The parallel would therefore be between the 'double-minded person' who is unstable in all their 'ways' and the rich individual who will perish in the midst of their 'ways'" (ibid., 207).

33. "But what is it that happens to the rich person? Μαραίνω is particularly fitting in this context, for it refers to both the withering of plants and the death of persons. Originally, then, the proverb meant that the rich person would die and all his deeds would crumble, leaving no trace of his former exaltation. Yet James implies something more . . . The rich will be scorched in the sun's heat, a scorching indicative of God's judgment which will follow and turn the 'fading away' into an eternal fact" (Davids, *James*, 78). "The verb μαρανθήσεται connotes the withering of flowers and the death of persons. James relentlessly connects the fate of the flower to the fate of the rich person. Both can be flourishing one day and gone the next. The eschatological judgment of God will cause the rich to perish . . . Thus, the rich man's 'humiliation' is the judgment he will suffer (v 10)" (Martin, *James*, 27-28).

b′) for *God* is *untempted* of evil things, and he himself *tempts* no one. But each one is *tempted* by his own desire, being dragged away and enticed. When the desire conceives, it gives birth to sin, and the sin having been brought to completion, brings birth to death (1:13b-15).

a′) Do not be led astray, my brothers *beloved* (1:16).

At the center of this chiastic sub-unit the audience experience a pivot of parallels involving the only occurrences in this sub-unit of expressions for "tempting" and the term "God." They hear a progression from "being tempted [πειραζόμενος]" and "being tempted [πειράζομαι] by God [θεοῦ]" in the b) sub-element (1:13a) to "God [θεός] is untempted [ἀπείραστός]," "tempts [πειράζει] no one" (1:13b), and "each one is tempted [πειράζεται]" (1:14) in the b′) sub-element. They then experience a progression of parallels involving the only occurrences in this sub-unit of expressions for "love." "To those who love [ἀγαπῶσιν] him" in the a) sub-element (1:12) progresses to "my brothers beloved [ἀγαπητοί]" in the a′) sub-element (1:16).

At this point the audience experience a number of parallel progressions from the A (1:1-8) to the A′ element (1:12-16) of this chiastic unit. "Of God (θεοῦ)" (1:1) and "the God [θεοῦ] who gives" (1:5) progress to "being tempted by God [θεοῦ]" and "God [θεός] is untempted" (1:13). The address to "my brothers [ἀδελφοί μου]" (1:2) progresses to the address to "my brothers [ἀδελφοί μου] beloved" (1:16). "Temptations [πειρασμοῖς]" (1:2) progresses to "temptation [πειρασμόν]" 1:12), "no one being tempted [πειραζόμενος]," "being tempted [πειράζομαι] by God," "God is untempted [ἀπείραστός]," "tempts [πειράζει] no one" (1:13), and "each one is tempted [πειράζεται]" (1:14).

"The testing (δοκίμιον) of your faith" (1:3) progresses to "having become tested [δόκιμος]" (1:12). "Produces endurance [ὑπομονήν]" (1:3) and "let endurance [ὑπομονή] have its perfect work" (1:4) progress to "endures [ὑπομένει] temptation" (1:12). And "a double-minded man [ἀνήρ]" (1:8) "will receive" (λήμψεται) nothing from the Lord (1:7) progresses to "a man [ἀνήρ] who endures temptation will receive [λήμψεται] the crown of life" (1:12).

Each member of the audience is persuaded to endure temptation in order to be "blessed" by God (1:12a). That James pronounces this divine blessedness with the authority of a servant speaking on behalf of God and of the Lord Jesus Christ (1:1) enhances its significance and attractiveness for the audience. The connotation of joy that can be celebrated within the liturgical gathering, as expressed with the address of "joyful greetings!" (1:1) and the exhortation for the audience to consider it all "joy" whenever they "tumble into teeming temptations [πειρασμοῖς]" (1:2), continues with the declaration that "blessed" is one who endures "temptation" (πειρασμόν).[34] Recalling that the "testing" (δοκίμιον) of their faith produces "endurance [ὑπομονήν]" (1:3), the "endurance" (ὑπομονή) that is to have its perfect work (1:4), each member of the audience is to be one who "endures" (ὑπομένει) temptation, and thus one who has become "tested [δόκιμος]" (1:12).

As the audience have heard, a double-minded "man [ἀνήρ]" (1:8) "will receive" (λήμψεταί) nothing from the Lord through prayer (1:7). But blessed is each member of the audience as he or she identifies with a "man" (ἀνήρ) who endures temptation, for having become tested, he "will receive" (λήμψεται) the crown of life that the Lord promised to those who love him (1:12). Enduring temptation and becoming tested thus amounts to ethical worship, the equivalent of a prayer that "will receive" an answer in terms of being divinely "blessed" with the "crown of life."

The audience are to realize that this triumphant "crown" of eschatological "life" represents the goal of the "perfect work" that their endurance is to have, so that they may be perfect and complete, lacking in nothing (1:4). They are to appreciate that this eschatological "crown of life" that they will receive at the last judgment stands in dramatic contrast to the final fate of the rich one, who "will pass away" (1:10c), be "destroyed" (1:11c), and ultimately "will die out" (1:11d). They will receive this crown of life that "he," that is, the Lord (cf. 1:7)—both the

---

34. The assonance in Greek among the terms "joyful greetings" (χαίρειν), "joy" (χαράν), and "blessed" (μακάριος) facilitates this connection. "[T]he word *blessed* does not mean quite the same as the English word *happy*. The latter refers mostly to a present emotional state, the former to the state of relationship with God, a 'wholeness,' as it were, that while truly a present reality, has its primary manifestation in the future" (McCartney, *James*, 100).

Lord God and the Lord Jesus Christ—promised to those who love him (1:12), a love to be manifested in and through both their liturgical and ethical worship.[35]

Whenever the audience "tumble into teeming temptations [πειρασμοῖς]" (1:2), no one who is being "tempted" (πειραζόμενος) among them should say, "I am being tempted [πειράζομαι] by God [θεοῦ]" (1:13a). The audience are to avoid the way of thinking of such an assertion, as it contradicts the exhortation for anyone of them who is lacking wisdom to ask from the "God" (θεοῦ) who gives to all unreservedly (1:5), and to ask in faith, disputing nothing with regard to God (1:6). For as James, a servant authorized by "God" (θεοῦ) himself (1:1), maintains, "God" (θεός) indeed is "untempted" (ἀπείραστός) of evil things, and he himself "tempts" (πειράζει) no one (1:13b).[36] The audience are to acknowledge that, rather than being tempted by God, each of them is "tempted" (πειράζεται) by his own desire, being dragged away and enticed (1:14), especially, in accord with the context, by the lure of the beautiful appearance of wealth (1:10-11).

With the imagery of giving birth James reveals the ultimate outcome of being tempted, dragged away, and enticed by one's own desire (1:14). When the desire "conceives," it "gives birth" to sin, and the sin, having been brought to completion, shockingly "brings birth" to death

---

35. "This future manifestation of wholeness and blessedness is here called the 'crown of life,' the result of successfully enduring persecution. It is the eschatological victory wreath bestowed upon those who are faithful in the love of God . . . The OT and much other Jewish literature use the word *life* to refer to the fullness of human destiny in personal relationship to God, particularly eschatological life" (ibid., 101). "The promise of the reward is made 'to those who love God.' The *Shema Israel* (Deut 6:4-5) expressed the foundation of Israel's faith in and relationship with God. To love God demonstrates that one is in the covenant relationship and will carry out God's will through obedience to the Torah" (Hartin, *James*, 90).

36. "The basic point is clear enough: God has nothing to do with evil" (Johnson, *James*, 193). "James's inclusion of the word 'himself' here is a way of acknowledging that although God is sovereign over the acts of his creatures, and although God may permit temptation and even use it in the believer's life, God himself is not the one who tempts to evil (which would make God the author of sin). God tests by allowing and even ordaining external pressure, but he himself does not try to lure people into sinning. . . . God does not tempt to evil, because to do so would be contrary to his character: he cannot himself be tempted by evil, and so he cannot be tempted to tempt" (McCartney, *James*, 105).

(1:15).³⁷ The sin "having been brought to its completion or perfection" (ἀποτελεσθεῖσα) ironically contrasts the "perfect" (τέλειον) work that the endurance of the audience is to have, so that they may be "perfect" (τέλειοι) and complete, lacking in nothing (1:4).³⁸

That sin given birth by desire brings birth to eschatological "death" (1:15) stands in striking contrast to the crown of eschatological "life," which the one who endures temptation will receive from God (1:12). This destiny of eschatological "death" thus brings to a climactic conclusion the previous references to the final destiny of the rich one—he "will pass away" (1:10c), be "destroyed" (1:11c), and "will die out" (1:11d). Consequently, the audience are not to be "led astray" (1:16a), especially by the alluring attraction of wealth, which ultimately leads to eternal death. Previously addressed as "my brothers [ἀδελφοί μου]" (1:2), the audience are now addressed as "my brothers beloved [ἀδελφοί μου ἀγαπητοί]" (1:16b).³⁹ That they are "beloved" not only by James but by the God who numbers them among "the twelve tribes" (1:1) of God's chosen and beloved people is to appropriately motivate them in return to "love" (ἀγαπῶσιν) the God who promises them the crown of eschatological life (1:12).

Summary on 1:1–16

As a "servant" who has been divinely authorized by both God and the Lord Jesus Christ, James addresses and thus also "serves" his audience, gathered together as a worshiping assembly to hear his epistolary homily. The address situates the letter's audience, characterized as "the twelve tribes, the ones in the diaspora," within a context of looking forward in

---

37. "The imagery is obviously shocking" (Johnson, *James*, 194).

38. Wilson, "Sin as Sex," 147–68. "When the human will yields to desire and gives credence to the lie, it gives birth to sin. And sin then grows up and 'brings forth' or 'births' death (using another word for 'giving birth,' which again manifests James's sharp irony). Just as endurance can achieve a 'perfect work,' fully equipping the believer for life (1:4), so sin, when it achieves its maturity or 'perfection' yields its natural fruit, death" (McCartney, *James*, 107).

39. "The address is an amplification of the form in 1:2, a characteristic of the homiletic style of the work. It shows that the author still considers himself addressing Christians; they have not yet left the faith" (Davids, *James*, 86).

hope to the final completion of their restoration as God's people, which would include their participation in the eternal life of the risen Lord Jesus Christ (1:1). As fellow servants, along with James, of God and of the Lord Jesus Christ, the audience may rejoice in knowing that the many temptations they must endure ultimately render them "perfect" for worship pleasing to God (1:2–4). Being "perfect and complete, lacking in nothing" will thus place them in a position of being worshipers pleasing to God, properly prepared for the fulfillment of their restoration as "the twelve tribes" at the final coming of the Lord Jesus Christ.

If anyone in the audience is lacking wisdom, he should perform a prayer of petition and ask from the God who gives to all unreservedly, indeed not reproaching for such asking, and it will be given to him (1:5). This implies that every member of the audience needs wisdom from God in order to be perfect for ethical worship. The one who asks in faith, lacking in nothing as one fit for proper worship (1:4), should ask disputing nothing regarding the wise ways of God, for the one who disputes with God detracts from the undivided focus of proper worship, becoming "like a wave of the sea blown and driven about by the wind" (1:6). A person who prays without a singularly focused and wholehearted faith must not expect to receive anything from the Lord (1:7)—either the Lord God or the Lord Jesus Christ—since such a person is double-minded and unstable in all his ways (1:8).

The exhortation to let the humble brother boast in his exaltedness invites each member of the audience to become a brother with a humble attitude who may boast or glory in the worshiping assembly presently in view of the future reversal of his lowliness into his exaltedness from God (1:9). But a rich person, despite his present socioeconomic wealth, may only boast or glory in his present lowliness before God in view of God's future reversal of the lofty status of his richness into his ultimate lowliness (1:10a). That a rich person "in his pursuits" will die out associates him with a double-minded man, unstable "in all his ways" (1:8), who may not suppose that he will receive anything from the Lord (1:7), either in prayer (1:5–6) or at the last judgment. And that the rich person in his pursuits with regard to wealth will pass away (1:10c), will be dried up (1:11b), will fall away (1:11c), will be destroyed (1:11c), and will die out (1:11d) reinforces the audience's realization that a rich person is destined for eternal death rather than eternal life.

Although a double-minded man (1:8) will receive nothing from the Lord through prayer (1:7), blessed by God is each member of the audience who identifies with a man enduring temptation. For having become tested, he will receive the crown of eschatological life that the Lord promised to those who love him (1:12), a love to be manifested by both their liturgical and ethical worship. The audience are to acknowledge that, rather than being tempted by God (1:13), each of them is tempted by his own desire, being dragged away and enticed (1:14), especially by the lure of the beautiful appearance, the appealing "flower," of wealth (1:10–11).

That sin given birth by desire brings birth to eschatological "death" (1:15) stands in striking contrast to the crown of eschatological "life," which the one who endures temptation will receive from God (1:12). This destiny of eschatological death thus brings to a climactic conclusion the previous references to the final destruction of the rich one (1:10–11). Consequently, the audience are not to be led astray (1:16a), especially by the alluring attraction of wealth, which ultimately leads to eternal death. That they are brothers "beloved" not only by James, but by the God who numbers them among the twelve tribes (1:1) of God's chosen and beloved people, is to appropriately motivate them in return to "love" the God who promises them the crown of eternal life (1:12). This first unit, then, fittingly introduces the main theme of the letter—to exhort its audience to a liturgical and ethical worship by which they are to live now and for all eternity.

James 1:17–27
Be Slow to Speak Not Deceiving the Heart for Useless Worship (B)

Worship to save your souls is to care for orphans
and widows in their affliction

A ¹⁷ Every good giving and every perfect gift from above is descending from the *Father* of lights, within whom there is no variation or shadow of turning.

    B ¹⁸ Having decided, he brought birth to us by a *word* of truth that we may be a kind of firstfruits of his creatures. ¹⁹ Know, my brothers beloved, let every person be quick to hear, slow to speak, slow to anger, ²⁰ for the anger of a man does not work the righteousness of God. ²¹ Therefore, putting away all filthiness and excess of evil, in humility welcome the implanted *word* that is able to save your souls. ²²ᵃ *Become doers* of the *word* and not only *hearers*,

    C ²²ᵇ deluding yourselves.

    B′ ²³ For if anyone is a *hearer* of the *word* but not a *doer*, this one is like a man observing the appearance of his birth in a mirror. ²⁴ For he observes himself and goes away and immediately forgets what sort he was. ²⁵ But one peering into the perfect law, the one of freedom, and persevering, having *become* not a *hearer* of forgetfulness but a *doer* of work, this one will be blessed in his *doing*.

A′ ²⁶ If anyone thinks he is religious, not bridling his tongue but deceiving his heart, the religion of this one is useless. ²⁷ Religion pure and undefiled before the God and *Father* is this: to care for orphans and widows in their affliction, to keep oneself spotless from the world.[1]

Audience Response to 1:17–27

1:17 (A): Every Perfect Gift from Above Is Descending from the Father of Lights

The audience hear the first element of this chiastic unit as an assertion about the remarkable giving of God the Father: "Every good giving and every perfect gift from above is descending from the Father of lights, within whom there is no variation or shadow of turning" (1:17). That every good "giving" (δόσις) and every perfect "gift" (δώρημα) from above, that is, from the heavenly realm, is descending from God as the Father of lights resonates with the previous exhortation that if anyone in the audience is lacking wisdom, let him ask from the God who "gives" (διδόντος) to all unreservedly, indeed not reproaching, and "it will be given" (δοθήσεται) to him (1:5).

The audience are to realize that wisdom, as a "perfect" (τέλειον) gift coming from God above, is a "perfect" (τέλειον) work that makes them "perfect" (τέλειοι) and complete, lacking in nothing with regard to their worship of God (1:4).[2] With the divine gift of the wisdom of knowing that while a rich one's destiny is eternal death (1:10–11), one who endures temptation regarding wealth will receive the crown of eternal life (1:12), the audience are not to be led astray by the attraction of riches (1:16).

That God is referred to here as the "Father of lights" (1:17a), that is, of the celestial bodies that give forth light, like the sun, makes explicit the divine origin of the eternal destruction of a rich person, compared to a flower of grass dried up by the light and heat of the sun (1:11).[3]

---

1. For the establishment of Jas 1:17–27 as a chiasm, see the Introduction.
2. Poirier, "Symbols of Wisdom," 57–75.
3. "This Jewish circumlocution ('Father of lights') refers to God as the creator of

In contrast to a rich one, who like a flower of grass "will pass away [παρελεύσεται]" (1:10), within God as the Father of lights there is no "variation" (παραλλαγή), as he remains eternally unchanged (1:17b).

Sin is conceived by the desire especially for wealth and, "having been brought to completion" (ἀποτελεσθεῖσα), it "brings birth" (ἀποκύει) to eternal death (1:15). In contrast, every perfect gift from above comes "from" (ἀπό) the Father of lights, in whom there is no "shadow" (ἀποσκίασμα) of turning (1:17b), like a shadow caused by the turning of a celestial body.[4] The Father of lights remains eternally unchanged in his giving of perfect gifts from above.[5] The audience are thus to be attracted to and to deepen their appreciation for the perfect gifts given by the eternally unchanging Father of lights, especially the gift of the crown of eternal life that the one who endures temptation will receive (1:12), rather than be led astray by the temptation to become rich, which leads to eternal death (1:13–16).[6]

1:18–22a (B): Become Doers of the Word and Not Only Hearers

The audience hear the B element (1:18–22a) of this chiastic unit as a chiastic pattern in itself:

a) Having decided, he brought birth to us by a *word* of truth that we may be a kind of firstfruits of his creatures (1:18).

    b) Know, my brothers beloved, let every person be quick to hear, *slow* to speak (1:19a),

---

the stars, especially the sun and moon" (Hartin, *James*, 93).

4. The alliteration in the Greek terms facilitates these connections to be made by the audience.

5. "[J]ust as God does not vary or generate shadows, his gifts are not subject to variation or trickery. They do not turn into something else when received, and they, unlike human gifts, never contain traps or enticements" (McCartney, *James*, 109). "James has made a similar point about God earlier in the same section, claiming that God gives to all who ask him with a single, undivided, intent (v. 5). Indeed, the integrity and undividedness of God—in contrast to the duality and instability of man (cf. vv. 7–8)—is a key motif of the letter as a whole" (Moo, *James*, 79).

6. The language of divine constancy in Jas 1:17 refers to the unwavering character of God's faithfulness in answering prayers, according to Verseput ("James 1:17," 177–91).

b′) *slow* to anger, for the anger of a man does not work the righteousness of God (1:19b-20).

a′) Therefore, putting away all filthiness and excess of evil, in humility welcome the implanted *word* that is able to save your souls. Become doers of the *word* and not only hearers (1:21-22a).

At the center of this chiastic sub-unit the audience experience a pivot of parallels involving the only occurrences in James of the adjective "slow." They hear a progression from "slow [βραδύς] to speak" in the b) sub-element (1:19a) to "slow [βραδύς] to anger" in the b′) sub-element (1:19b-20). They then experience a progression of parallels involving the only occurrences in this sub-unit of the term "word." "He brought birth to us by a word [λόγῳ] of truth" in the a sub-element (1:18) progresses to "welcome the implanted word [λόγον]" (1:21) and "become doers of the word [λόγου]" (1:22a) in the a′) sub-element (1:21-22a).

When the audience hear that God as the Father of lights, having "decided" or "willed" (βουληθείς), brought birth to us by a word of truth (1:18a), they realize the immutable and definite character of this decision based upon God's unchangeableness (1:17). With the verb "brought birth to" (ἀπεκύησεν) they hear the transitional word that links this second unit (1:17-27) to the first unit (1:1-16), whose closing assertion that sin "brings birth to" (ἀποκύει) death (1:15) contains the only other occurrence in James of this verb. In contrast to the sin conceived by one's own desire, especially for wealth, that brings birth to eternal death, God as the Father of lights brought birth to us, with the implication that this is a divine birth enabling us to live a new and eternal life.[7]

This divine birth to a new life thus represents another "perfect gift" that comes from God's good giving (1:17). As among the twelve tribes of God's chosen people, and as fellow servants with James of God and of the Lord Jesus Christ (1:1), the audience are to appreciate that they were brought to birth for this eschatological life by God's "word of truth" to them, the gospel as the creative word of God that initially brought them to faith and that they continue to hear during their liturgical worship.[8]

---

7. Miller, "Can the 'Father of Lights' Give Birth?"; "Whereas in 1:15 the reference was to sin giving birth to death, here God gives birth to life" (Hartin, *James*, 93).

8. "Just as God deliberately brought forth the heavenly lights by a word (Gen. 1), so he brings forth believers by 'the word of truth' . . . In the NT this word of truth is

The audience, brought to birth by God for a new and eternal life, are to be "a kind of firstfruits [ἀπαρχήν] of his creatures" (1:18b). This resonates with the audience being "the twelve tribes" (1:1) of God's chosen people Israel, since Israel as a whole was designated as God's "firstborn" (Exod 4:22). In the biblical tradition the cultic term "firstfruits" referred to the first portion of a harvest specially chosen and set apart to be holy. The sacred firstfruits were offered and dedicated to God in worship. The hope of offering the firstfruits, as the part that represents the whole, was that a bountiful harvest of further fruit would follow. This cultic imagery of the audience as the firstfruits thus invites them to offer themselves in worship to the God who brought them to birth for eternal, eschatological life, so that more creatures of God will follow them into this divine life.[9]

Having been exhorted, as "my brothers beloved" (ἀδελφοί μου ἀγαπητοί), not to be led astray (1:16), the audience are now exhorted: "Know, my brothers beloved [ἀδελφοί μου ἀγαπητοί], let every person be quick to hear, slow to speak, slow to anger, for the anger of a man does not work the righteousness of God" (1:19-20). In the context this is an exhortation for every person in the audience to be quick to hear and thus to believe the word of God—the word of truth by which God brought them to birth for a new, eternal life (1:18), and the word of God they continue to hear in their liturgical worship.[10]

While everyone in the audience should be quick to hear the word of God, they should be slow to speak their own words, as this will help them to be slow in becoming angry with others. The audience are to

---

the gospel" (McCartney, *James*, 110).

9. "The noun ἀπαρχή is widely attested for 'beginning sacrifice' or for the 'first part of a sacrifice'" (Johnson, *James*, 198). "'Firstfruits' were the first harvest or finest produce that was set apart as an offering to God and was considered God's special possession (Exod. 23:19). The firstfruits offering sanctified the whole harvest . . . The term therefore is eschatological as well as cultic, and James's designation of believers as 'firstfruits' not only declares them to be holy, but also places them in the category of those who are already experiencing the full redemption that the rest of creation still awaits. A further implication of this is that the 'firstfruits' are the exemplars who reflect God's character to the world" (McCartney, *James*, 110-11).

10. "James is not just giving good advice for living; he has something specific in mind: being quick to hear 'the word of truth,' which is synonymous with believing it" (ibid., 115).

avoid anger, since anger does not work the righteousness of God—the right and just way of moral behavior that is pleasing to God. In other words, anger does not place them in a right relationship with God as those called to be obedient servants of God and of the Lord Jesus Christ (1:1).[11] That anger does not "work" (ἐργάζεται) the righteousness of God means that it contradicts the perfect "work" (ἔργον) that endurance is to have, the endurance that the testing of faith "produces" or "works out [κατεργάζεται]" (1:3), and that makes the audience perfect and complete for worship (1:4).

That the audience are to be "putting away all filthiness and excess of evil" (1:21a) develops the exhortation for them not to be led astray (1:16) by the desire, especially for wealth, that leads to sin and death (1:15). With its cultic connotations, putting away all "filthiness" (ῥυπαρίαν) and excess of evil would render the audience pure and clean for both their liturgical and ethical worship.[12]

In the humility involved in accepting the gracious gifts of God (1:17) and that stands in contrast to the anger that does not work the righteousness of God (1:20), the audience are to welcome the "implanted word" (1:21b), that is, God's "word of truth" by which God graciously gave them a new birth to eternal life (1:18a). They continue to hear and thus may welcome this word during their liturgical worship.[13]

That this word is "implanted" (ἔμφυτον) like a life-giving seed appropriately resonates with the word of truth that gives birth to a new and eternal life, as well as with the agricultural imagery of the audience

---

11. "James's point, then, is that although the wrath of a human being may indeed work what looks like 'justice' to humans, it does not bring about the divine justice; it does not reflect the righteous character of God, nor does it accomplish that which God would regard as true righteousness" (ibid., 115–16).

12. "What one removes is ῥυπαρία, dirt, filth, moral uncleanness, especially greediness" (Davids, *James*, 94). "Putting off filthiness is a challenge to repent from the pollution resulting from adopting the alien values and behavior of a different 'world,' one contrary to God's righteousness" (Lockett, *Purity*, 139).

13. "The call to receive the word of the gospel which they have already implanted in them sounds contradictory. But the stock characteristic of the language of receiving the word and the fact that the gospel consists of both a word about Jesus and ethical content point to the sense 'act upon the word you accepted at conversion'" (Davids, *James*, 95).

being a kind of "firstfruits" of God's creatures (1:18b).[14] The audience are to appreciate that this implanted, life-giving word is able to save their souls (1:21b) from the eternal death that is brought to birth by the sin that is conceived by desire (1:15).[15]

The audience are to become doers and not only hearers of the word (1:22a) that has been implanted within them and by which God brought them to birth for eschatological life (1:18). This further specifies what it means for the audience to welcome the implanted word that is able to save their souls (1:21) from eternal death (1:15). By doing the word of God which they hear as a liturgical assembly, they demonstrate a moral behavior that complements their liturgical worship with a corresponding ethical worship.

1:22b (C): Deluding Yourselves

For the audience to hear the word of God but not do it would be a matter of "deluding yourselves" (1:22b). The audience are to sense the seriousness of this matter through a subtle but poignant play on words here. If they are hearers but not doers of the "word" (λόγου), they are "deluding," or one might say "de-wording" (παρα-λογι-ζόμενοι), themselves, missing the full significance the word has for them.[16]

1:23–25 (B'): The Hearer Who Becomes a Doer Will Be Blessed in His Doing

The audience hear the B' element (1:23–25) of this chiastic unit as a chiastic pattern in itself:

---

14. "'The *implanted* word has in mind the word of the gospel, which they received after their natural birth but which gave them a rebirth. It refers back to 1:18, where James's hearers are reminded that they are given rebirth 'by the word of truth' and become 'the first fruits of his (God's) creatures'" (Hartin, *James*, 98).

15. Baker, "Who's Your Daddy?," 195–207.

16. "Scripture was regularly read in the synagogue and subsequently in the church assemblies, but those who only hear the word and fail to act on it in faith derive no benefit and, indeed, delude themselves . . . The point is that being a hearer only and not a doer leads a person to a false self-reckoning" (McCartney, *James*, 120).

a) For if anyone is a *hearer* of the word but not a *doer*, *this one* is like (1:23a)

b) a man *observing* the appearance of his birth in a mirror (1:23b).

b′) For he *observes* himself and goes away and immediately forgets what sort he was (1:24).

a′) But one peering into the perfect law, the one of freedom, and persevering, having become not a *hearer* of forgetfulness but a *doer* of work, *this one* will be blessed in his *doing* (1:25).

At the center of this chiastic sub-unit the audience experience a pivot of parallels involving the only occurrences in James of the verb "observe." They hear a progression from "a man observing [κατανοοῦντι] the appearance of his birth" in the b) sub-element (1:23b) to "he observes [κατενόησεν] himself" in the b′) sub-element (1:24). They then experience a progression of parallels involving the only occurrences in this sub-unit of the terms "hearer," "doer/doing," and "this one." "If anyone is a hearer [ἀκροατής] of the word but not a doer [ποιητής], this one [οὗτος]" in the a) sub-element (1:23a) progresses to "having become not a hearer (ἀκροατής) of forgetfulness but a doer (ποιητής) of work, this one (οὗτος) will be blessed in his doing (ποιήσει)" in the a′) sub-element (1:25).

After the central and unparalleled C element, "deluding yourselves" (1:22b), the audience experience a pivot of parallels from the B (1:18–22a) to the B′ element (1:23-25) of this chiastic unit. "A word [λόγῳ] of truth" (1:18), "the implanted word [λόγον]" (1:21) and "become [γίνεσθε] doers [ποιηταί] of the word [λόγου] and not only hearers [ἀκροαταί]" (1:22a), progress to "a hearer [ἀκροατής] of the word [λόγου] but not a doer [ποιητής]" (1:23), and, "having become [γενόμενος] not a hearer [ἀκροατής] of forgetfulness but a doer (ποιητής) of work, this one will be blessed in his doing [ποιήσει]" (1:25).

The audience are further persuaded not to delude themselves (1:22b) by becoming only hearers but not doers of the word (1:22a). If anyone of them is a hearer of the word of God, the implanted word that is able to save their souls (1:21), and the word of truth by which God brought birth to them for a new eternal life (1:18), this one is like a man observing the appearance of his new birth to eternal life in a mirror

(1:23). By hearing the word of God, he sees and realizes his new identity as one born into eternal life. But if he does not act on this word, it is the same as observing himself, with his new identity, in a mirror, but going away and immediately forgetting what sort he is, namely one whom God has given new birth for eternal life (1:24).[17]

The audience are to realize, then, that when each of them hears the word of God, he is not only "observing" his new identity as one born into eternal life (1:23-24), but also "peering" into the perfect law of God, the one of freedom (1:25a).[18] This "perfect" (τέλειον) law is thus another "perfect" (τέλειον) gift from above (1:17), given by God for endurance to have its "perfect" (τέλειον) work, so that the audience may be "perfect" (τέλειοι) and complete, lacking in nothing with regard to their worship (1:4).[19] This perfect law, as the word of God, is one of freedom, further describing the implanted word that is able to save and thus free the souls (1:21) of the audience from eternal death (1:15).

By persevering in doing the word of God which they hear during their liturgical worship, the audience may become not hearers of

---

17. Johnson, "Mirror of Remembrance," 632-45. "To 'forget' (ἐπιλανθάνομαι) refers not just to failing to remember, but to allowing something to escape by inattention or neglect (BDAG, 374), to leave it disregarded" (McCartney, *James*, 121).

18. Marucci, "Das Gesetz," 317-31. "Why the shift from mentioning God's word (1:21) to God's law (1:25)? They actually refer to the same thing. The word νόμος (*nomos*, law) is the Greek equivalent of Torah, and Torah comprises not just legal statutes and mandates; it is the teaching of Scripture. Thus, to equate the word and law is by no means to limit the word to God's moral demands; rather, it equates the law of God with the totality of his saving revelation through Scripture. The reason for the shift in terms is the new focus on the instructional character of the λόγος/ νόμος, because it makes a reader aware of who he or she is and who God is. The 'perfect law of freedom' is therefore the same as the word of truth, the gospel, which is instrumental in the bringing forth and maturation of believers" (McCartney, *James*, 122-23). "The 'law' of v. 25 must be substantially equivalent to the 'word' of vv. 22-23. Yet that 'word' must also be closely related to, if not identical to, the 'word of truth' through which men and women are regenerated to salvation (v. 18). Taken together, these points suggest that James's 'law' does not refer to the law of Moses as such, but to the law of Moses as interpreted and supplemented by Christ" (Moo, *James*, 94).

19. "The use of the word τέλειος must be connected with the same usage in 1:4 and 1:17. 'Every perfect gift' (1:17) comes down from God. Without doubt the law is truly the gift from God that brings wholeness and completeness" (Hartin, *James*, 100).

forgetfulness, forgetting their new birth and identity (1:24), but doers of "work [ἔργου]" (1:25b), the perfect "work" (ἔργον) that makes them perfect by completing their liturgical worship with their ethical worship (1:4).[20] Each member of the audience who perseveres in doing the word of God may look forward to being "blessed" (μακάριος) by God (1:25c), recalling that "blessed" (μακάριος) is a man who endures temptation, for having become tested, he will receive at the last judgment the triumphant crown of eschatological life that the Lord promised to those who love him (1:12).

1:26–27 (A′): Religion Pure and Undefiled before the God and Father

The audience hear the A′ element (1:26–27) of this chiastic unit as a chiastic pattern in itself:

a) If anyone thinks he is religious, not bridling *his* tongue but deceiving *his* heart (1:26a),

  b) the *religion* of this one is useless (1:26b).

  b′) *Religion* pure and undefiled before the God and Father is this (1:27a):

a′) to care for orphans and widows in *their* affliction, to keep oneself spotless from the world (1:27b).

At the center of this chiastic sub-unit the audience experience a pivot of parallels involving the only occurrences in James of the noun "religion." They hear a progression from "the religion [θρησκεία] of this one" in the b) sub-element (1:26b) to "religion [θρησκεία] pure and undefiled" in the b′) sub-element. They then experience a progression of parallels involving the only occurrences in this sub-unit of personal pronouns. "His [αὐτοῦ] tongue" and "his [αὐτοῦ] heart" in the a) sub-element (1:26a) progress to "their [αὐτῶν] affliction" in the a′) sub-element (1:27b).

---

20. "'A hearer of the law or of the word' implies that the Scriptures are being read in public in the context of a liturgical assembly" (ibid., 98).

At this point the audience also experience a progression, via the chiastic parallels, from the A (1:17) to the A' element (1:26-27) of this chiastic unit. "The Father [πατρός] of lights" (1:17) progresses to "the God and Father [πατρί]" (1:27).

The audience are to acknowledge that if anyone of them thinks he is "religious" (θρησκός), that is, one who worships God both liturgically and ethically, not bridling his tongue but deceiving his heart, the "religion" (θρησκεία)—the practice of both liturgical and ethical worship—of this one is useless as worship that is pleasing to God (1:26).[21] That the religious worship of one who does not "bridle his tongue" is useless develops and reinforces the previous exhortation for every person in the audience to be quick to hear, but "slow to speak, and slow to anger" (1:19), for the anger of a person does not work the righteousness of God (1:20).[22] And that the religious worship of one who does not bridle his tongue but "deceives" his heart is useless resonates with the previous exhortation for the audience to become ethical doers of the word of God that they hear in their liturgical worship and not just hearers, "deluding" themselves (1:22).

For religious worship to be useful and meaningful as worship pleasing to God (1:26), it must be "pure and undefiled" (καθαρὰ καὶ ἀμίαντος), like a ritually acceptable cultic sacrifice that is offered before

---

21. "The ritual and liturgical meaning of θρησκεία is its basic and most attested sense: acts of worship, ritual function, liturgy, religious observance, ceremony . . . θρησκεία takes on ethical connotations in Jas 1:26" (Spicq, "θρησκεία," 2:201, 203). "While the adjective 'religious' (θρησκός) is not found elsewhere in the New Testament, the meaning is clear. It is derived from the noun θρησκεία (1:26, 27), meaning 'religious worship,' which includes rituals as well as pious practices such as almsgiving, prayer, and fasting (Matt 6:1-18). James's hearers/readers would be aware of numerous religious practices in which they participated. The English translation 'religious' or 'religion' must be understood in the sense of external observances of worship" (Hartin, *James*, 100-101). "The notion of 'religion' being worked out here is that of observable, outward religious activity such as worship, prayer, and good deeds, yet also includes the total religious system to which each individual must give assent" (Lockett, *Purity*, 97).

22. "Failure to control one's speech, James asserts, means that one is 'deceiving' oneself about having true religion (see v. 22); that kind of religion is *worthless*. This word translates a Greek word (μάταιος) that is often used in Scripture to characterize idolatry as 'vain' or 'meaningless.' The 'religion' that people who do not control their speech have is no better, James suggests, than idolatry" (Moo, *James*, 96).

the God and Father (1:27a).²³ This would be an appropriate worshipful response to the God and Father, the "Father of lights," who gives every perfect gift from above (1:17). The audience are to offer this kind of religious worship by caring for orphans and widows in their affliction, and thus keeping themselves "spotless" or "unstained" (ἄσπιλον) from the world (1:27b), remaining pure for proper worship, separated from what is profane and made holy like a cultic sacrifice consecrated to God.²⁴

Everyone in the audience who wants to offer proper religious worship must not only bridle "his" (αὐτοῦ) tongue and not deceive "his" (αὐτοῦ) heart (1:26a), but also take care of orphans and widows in "their" (αὐτῶν) affliction (1:27b).²⁵ In sum, this is what it means for the audience to be truly and fully religious as a worshiping assembly. They are to complete their liturgical worship of hearing the word of God with an ethical worship of becoming doers of the word of God (1:22) by which they were brought to a new birth for eternal life (1:18).²⁶

23. "Both in the LXX and the NT, καθαρός refers to physical purity (e.g., ritual purity qualifying one for cultic use) and to moral purity . . . Likewise, the term 'undefiled' (ἀμίαντος) is used in the LXX with reference to the ritually undefiled temple and to moral purity" (Lockett, *Purity*, 114–15). "'Pure and undefiled' in 1:27 probably is a hendiadys, using two words to express the same thing, in this case positively and negatively. In context, it refers not to the ritual purity of the OT cultic requirements, but to ethical purity (although, of course, ethical purity extends to behavior in worship assembly, as is clear in 2:1–4)" (McCartney, *James*, 128). "They ['pure and undefiled'] are naturally associated with 'religion' (θρησκεία) because in the ancient world purity rules demanded that both the worshipper and the offering must be ritually pure and without stain" (Hartin, *James*, 101).

24. "James's audience is to keep ἄσπιλος with respect to 'the world,' that is, to maintain a particular purity boundary between them and 'the world'" (Lockett, *Purity*, 116). According to Martin (*James*, 52), "spotless" (ἄσπιλος) is another cultic term matching "undefiled" (ἀμίαντος) in the first part of the verse. "The term 'world' (κόσμος) is used in various ways in the NT. Here, as at 3:6 and 4:4, it signifies the human environment standing in opposition to God, which acts as a corrupting agent. Therefore, to keep oneself unstained from the world is not to withdraw from the world, but to avoid being unduly influenced by the world's values" (McCartney, *James*, 129–30).

25. "[I]n the OT God is especially a father to the fatherless and a protector of widows (Ps. 68:5; see also, among many other OT examples, Ps. 10:14, 18). Hence, those who are genuinely religious and bear the character traits of God will also take special interest in orphans and widows" (ibid., 129).

26. This passage is particularly concerned with the way the audience are to wor-

Summary on 1:17–27

The audience are to be attracted to and to deepen their appreciation for the perfect gifts given by the eternally unchanging Father of lights (1:17), especially the gift of the crown of eternal life that the one who endures temptation will receive (1:12). They are not to be led astray by the temptation to become rich, which leads to eternal death (1:13–16).

As among the twelve tribes of God's chosen people, and as fellow servants with James of God and of the Lord Jesus Christ (1:1), the audience are to appreciate that they were brought to birth for eternal life by God's "word of truth" to them (1:18a), the gospel as the creative word of God that initially brought them to faith and which they continue to hear during their liturgical worship. The cultic imagery of the audience as the "firstfruits" (1:18b) invites them to offer themselves in worship to the God who brought them to birth for eternal, eschatological life, so that more creatures of God will follow them into this divine life.

With its cultic connotations, putting away all "filthiness" and excess of evil would render the audience pure and clean for both their liturgical and ethical worship (1:21a). In the humility involved in accepting the gracious gifts of God (1:17) and which stands in contrast to the anger that does not work the righteousness of God (1:20), the audience are to welcome the "implanted word," that is, God's "word of truth" by which God graciously gave them a new birth to eternal life (1:18a). The audience are to appreciate that this implanted, life-giving word is able to save their souls (1:21b) from the eternal death that is brought to birth by the sin that is conceived by desire, especially the desire for wealth (1:15). By doing the word of God which they hear as a liturgical assembly (1:22), the audience demonstrate a moral behavior that complements their liturgical worship with a corresponding ethical worship.

The audience are to realize that when each of them hears the word of God, he is not only "observing" his new identity as one born into eternal life (1:23–24), but also "peering" into the perfect law of God, the

---

ship, according to Collins ("Coherence in James 1:19–27"). "James is not polemicizing against religious ritual per se but against a ritual that goes no further than outward show and mere words. He is probably somewhat dependent on a widespread pagan and Jewish tradition that emphasized that proper cultic worship must be accompanied by ethical conduct" (Moo, *James*, 96). See also Verseput, "Reworking," 101–4.

one of freedom (1:25) that is able to save and thus free their souls (1:21) from eternal death (1:15). Each member of the audience who perseveres in doing the word of God may look forward to being "blessed" by God (1:25), recalling that "blessed" is a man who endures temptation, for having become tested, he will receive at the last judgment the triumphant crown of eschatological life that the Lord promised to those who love him (1:12).

The audience are to acknowledge that if anyone of them thinks he is "religious," that is, one who worships God both liturgically and ethically, not bridling his tongue but deceiving his heart, the "religion," the practice of both liturgical and ethical worship, of this one is useless as worship that is pleasing to God (1:26). For religious worship to be useful and meaningful as worship pleasing to God, it must be "pure and undefiled," like a ritually acceptable cultic sacrifice that is offered before the God and Father (1:27a). The audience are to offer this kind of religious worship by caring for orphans and widows in their affliction, and thus keeping themselves "undefiled" or "unstained" from the world (1:27b), remaining pure for proper worship, separated from what is profane and made holy like a cultic sacrifice consecrated to God. The audience, then, are to complete their liturgical worship of hearing the word of God with an ethical worship of becoming doers of the word (1:22), the word of the God and Father who brought them to new birth for eternal life (1:18).

James 2:1–13

A Rich One Enters for Worship but the Poor Who Enters Is Rich in Faith (C)

The doing of mercy results in life

A ^{2:1} My brothers, do not with partiality have the faith in our Lord Jesus Christ of glory. ² For if a man with a gold ring and in fine clothing enters into your assembly, and a poor one enters in filthy clothing, ³ and you pay attention to the one wearing the fine clothing and say, "you rightly sit here," and to the poor one say, "you stand there or sit at my footstool," ⁴ have you not been divided among yourselves and become *judges* with evil designs? ⁵ Hear this, my brothers beloved, did not God choose the poor in this world to be rich in faith and heirs of the kingdom that he promised to those who love him? ⁶ But you have dishonored the poor one. Are not the rich oppressing you and they themselves dragging you into *courts*? ⁷ Do they not blaspheme the praiseworthy name that was invoked over you?

B ⁸ If however you complete the royal law according to the scripture, "You shall love your neighbor as yourself" (Lev 19:18), you are doing rightly. ⁹ But if you show partiality, you are working sin, convicted by the law as *transgressor*. ¹⁰ For whoever keeps the whole law, but stumbles in one point, has *become* guilty of all of it.

> **C** ¹¹ᵃ For the one who said, "Do not *commit adultery*" (Exod 20:14; Deut 5:18), said also, "Do not *murder*" (Exod 20:13; Deut 5:17).
>
> **C′** ¹¹ᵇ If then you do not *commit adultery* but you *murder*,
>
> **B′** ¹¹ᶜ you have *become* a *transgressor* of the law.
>
> **A′** ¹² So speak and so do as those about to be *judged* through a law of freedom. ¹³ For the *judgment* is merciless for the one not doing mercy; *mercy* boasts over judgment.[1]

Audience Response to 2:1–13

2:1–7 (A): Do Not Become Judges as Those Dragged into Courts

The audience hear the A element (2:1–7) of this chiastic unit as a chiastic pattern in itself:

a) *My brothers*, do not with partiality have the *faith* in our Lord Jesus Christ of glory (2:1).

> **b)** For if a man with a gold ring and in fine clothing enters into your assembly, and a poor one enters in filthy clothing, and you pay attention to the one wearing the fine clothing and *say*, "*you* rightly *sit* here" (2:2–3a),
>
> **b′)** and to the poor one *say*, "*you* stand there or *sit* at my footstool," have you not been divided among yourselves and become judges with evil designs (2:3b–4)?

a′) Hear this, *my brothers* beloved, did not God choose the poor in this world to be rich in *faith* and heirs of the kingdom that he promised to those who love him? But you have dishonored the poor one. Are not the rich oppressing you and they themselves dragging you into courts? Do they not blaspheme the praiseworthy name that was invoked over you (2:5–7)?

At the center of this chiastic sub-unit the audience experience a pivot of parallels involving the only occurrences in James of the verb "to

---

1. For the establishment of Jas 2:1–13 as a chiasm, see the Introduction.

sit" and of the second-person plural aorist active subjunctive of the verb "to say," as well as the only occurrences in this sub-unit of the singular personal pronoun "you." They hear a progression from "say [εἴπητε], 'you (σύ) rightly sit [κάθου] here'" in the b) sub-element (2:3a) to "say [εἴπητε], 'you [σύ] stand there or sit [κάθου] at my footstool'" in the b') sub-element (2:3b). They then experience a progression of parallels involving the only occurrences in this sub-unit of the terms "my brothers" and "faith." "My brothers [ἀδελφοί μου], do not with partiality have the faith [πίστιν]" in the a) sub-element (2:1) progresses to "my brothers [ἀδελφοί μου] beloved, did not God choose the poor in this world to be rich in faith [πίστει]" in the a') sub-element (2:5).

Having been most recently addressed as "my brothers beloved" (1:16, 19), the audience are again addressed as "my brothers" (2:1), just as they were addressed at the beginning of the letter (1:2), recalling that as "brothers" of James they are fellow servants with him of God and of the Lord Jesus Christ (1:1). As brothers who share the same faith as James, the audience are not with partiality to have the faith in our Lord Jesus Christ of glory (2:1). The audience are to have "faith" (πίστιν) without partiality as part of the wisdom for which they are to ask in "faith [πίστει]" (1:6), and as part of the testing of their "faith" (πίστεως) that produces the endurance (1:3) for which they will receive the crown of eternal life (1:12).

Not with partiality are the audience to have the faith in our Lord Jesus Christ "of glory [δόξης]" (2:1), alluding not only to his glory as the one who became our Lord Jesus Christ by being raised from the dead to eternal life but to his glory as the who will come again as our Lord Jesus Christ to carry out the final judgment that will bestow that life on others.[2] That he is the Lord of glory thus reinforces his promise to give the crown of eternal life to the audience as those who love him (1:12), that is, those who acknowledge his glory or glorify him through their

2. "Describing Jesus as *the Lord of glory* suggests particularly the heavenly sphere to which he has been exalted and from which he will come at the end of history to save and to judge (cf. Jas. 5:9). This reminder is particularly appropriate in a situation where Christians are giving too much 'glory' to human beings" (Moo, *James*, 101). See also Davids, *James*, 107. Freeborn ("Lord of Glory") maintains that the early, undeveloped use of the title "Lord of Glory" was associated with caring for the poor without partiality.

worship, rather than giving glory to others through acts of partiality. The audience are to have the "faith" in our "Lord" (κυρίου) Jesus Christ of glory, as the divine "Lord" (κυρίου) who gives (1:7) to those who ask in "faith" (1:6).

The audience are then presented with a hypothetical situation involving a rich man with a gold ring and in fine clothing entering into their "assembly" (συναγωγήν), that is, their communal gathering which would include worship, and a poor man entering in filthy clothing (2:2).[3] The hypothetical suggestion of their paying attention to the one wearing the fine clothing (2:3a) provides the transitional term linking this unit (2:1–13) with the previous unit (1:17–27). Through its alliteration and similar meaning, the verb "you pay attention to" (ἐπιβλέψητε) recalls the verb "to care for [ἐπισκέπτεσθαι]" (1:27), which occurs at the conclusion of the previous unit.[4] The audience are thus made aware that their paying attention to the rich man within a context of their liturgical worship would contradict their caring for orphans and widows as their ethical worship that is part of a pure and undefiled religion (1:27).

If the audience were to honor the rich man with a favored position by saying to him, "you rightly sit here," but to the poor one would say, "you stand there or sit at my footstool" (2:3), they must admit that they would then have been divided among themselves and have become judges with evil designs (2:4).[5] That "you have been divided" (διεκρίθητε) among yourselves in the worshiping assembly resonates with the admonition that one must pray to God in faith, "disputing" (διακρινόμενος) nothing, for the person who "disputes" (διακρινόμενος) is like a wind-blown wave (1:6), double-minded, unstable (1:8), and thus divided within oneself. Being in dispute or divided among them-

---

3. "If James is an early letter, then 'your synagogue' is perfectly understandable as a reference to an early Christian church's local gathering for worship, in echo of synagogue worship in Judaism generally" (McCartney, *James*, 138).

4. Within the letter of James the verb "you pay attention to" (2:3a) is the next word to begin with ἐπι- after the verb "to care for" (1:27).

5. Van der Watt ("Jacobus 2:1–4," 210–29) argues that a large ancient house that served as a gathering place for the Christian community is envisioned as the location for this hypothetical situation. The rich man receives a place on the couches, while the poor person is asked to stand in the courtyard or sit on the ground in the sitting room.

selves would thus render the audience imperfect and incomplete (1:4) for their worship of God.⁶ And becoming "judges" with evil designs would contradict their faith in our Lord Jesus Christ of glory (2:1), as the one who is to come as final judge of all.

Having been most recently addressed as "my brothers" (2:1), the audience are again addressed as "my brothers beloved" (2:5a), reminding them that they have been beloved by the God who brought us to birth to eternal life by a word of truth (1:18). Previously exhorted to be quick to "hear" (ἀκοῦσαι) as "my brothers beloved" (1:19), the audience are now urged as "my brothers beloved" to "hear [ἀκούσατε]" (2:5a) another word of truth about God. They are to hear and acknowledge that God has chosen the poor in this world to be rich "in faith" (ἐν πίστει) and heirs of the kingdom that God promised to those who love him (2:5).⁷ This acknowledgement reinforces the exhortation that they are not with partiality against the poor to have the "faith" (πίστιν) in our Lord Jesus Christ of glory (2:1). As those called to identify with the poor, the audience are to desire to be rich in faith rather than in money or material things, recalling that they are, "in faith" (ἐν πίστει), to ask God (1:6) for the wisdom (1:5) that those who would be rich materially are destined for eternal death (1:10–11, 15) rather than eternal life (1:12).

That God chose the poor in this world to be heirs of the heavenly kingdom that he promised to those who "love" (ἀγαπῶσιν) him further motivates the audience, as brothers "beloved" (ἀγαπητοί) by God (2:5), to reciprocate God's love for them by loving God with an ethical worship that does not demonstrate partiality toward the rich and against the poor (2:1–4). The audience are to appreciate that the poor being heirs of the heavenly kingdom that God "promised to those who love him [ἐπηγγείλατο τοῖς ἀγαπῶσιν αὐτόν]" (2:5) is synonymous with

---

6. "James's point being that the discrimination exhibited in the community is another manifestation of a wavering, divided attitude toward God. The improper 'division' being made between rich and poor reflects the improper 'divisions' harbored in the mind of the believers" (Moo, *James*, 104).

7. Frick ("James 2:5," 99–103) proposes reading τῷ κόσμῳ in 2:5 as a causal dative, implying that poor people and their poverty are caused "by the world."

their receiving the crown of eternal life that the Lord "promised to those who love him [ἐπηγγείλατο τοῖς ἀγαπῶσιν αὐτόν]" (1:12).[8]

The audience are to realize that by favoring the rich over the poor they have dishonored the poor one (2:6a), with the implication that they have thereby dishonored rather than properly worshiped the God who chose the poor to be rich in faith and heirs of God's heavenly kingdom (2:5).[9] They are to acknowledge that the rich toward whom they would show partiality are actually the ones who are oppressing them. They are thus to appreciate the ironic incongruity of their becoming "judges" (κριταί) who honor the rich over the poor (2:4), when the rich themselves are dragging them into "courts" (κριτήρια) for judgments against them (2:6b).[10]

The audience are to realize that the rich, by oppressing and dragging them into courts, are actually blaspheming rather than properly worshiping the praiseworthy divine name, the name of our Lord Jesus Christ of glory (2:1), which was ritually "invoked" over them at their baptism (2:7), and which they acknowledge in their worship. This further motivates the audience not with partiality to have the faith in our Lord Jesus Christ of glory (2:1), in order to glorify him with proper worship.[11]

---

8. "'Kingdom' parallels 'crown of life.' This lends further support for understanding the kingdom as equivalent to 'eternal life'" (Hartin, *James*, 120).

9. "According to Prov. 17:5 (cf. Prov. 14:31), to dishonor poor people is to dishonor their maker, so this discriminatory conduct not only is a behavior of unbelief, it is an insult to God" (McCartney, *James*, 142).

10. Jas 2:1–13 is directed not just at the issues of partiality of rich versus poor but at the practice of patronage and its effects on social interaction, according to Kloppenborg Verbin ("Patronage," 755–94).

11. "The name of Jesus was called over the believer at baptism (Acts 8:16; 10:48). The blasphemy, then, is the slandering of Jesus' name by the rich, the very name in which believers were baptized" (Hartin, *James*, 121). "There is a long line of development from the practice of baptism 'in/into the name of Jesus' (Acts 2:38; 10:48) to the receiving of the (new) name in baptism and the use of the Lord's name invoked over the candidate in the rite" (Martin, *James*, 67). "'The name invoked upon you' is the name by which believers are called and recognized. Here it can signify no other than the name of Jesus Christ . . . That the name of Christ 'has been invoked upon' them means that they are 'named' as those who belong to and acknowledge Jesus as Lord and Christ (2:1)" (McCartney, *James*, 143).

2:8–10 (B): Transgressors Who Have Become Guilty of All of the Law

The audience continue to be warned against practicing partiality: "If however you complete the royal law according to the scripture, 'You shall love your neighbor as yourself' (Lev 19:18), you are doing rightly. But if you show partiality, you are working sin, convicted by the law as transgressors. For whoever keeps the whole law, but stumbles in one point, has become guilty of all of it" (2:8–10).

The condition that if "you complete the law" (νόμον τελεῖτε), that is, bring the law to its "perfection" or "completion" by doing it (2:8), resonates with the "perfect law" (νόμον τέλειον), the one of freedom (1:25), the one that is synonymous with the word of God, which saves one from eternal death (1:21).[12] This is the "royal" (βασιλικόν) law (2:8) that comes from God as the divine King and is to be practiced by the poor in this world, who are to be rich in faith and heirs of God's heavenly "kingdom" (βασιλείας), those to whom God promised the crown of eternal life (2:5; 1:12).[13]

The audience are to complete this royal law according to the scripture in Lev 19:18, which states that "you shall love your neighbor as yourself" (2:8). In the context, the "neighbor" the audience are to love is the poor person they are not to dishonor by showing partiality to the rich (2:1–7). That "you shall love" (ἀγαπήσεις) this neighbor as the poor one whom God has chosen (2:5) and thus loved amounts to loving God himself, and thus becoming heirs of the kingdom, recipients of the crown of eternal life, which God promised to those who "love" (ἀγαπῶσιν) him (2:5; 1:12).

---

12 "When James wishes to speak of the OT law (or one of its commandments) he simply uses νόμος (see vv 10–11). However, when he is referring to the Christian understanding of 'law' he qualifies νόμος, as in 1:25 and 2:12: 'the law of freedom'" (Martin, *James*, 67). "The verb 'fulfill' (τελεῖτε) returns again to the theme of perfection that recurs throughout the letter. The concept implies that the reader carries out the Law fully, wholly, or totally" (Hartin, *James*, 121).

13. "This law summarized in love is 'royal' because it is the 'law' of the kingdom of God, the kingdom promised to the poor who love him (2:5)" (McCartney, *James*, 147).

The command to love one's (poor) neighbor as if loving oneself further motivates the audience to desire to become poor rather than rich in this world. In contrast to the partiality evident in telling a rich man, "you rightly [καλῶς] sit here" (2:3), by loving their neighbor the audience "are doing rightly [καλῶς]" (2:8). And by thus "doing" (ποιεῖτε) rightly, the audience become "doers" (ποιηταί) of the word of God and not only hearers (1:22), each of them a "doer [ποιητής]" (1:23, 25) who, in his "doing" (ποιήσει), will be divinely blessed (1:25) by receiving the crown of eternal life (1:12).

If the audience show partiality toward the rich and against the poor, they are working "sin" (ἁμαρτίαν), convicted by the law as transgressors (2:9).[14] Such partiality contributes to eternal death. The desire to become rich is evident in partiality toward the rich. And, as the audience are to recall, when the desire for wealth conceives, it gives birth to "sin" (ἁμαρτίαν), and the "sin" (ἁμαρτία) having been brought to completion, brings birth to death (1:15).

As the anger of a man does not "work" (ἐργάζεται) the righteousness of God (1:20), so the audience are told that by their partiality toward the rich, "you are working" (ἐργάζεσθε) sin (2:9), the sin that brings about eternal death, rather than the righteousness of God that leads to eternal life. For the audience to "work" sin contradicts their being a doer of "work" (ἔργου), one who will be blessed in his doing (1:25) with eternal life (1:12). And it contradicts the perfect "work" (ἔργον) their endurance is to have, so that they may be perfect and complete, lacking in nothing (1:4).[15] As religion that is pure and undefiled before the God and Father involves "keeping" (τηρεῖν) oneself spotless from the world (1:27), so doing rightly the law of God requires that one "keeps" (τηρήσῃ) the whole law, since to stumble in any one part of it is to transgress all of it (2:10).

---

14. "The sin of partiality, as an act committed against the poor, is condemned in the OT. In Lev 19:15 (in close proximity to Lev 19:18) the Israelite is exhorted to refrain from discriminating against the poor and urged to treat one's neighbor fairly (see also Deut 16:19)" (Martin, *James*, 68).

15. "Literally, those who show favoritism 'work' sin. Works can be sinful as well as faithful" (McCartney, *James*, 148).

2:11a (C): Do Not Commit Adultery and Do Not Murder

The audience are then presented with an example of two of the commandments of the law: "For the one who said, 'Do not commit adultery' (Exod 20:14; Deut 5:18), said also, 'Do not murder' (Exod 20:13; Deut 5:17)" (2:11a). The hypothetical example previously proposed to the audience would create divisions among them (2:4) by the different things they "say"—if to the rich one "you say" (εἴπητε), "you rightly sit here," and if to the poor one "you say" (εἴπητε), "you stand there or sit at my footstool" (2:3). But the audience cannot treat differently these two successive commandments of the law that God himself "says"—the one who "said" (εἰπών), "Do not commit adultery," also "said" (εἶπεν), "Do not murder."[16]

2:11b (C'): If You Do Not Commit Adultery but You Murder

The audience are then presented with another hypothetical situation: "If then you do not commit adultery but you murder" (2:11b). At this point the audience experience the pivot of parallels at the center of this chiastic unit from "do not commit adultery [μοιχεύσῃς]" and "do not murder [φονεύσῃς]" in the C element (2:11a) to "you do not commit adultery [μοιχεύεις] but you murder [φονεύεις]" in the C' element (2:11b). In other words, in this case the audience would not have fulfilled both of these commandments of the law spoken successively by God. There may also be the implication that the audience's partiality against the poor, a form of hating rather than loving them (2:8), would be tantamount to "murdering" them.[17]

---

16. "Both commandments, against adultery and killing, have their origin in the person of God" (Hartin, *James*, 122). "'The one who said ... also said ...' emphasizes that the unity of the law lies in its personal character. The law is not an abstract social contract; it reflects God's character and is thus bound up with the relationship of God with his people" (McCartney, *James*, 149).

17. "Murder, however, is frequently associated with discrimination against the poor and failure to love the neighbor (Je. 7:6; 22:3; Sir. 34:26; Test. Gad 4:6–7; 1 Jn. 3:15; Am. 8:4). Thus, while the commandments serve as an example, the 'if' in the context of the accusation James is making is a very real possibility (cf. 4:2; 5:4–6)" (Davids, *James*, 117). "The prohibition of 'murder' ... is cited not haphazardly as a well-known example but because James finds it to be particular apropos to the

2:11c (B'): You Have Become a Transgressor of the Law

The audience are confronted with the consequence of their not observing both the divine commandment against adultery and the divine commandment against murder: "You have become a transgressor of the law" (2:11c). At this point the audience experience a progression, via the chiastic parallels, from "convicted by the law as transgressors [παραβάται]" (2:9) and "has become [γέγονεν] guilty of all of it" (2:10) in the B element to "you have become [γέγονας] a transgressor [παραβάτης] of the law" (2:11c) in the B' element. The audience are thus to realize that if, by showing partiality toward the rich and against the poor, they fail to complete the commandment of the law that says, "You shall love your neighbor as yourself (Lev 19:18)" (2:8), then they become guilty of transgressing all of the law spoken by God himself (2:9–11).

2:12–13 (A'): For Those About to Be Judged Mercy Boasts over Judgment

Consequently, the audience are exhorted: "So speak and so do as those about to be judged through a law of freedom, For the judgment is merciless for the one not doing mercy; mercy boasts over judgment" (2:12–13). At this point the audience experience a progression, via the chiastic parallels, involving various expressions for "judging" and "judgment." "Become judges [κριταί] with evil designs" (2:4) and "dragging you into courts [κριτήρια]" (2:6), as expressions for human judgment, in the A element (2:1–7) progress to "those about to be judged [κρίνεσθαι]" (2:12), "the judgment [κρίσις] is merciless" (2:13a), and "mercy boasts over judgment [κρίσεως]" (2:13b), as expressions for divine judgment, in the A' element (2:12–13).

Having been exhorted to be slow to "speak" (λαλῆσαι) in order to avoid anger (1:19), the audience are now exhorted that "you are to

situation of his readers ... It is more likely that James's reference to the prohibition of murder presumes the 'deepening' of its sense that Jesus gave it (Matt. 5:21–26). Anger, Jesus taught, is also 'covered' in his reinterpretation of the commandment; and James may see the favoritism being shown in the community as an instance of this kind of anger, or disregard of others, and so tantamount to 'murder'" (Moo, *James*, 115).

speak" (λαλεῖτε) to the poor without the partiality (2:3) that can lead to anger (2:12). And "you are to do" (ποιεῖτε) to the poor (2:12) as those who love their (poor) neighbor as themselves, so that "you are doing" (ποιεῖτε) rightly (2:8). They are thus to complete the royal "law" (νόμον) of loving their neighbor as themselves (2:8), since they are destined to be judged by God through a "law of freedom [νόμου ἐλευθερίας]" (2:12), that is, the perfect "law" (νόμον), the one of "freedom [ἐλευθερίας]" (1:25), the one that frees and thus saves their souls (1:21) from eternal death (1:15) by bringing them to a new birth (1:18) to eternal life (1:12).[18]

By showing partiality toward the rich, the audience would become "judges" (κριταί) with evil designs (2:4) against the poor, even though the rich are the ones dragging them into "courts" (κριτήρια) for judgment (2:6). But the audience are about to be divinely "judged" (κρίνεσθαι) by a law of freedom (2:12).[19] And they are warned that such "judgment" (κρίσις) is merciless for one not doing mercy, but mercy boasts over "judgment [κρίσεως]" (2:13). The audience may "do" (ποιήσαντι) mercy by "doing" (ποιεῖτε; cf. 2:12) rightly in loving their neighbor, the poor person, as themselves (2:8).

Such mercy "boasts over" or "triumphs over" (κατακαυχᾶται) the reception of a merciless judgment from God in the final judgment (2:13).[20] Just as the humble brother who is poor may "boast" (καυχάσθω) in his exaltedness (1:9), so one showing mercy may "boast over" judgment.[21] In other words, by their showing of mercy, rather than partiality, toward the poor, the audience, as a worshiping assembly,

---

18. "James has described the law as 'perfect law' (1:25), 'royal law' (2:8), and 'law of freedom' (1:25; 2:12) not because there are three different laws, but because the law of God is complete, kingly, and liberating" (McCartney, *James*, 149).

19. "The participle μέλλοντες ('going to be') has a future eschatological ring to it. However, James says nothing about the imminence of the judgment (although 5:7-8 implies that it is at hand). What his expression captures is the certainty that judgment will occur" (Hartin, *James*, 123).

20. "Certainly the connection must be that in humiliating the poor (whom God honors) and in transgressing the law of love (thus breaking the law) they are also failing to show mercy. As such they could expect no mercy in the final judgment" (Davids, *James*, 119).

21. Wall, *Community*, 129.

may joyously and triumphantly "boast" or "exult" presently in view of their ultimately receiving divine mercy at the eschatological judgment. And receiving divine mercy includes receiving the triumphant crown of eternal life that the Lord promised to those who love him (1:12) by loving their neighbor as themselves (2:8).

Summary on 2:1–13

The audience are to have "faith" in our Lord Jesus Christ of glory without partiality (2:1) as part of the wisdom for which they are to ask in "faith" (1:6), and as part of the testing of their "faith" that produces the endurance (1:3) for which they will receive the crown of eternal life (1:12). That Jesus Christ is the Lord of "glory" reinforces his promise to give the crown of eternal life to the audience as those who love him (1:12), that is, those who acknowledge his glory or glorify him through their worship, rather than giving glory to others through acts of partiality.

For the audience to pay attention to the rich man within a context of their liturgical worship (2:2–3) would contradict their caring for orphans and widows as their ethical worship that is part of a pure and undefiled religion (1:27). Being in dispute or divided among themselves by showing partiality toward the rich and against the poor (2:4) would render the audience imperfect and incomplete (1:4) for their worship of God. As those called to identify with the poor, the audience are to desire to be rich in faith rather than in money or material things (2:5), recalling that they are "in faith" to ask God (1:6) for the wisdom (1:5) that those who would be rich materially are destined for eternal death (1:10–11, 15) rather than eternal life (1:12).

That God chose the poor in this world to be heirs of the heavenly kingdom that he promised to those who "love" him further motivates the audience, as brothers "beloved" by God (2:5), to reciprocate God's love for them by loving God with an ethical worship that does not demonstrate partiality toward the rich and against the poor (2:1–4). The audience are to appreciate that the poor being heirs of the heavenly kingdom that God "promised to those who love him" (2:5) is synonymous with their receiving the crown of eternal life that the Lord "promised to those who love him" (1:12).

The audience are to realize that the rich, by oppressing and dragging them into courts (2:6), are actually blaspheming rather than properly worshiping the praiseworthy divine name, the name of our Lord Jesus Christ of glory (2:1), which was ritually invoked over them at their baptism (2:7) and which they acknowledge in their worship. They are thus further motivated not with partiality to have the faith in our Lord Jesus Christ of glory (2:1), in order to glorify him with proper worship.

For the audience to "love" their neighbor (2:8) as the poor one whom God has chosen (2:5) amounts to loving God himself, and thus becoming heirs of the kingdom, recipients of the crown of eternal life, which God promised to those who "love" him (2:5; 1:12). As the anger of a man does not "work" the righteousness of God (1:20), so the audience are told that by their partiality toward the rich, "you are working" sin (2:9), the sin that brings about eternal death, rather than the righteousness of God that leads to eternal life. For the audience to "work" sin contradicts their being a doer of "work," one who will be blessed in his doing (1:25) with eternal life (1:12). The audience are thus to realize that if, by showing partiality toward the rich and against the poor, they fail to complete the commandment of the law that says, "You shall love your neighbor as yourself [Lev 19:18]" (2:8), then they become guilty of transgressing all of the law spoken by God himself (2:9–11).

The audience are to complete the royal "law" of loving their neighbor as themselves (2:8), since they are destined to be judged by God through a "law of freedom" (2:12), that is, the perfect "law," the one of "freedom" (1:25), the one that frees and thus saves their souls (1:21) from eternal death (1:15) by bringing them to a new birth (1:18) to eternal life (1:12). By their showing of mercy, rather than partiality, toward the poor, the audience, as a worshiping assembly, may joyously and triumphantly "boast" or "exult" presently in view of their ultimately receiving divine mercy at the eschatological judgment (2:13). And receiving divine mercy includes receiving the triumphant crown of eternal life that the Lord promised to those who love him (1:12) by loving their neighbor as themselves (2:8).

James 2:14–26

You Want To Know That Faith without Works Is Useless for Life (D)

Faith without works is dead

A **14** What is the benefit, my brothers, if someone says he has faith but does not have works? That faith is not able to save him, is it? **15** If a brother or sister is without clothing and lacking daily food, **16** and one of you says to them, "Go in peace, keep warm and be well fed," but you do not give them what is necessary for the *body*, what is the benefit? **17** So also faith, if it does not have works, is *dead* by itself.

B **18** But someone will say, "You have faith and I have works." Show me your faith without works, and I will show you, from my works, faith. **19a** You *believe* that *God* is one. You are doing rightly. Even the demons are *believing*

C **19b** but shuddering.

B′ **20** Do you want to know, O senseless person, that faith without works is useless? **21** Was not Abraham our father justified from works, having offered Isaac his son on the altar? **22** You notice that faith was working together with his works and from the works the faith was perfected, **23** and the scripture was fulfilled that says, "Abraham *believed God*, and it was reckoned to him as righteousness" (Gen 15:6) and friend of *God* he was called. **24** See that from works a person is justified and not from faith alone. **25** And likewise was not also

Rahab the prostitute justified from works, having welcomed the messengers and sent them out by a different way?

A′ ²⁶ For just as the *body* without a spirit is *dead*, so also faith without works is *dead*.¹

Audience Response to 2:14-26

2:14-17 (A): Do What Is Necessary for the Body for Faith without Works Is Dead

The audience hear the A element (2:14-17) of this chiastic unit as a chiastic pattern in itself:

a) *What is the benefit*, my brothers, if someone says he has faith but does not have works? That faith is not able to save him is it? If a brother or sister is without clothing and lacking daily food (2:14-15),

    b) and one of you says to *them* (2:16a),

        c) "Go in peace, keep warm and be well fed" (2:16b),

    b′) but you do not give *them* what is necessary for the body (2:16c),

a′) *what is the benefit*? So also faith, if it does not have works, is dead by itself (2:16d-17).

The audience hear the command, "Go in peace, keep warm and be well fed" (2:16b), as the unparalleled central and pivotal sub-element in this chiastic sub-unit. They then experience a pivot of parallels involving the only occurrences in James of the personal pronoun in the dative masculine plural. They hear a progression of parallels from "one of you says to them (αὐτοῖς)" in the b) sub-element (2:16a) to "do not give them [αὐτοῖς]" in the b′) sub-element (2:16c). Finally, they experience another progression via the chiastic parallels determined by the only occurrences in James of the question, "What is the benefit?" The introductory question, "What is the benefit?" (τί τὸ ὄφελος), in the a) sub-element (2:14-15) progresses to a repetition of the same question,

---

1. For the establishment of Jas 2:14-26 as a chiasm, see the Introduction.

"What is the benefit?" (τί τὸ ὄφελος), at the conclusion of the a') sub-element (2:16d–17).

The term "benefit [ὄφελος]" (2:14) in the question that opens this unit (2:14–26) serves as the transitional term that links this unit with the preceding unit (2:1–13) by way of its assonance with the term "mercy [ἔλεος]" (2:13), which occurs twice at the conclusion of the preceding unit. There is also a conceptual link, as the eschatological connotation of the assertion that "mercy boasts over judgment" (2:13b) carries over to the question, "What is the benefit?" (2:14a). In other words, the implication of the question for the audience is, "What or where is the mercy that will be of benefit for the final judgment?"[2]

The audience, again addressed as "my brothers" (cf. 1:2, 16, 19; 2:1, 5), are asked to ponder what the benefit is if anyone of them should say that he has faith but does not have works (2:14a).[3] For anyone of them to say that he does not have "works" (ἔργα) would mean that he is not a doer of "work" (ἔργου), who will be blessed in his doing (1:25) by receiving the crown of eternal life (1:12) from God.[4] Indeed, he would not have the perfect "work" (ἔργον) that comes from endurance, so that one may be perfect and complete, lacking in nothing (1:4), and thus properly qualified for worship. The audience are then induced to admit that faith without works is not "able" (δύναται) to "save" (σῶσαι) one (2:14b). This resonates with and reinforces the exhortation for the audience to become doers of the word (1:22), the implanted word that is "able" (δυνάμενον) to "save" (σῶσαι) their souls (1:21) from eternal death (1:15), as it is a word of truth by which God brought us to a new birth to eternal life (1:18).[5]

---

2. "What James is asking is whether a certain faith will help one in the final judgment (the κρίσις of 2:13)" (Davids, *James*, 120).

3. "[A]lthough the irony is sharp, James also reiterates his connection with them as the people of God by addressing them as 'my brothers'" (McCartney, *James*, 155).

4. "James uses 'works' in a general sense to refer to actions done in obedience to God" (Moo, *James*, 123).

5. Heide, "Soteriology," 69–97. "It is the 'word of truth' implanted by God that is 'able to save their souls' (1:18), but only, as 1:22–25 argues, if they are 'doers of the word and not hearers only'" (Johnson, *James*, 238). "The 'saving' in view . . . refers to the deliverance from eschatological judgment and hence deliverance from death, and the reception of the 'crown of life' (1:12) from God" (McCartney, *James*, 156).

The audience are then presented with another hypothetical situation in which a fellow believer—a brother or sister—is without clothing and "lacking" (λειπόμενοι) daily food (2:15), recalling that a believer is to be "lacking" (λειπόμενοι) nothing as part of being perfect and complete for worship (1:4). If someone were merely to greet them with language resembling a prayerful wish, "Go in peace, keep warm and be well fed," then this would be a kind of incomplete, inauthentic worship.[6] If "you do not give [δῶτε]" them what is necessary for their body (2:16), then the audience are to recall how this contradicts the behavior of God who "gives" (διδόντος) to all unreservedly, especially to a believer who "will be given" (δοθήσεται) the wisdom he is "lacking [λείπεται]" (1:5). Such behavior, the audience are to realize, represents useless religion, as it fails to demonstrate the ethical worship exemplified by caring for orphans and widows in their affliction (1:26–27).[7]

The repetition of the question, "What is the benefit?" (2:16; cf. 2:14), reinforces the audience's realization that such behavior fails to do the mercy that boasts over judgment (2:13). It is thus of no benefit for the final judgment.[8] The audience must admit that a faith without works is "dead" by itself (2:17), leading not only to the "death" of those in need but also to the eternal "death" (1:15) rather than to the crown of eternal life (1:12) for those who fail to help them.[9]

---

6. "Each verb is in the imperative, resembling a wish-prayer" (Martin, *James*, 84).

7. "Here is the example of the person who 'thinks himself religious' but who shows both a failure to 'control the tongue' and refuses to feed 'orphans and widows in their trial' (1:26–27)" (Johnson, *James*, 239).

8. "[T]he issue is not that of faith being unproductive, or inwardly dead with no signs of life, but faith's inability to save on its own merit when unaccompanied by works. Existing alone outside of the marriage with works, faith is of no profit before the judgment" (Verseput, "Reworking," 106–7).

9. "The image of death is particularly striking because of the example provided. If the verbal profession of faith does not come to life in acts applicable to those naked and hungry and living on the margins, *they* will die!" (Johnson, *James* 239, emphasis original).

2:18–19a (B): You Believe That God Is One

The audience hear the B element (2:18–19a) of this chiastic unit as a chiastic pattern in itself:

a) But someone will say, "*You* have faith and I have works" (2:18a).

    b) *Show* me your faith without works (2:18b),

    b′) and I will *show* you, from my works, faith (2:18c).

a′) *You* believe that God is one. You are doing rightly. Even the demons are believing (2:19a).

At the center of this chiastic sub-unit the audience experience a pivot of parallels involving the only occurrences in this unit of the verb "to show." They hear a progression from "show [δεῖξόν] me your faith without works" in the b) sub-element (2:18b) to "I will show [δείξω] you, from my works, faith" in the b′) sub-element (2:18c). They then experience a progression of parallels involving the only occurrences in this unit of the second person singular personal pronoun in the nominative. "You [σύ] have faith" in the a) sub-element (2:18a) progresses to "you [σύ] believe" in the a′) sub-element (2:19a).

As a further development to the hypothetical situation in which "someone" (τις) says he has faith but does not have works (2:14), the audience are now presented with another hypothetical situation in which an imaginary "someone" (τις) will present two different positions regarding faith and works with the implication that they are equally valid—"You have faith and I have works" (2:18a).[10] But the author counters this with an assertion that indicates the inseparability of an authentic faith with the doing of works: "Show me your faith without works (2:18b), and I will show you, from my works, faith" (2:18c). The

---

10. McKnight, "James 2:18a," 355–64. "Taking up the challenge offered by James's harsh judgment against 'faith by itself' in vv. 14–17, the τις in v. 18a defiantly contends that participation in the worship of the community and ethical behaviour are not necessarily wedded in securing salvation, but rather, distinct and equally becoming qualities . . . The one has piety while the other displays a purity of life, the imaginary opponent insists, but are not both equally valid expressions of religion?" (Verseput, "Reworking," 109).

audience are to appreciate that only the doing of works demonstrates one's possession of a genuine faith.[11]

Continuing to address the hypothetical individual, the author asserts, "You believe that God is one" (2:19a), an allusion to the Shema (Deut 6:4), the creedal prayer recited in communal worship.[12] The implication for the audience is that the absolute unity of God in whom they believe further establishes the inseparable combination of a valid faith with the doing of works. Just as the audience were assured, "You are doing rightly" (καλῶς ποιεῖτε), if they complete the royal law of the one God who said, "You shall love your neighbor as yourself [Lev 19:18]" (2:8), so the individual is assured, "You are doing rightly" (καλῶς ποιεῖς), if he believes that God is one, as, indeed, even the demons are believing this (2:19a).[13] In "doing rightly" by loving their neighbor in accord with their faith in the one God, the audience are doing a work that demonstrates the inseparability of their faith and their works. Now they are to realize, with a subtle irony, that their faith that God is absolutely one includes a work of "doing rightly." In other words, believing and doing are an inseparable combination.

2:19b (C): But Shuddering

To the notion that even the demons are believing that God is one (2:19a) the author adds, "but shuddering" (2:19b). Rather than doing rightly in believing that God is one, the demons are "shuddering" (φρίσσουσιν)

---

11. "One cannot show faith by any means other than works, and thus faith and works cannot be separated" (McCartney, *James*, 160). According to Moo (*James*, 130), James "may not be challenging the objector to reveal faith by actions, but to prove that he has faith by what he does."

12. "[I]t is not entirely implausible that the allusion to the Shema in v. 19 owes less to the precise content of the recited confession than to its customary role as a central act of worship in the life of the Christian community" (Verseput, "Reworking," 110–11).

13. "The important thing James expresses in this verse is that while the demons know who God is, this knowledge does not bring salvation" (Hartin, *James*, 152–53). "One who considers his pious participation in Christian worship to be acceptable before God without righteous living, James says, must face the devastating truth that even the demons could share his beloved confession—a belief clearly without salvatory effect in view of their unspeakable wickedness" (Verseput, "Reworking," 111).

The Letter of James

in awe and fear of the God whose absolute oneness completely overwhelms them. The awesomely profound unity of God signals their ultimate defeat. The audience are thus to appreciate that merely believing that God is one, like the demons, but without doing the works God wants from them, is not enough to secure their reception of the crown of eternal life (1:12).[14]

2:20–25 (B'): Abraham Believed God and Friend of God He Was Called

The audience hear the B' element (2:20–25) of this chiastic unit as a chiastic pattern in itself:

a) Do you want to know, O senseless *person*, that faith without works is useless? Was not Abraham our father *justified* from works, having offered Isaac his son on the altar? You notice that faith was working together with his works and from the works the faith was perfected, and the scripture was fulfilled that says (2:20–23a),

> **b)** "Abraham believed *God* (2:23b),
>
>> **c)** and it was reckoned to him as righteousness [Gen 15:6]" (2:23c)
>
> **b')** and friend of *God* he was called (2:23d).

a') See that from works a *person* is *justified* and not from faith alone. And likewise was not also Rahab the prostitute *justified* from works, having welcomed the messengers and sent them out by a different way (2:24–25)?

The audience hear the scriptural statement, "and it was reckoned to him as righteousness" (2:23c), as the unparalleled central and

---

14. According to Johnson (*James*, 241), the word "shudder" (φρίσσω) refers to "the involuntary reaction of the body in shaking, as in a fever, and is frequently used for reactions of fear. It can be used of a 'holy awe' . . . Whether the response is that of terror or awe, the 'faith' of demons plainly shows that one can confess God without doing the deeds that God commands." "The word 'shudder' can also be applied to the dread experienced by sinful people who know they are deserving of judgment to come. So James might be implying, as demons, knowing something of the true God, yet lacking true faith, shudder in fear of judgment, so also ought people whose verbal profession is not followed up with actions" (Moo, *James*, 131).

pivotal sub-element in this chiastic sub-unit. They then experience a pivot of parallels involving the only occurrences in this sub-unit of the term "God." They hear a progression of parallels from "Abraham believed God [θεῷ]" (2:23b) in the b) sub-element to "and friend of God [θεοῦ] he was called" (2:23d) in the b') sub-element. Finally, they experience another progression via the chiastic parallels determined by the only occurrences in this unit of the term "person" and the only occurrences in James of the term "justified." The address, "O senseless person [ἄνθρωπε]" (2:20), and the question of whether Abraham was "justified" (ἐδικαιώθη) from works (2:21) in the a) sub-element progress to the statement that "from works a person [ἄνθρωπος] is justified [δικαιοῦται]" (2:24), and the question of whether Rahab the prostitute was "justified" (ἐδικαιώθη) from works (2:25) in the a') sub-element.

After the central and unparalleled C element, "but shuddering" (2:19b), the audience experience a pivot of chiastic parallels from the B (2:18-19a) to the B' element (2:20-25) of this chiastic unit. "You believe [πιστεύεις] that God [θεός] is one" and "even the demons are believing [πιστεύουσιν]" (2:19a) progress to "Abraham believed [ἐπίστευσεν] God [θεῷ]" (2:23b) and "friend of God [θεοῦ] he was called" (2:23d).

In a reproachful response to the imaginary "someone," a person who maintains that faith and the doing of works are two separate but equally valid ways of behaving (2:18), a position potentially taken by anyone in the audience, James proposes a provocative question, "Do you want to know, O senseless person, that faith without works is useless?" (2:20). An alliterative wordplay ironically underlines how the "senseless" (κενέ) person needs to "know" (γνῶναι) that faith without works is useless. And the artfully alliterative wordplay between "without works" (χωρὶς τῶν ἔργων) and "useless" (ἀργή) underscores for the audience that faith without works is utterly "useless," that is, of no benefit for one's salvation (2:14; cf. 2:16).[15]

The imaginary "senseless person," as well as the audience, must admit that Abraham our father was "justified," that is, acknowledged to be in a right relationship with God, a relationship that pleases God and thus amounts to a proper worship of God, from works, having offered Isaac his son on the altar (2:21). The audience are to appreciate that

---

15. McCartney, *James*, 161; Brosend, *James*, 75.

Abraham's faith in God motivated his obedient willingness to do the work of offering his beloved son Isaac as a cultic act of sacrificial worship. Although God did not require him to actually carry out the cultic act of sacrifice, Abraham's obedient behavior, his works that demonstrated his willingness to do so, amounted to an act of ethical or moral worship that was pleasing to God (Gen 22:9–12).

"You"—the imaginary senseless person (2:20) as well as every individual in the audience—are to notice that faith was working together with Abraham's works, his behavior in being willing to offer his son Isaac on the altar (2:21; cf. Gen 22:12; Heb 11:17–19) as an act of sacrificial worship, and from the works the faith was perfected (2:22). In contrast to sin, which, "having been brought to completion" (ἀποτελεσθεῖσα), brings birth to eternal death (1:15), faith "was perfected" or "brought to completion" (ἐτελειώθη) from works, so that it is not "dead" (2:17). Abraham is presented to the audience as a model for how one's faith is "perfected" from one's "works" (ἔργων), that is, for how one's doing of works perfects and completes one's faith for the proper worship of God. The prominent example of Abraham thus reinforces the exhortation for the audience to let endurance have its "perfect" (τέλειον) "work" (ἔργον), so that they may be "perfect" (τέλειοι) and complete, lacking in nothing with regard to their worship of God (1:4).[16]

In contrast to the imaginary someone within the audience who "says" (λέγῃ) he has faith but does not have works (2:14), in the case of Abraham the scripture was fulfilled that "says" (λέγουσα), "Abraham believed God and it was reckoned to him as righteousness" (Gen 15:6) and friend of God he was called (2:23).[17] Whereas the anger of a man does not "work" (ἐργάζεται) the "righteousness" (δικαιοσύνην) of God (1:20), the audience are to appreciate that Abraham's faith "working together" (συνήργει) with his "works [ἔργοις]" (2:22) was reckoned to him by God as "righteousness" (δικαιοσύνην). With the divine author-

---

16. According to Hartin (*James*, 154), the verb "was perfected" in 2:22 "clearly connects back to 1:3–4, where faith is brought to perfection through works of testing and suffering, while in 2:22 Abraham's faith is perfected through the testing he endured in being asked to offer his son." See also Johnson, *James*, 243.

17. '[F]ulfill' in the NT involves more the notion of 'full realization' than simply connecting a NT event to an OT prediction" (McCartney, *James*, 169). See also Moo, *James*, 138.

ity of scripture this confirms for the audience that Abraham was "justified" (ἐδικαιώθη) by God from the "works" (ἔργων) involved in being willing to offer Isaac his son on the altar (2:21).

The Abraham who believed "God" was called a "friend of God" (φίλος θεοῦ) by God himself (2:23d), in accord with Wis 7:27, where it is the wisdom of God that produces "friends of God" (φίλους θεοῦ). The audience are to appreciate the OT (LXX) allusions to Abraham as God's "beloved" (ἠγαπημένῳ in 2 Chr 20:7; ἠγαπημένον in Dan 3:35) and to God referring to Abraham as the one whom "I have loved" (ἠγάπησα in Isa 41:8; 51:2). As a "friend" who was both loved by God and who loved God as evident by his faith in God that was working together with his works (2:22), Abraham provides the audience with a model of one of those who "love" God by a faith combined with the doing of works. The audience, as brothers "beloved" (ἀγαπητοί) by God (1:16, 19; 2:5), are to imitate Abraham by being rich in the faith that is combined with the doing of works and thereby become heirs of the heavenly kingdom and recipients of the crown of eternal life that God promised to those who "love" (ἀγαπῶσιν) him (2:5; 1:12).[18]

Again addressed directly, rather than through an imaginary "senseless person" (2:20), the audience, who, as the "senseless person," were to "notice" (βλέπεις) that faith was working together with Abraham's works and from the works the faith was perfected (2:22), are now to "see" (ὁρᾶτε) that from works a person is justified and not from faith alone (2:24). The audience are to realize that the specific example of Abraham as one who was "justified" (ἐδικαιώθη) from works (2:21) together with faith (2:22–23) extends in a general way to everyone. Not only Abraham but every person is "justified" (δικαιοῦται) from works and not from faith alone. Having been invited to identify with an imaginary senseless "person" (ἄνθρωπε), each member of the audience is now to see himself as a real "person" (ἄνθρωπος) who is to be justified, and thus made righteous for the proper worship of God, from the doing of works and not from faith alone.

The audience are to acknowledge that another exemplary biblical figure, Rahab the Canaanite prostitute (Josh 2:1–21; 6:22–25), was

18. "To be God's friend is to be in the people of God, to be in the right, to be saved, and to be a person who in fellowship with God lives out the life God designs for those on earth . . . friendship with God involves love" (McKnight, *James*, 255).

likewise justified from works, having welcomed the Israelite messengers and sent them out by a different way (Jas 2:25; cf. Heb 11:31). Her faith in the God of Israel (Josh 2:11-12) was combined with her works in protecting the Israelite spies.[19] The example of Rahab the prostitute, who was "justified" (ἐδικαιώθη) from works (Jas 2:25), complements the example of Abraham our father, who was likewise "justified" (ἐδικαιώθη) from works (2:21). Together they provide the audience with a complete and convincing scriptural authorization that every person is "justified" (δικαιοῦται) from works and not from faith alone (2:24).[20] The audience are likewise to combine their faith with their doing of works in order to be justified by God and made righteous for a proper and complete worship of God, a worship that includes not only the liturgical profession of faith but also the ethical behavior involved in the doing of works.

2:26 (A'): As the Body without a Spirit Is Dead so Faith without Works Is Dead

The audience are presented with the climactic conclusion of the discussion concerning faith without works: "For just as the body without a spirit is dead, so also faith without works is dead" (2:26). At this point the audience experience a progression, via the chiastic parallels, from the A (2:14-17) to the A' (2:26) element of this chiastic unit. "What is necessary for the body [σώματος]" (2:16) and "faith, if it does not have works, is dead [νεκρά]" (2:17) progress to "just as the body [σῶμα]

---

19. "Rahab's justifying works in view, then, are not a righteous life generally, but those acts based upon her recognition (i.e., nascent belief) that the God of Israel was the true and mighty God, and that her Canaanite society was doomed. Thus, like Abraham, she was justified by her faith-deed and the events that followed" (McCartney, *James*, 171).

20. "So alongside the famous and celebrated ancestor of the Jewish people, a man, 'the friend of God,' he places an obscure Gentile woman of low moral character. Thus he implies that anyone is capable of acting on his or her faith—whether a patriarch or a prostitute" (Moo, *James*, 143). "James, then, is not raising the issue of how God can save the ungodly, nor is he asking how Abraham and Rahab became righteous; he simply sets forth Abraham and Rahab as examples of righteous people who were proven and acknowledged by God as righteous through their deeds of faith, thereby obliterating the entirely mistaken and dangerous notion that a faith without deeds has any value or power" (McCartney, *James*, 172).

without a spirit is dead [νεκρόν], so also faith without works is dead [νεκρά]" (2:26).

The assertion that the "body" without a spirit is dead (2:26a) reinforces the need for the audience to give a brother or sister without clothing and lacking daily food (2:15) what is necessary for the "body" (2:16) to maintain its life-giving spirit, and thus to keep the brother or sister alive.[21] The comparison of the body without a spirit being "dead" to faith without works being "dead" (2:26) emphatically restates the assertion that faith, if it does not have works, is "dead" by itself (2:17). The audience are thus exhorted to combine the faith they profess during their liturgical worship with their doing of good works, especially in the assisting of the poor and needy among them, as part of their ethical worship. This combination will make their worship complete, as it will be immediately life-giving to those in need and ultimately life-giving to those who help them. By combining their faith with the doing of works for the complete worship that demonstrates the love of God, the audience may become heirs of the heavenly kingdom and recipients of the crown of eternal life that God promised to those who love him (2:5; 1:12).[22]

Summary on 2:14–26

The audience are asked to ponder what is the benefit for salvation in the final judgment if anyone of them should say that he has faith but does not have works (2:14a). They are then induced to admit that faith without works is not "able" to "save" one (2:14b). This resonates with and reinforces the exhortation for the audience to become doers of the word (1:22), the implanted word that is "able" to "save" their souls (1:21) from eternal death (1:15), as it is a word of truth by which God brought us to a new birth to eternal life (1:18).

If someone in the audience were merely to greet a fellow brother or sister who is "lacking" the material necessities for life (2:15) with

21. "The πνεῦμα (without definite article) here means simply 'spirit' in the sense of life-principle, that which animates the body" (Johnson, *James*, 245).

22. For discussions of Jas 2:14–26 as a whole, and including comparisons with Paul, see Laato, "Justification," 43–84; Proctor, "Faith," 307–31.

language resembling a prayerful wish, "Go in peace, keep warm and be well fed," then this would be an incomplete, inauthentic worship. Not to "give" them what is necessary for their body (2:16) would contradict the behavior of God who "gives" to all unreservedly, especially to a believer who "will be given" the wisdom he is "lacking" (1:5). Such behavior represents useless religion, as it fails to demonstrate the ethical worship exemplified by caring for orphans and widows in their affliction (1:26–27). The repetition of the question, "What is the benefit?" (2:16; cf. 2:14), reinforces the audience's realization that such behavior fails to do the mercy that boasts over judgment (2:13). It is thus of no benefit for the final judgment. The audience must admit that a faith without works is "dead" by itself (2:17), leading not only to the "death" of those in need but also to the eternal "death" (1:15) rather than to the crown of eternal life (1:12) for those who fail to help them.

The audience are to appreciate that only their doing of works demonstrates their possession of a genuine faith (2:18). In "doing rightly" by loving their neighbor in accord with their faith in the one God (2:8), the audience are doing a work that demonstrates the inseparability of their faith and their works. They are thus to realize that their faith that God is absolutely one includes a work of "doing rightly." In other words, believing and doing are an inseparable combination. The audience are to appreciate merely believing that God is one, like the demons (2:19), but without doing the works God wants from them, is not enough to secure their reception of the crown of eternal life (1:12).

Any individual in the audience who would think that faith can be separated from works (2:20) is to notice that faith was working together with Abraham's works, his obedient behavior in being willing to offer his son Isaac on the altar (2:21) as an act of sacrificial worship, and from the works the faith was perfected (2:22). Abraham is presented to the audience as a model for how one's doing of "works" actually "perfects" and completes one's faith for the complete and proper worship of God. The prominent example of Abraham thus reinforces the exhortation for the audience to let endurance have its "perfect work," so that they may be "perfect" and complete, lacking in nothing with regard to their worship of God (1:4).

The divine authority of scripture (Gen 15:6) confirms for the audience that Abraham was "justified," that is, acknowledged to be in a right relationship with God, a relationship that pleases God and thus amounts to a proper worship of God, from the "works" involved in being willing to offer Isaac his son on the altar (2:21). As a "friend of God" who was both loved by God and who loved God as evident by his faith in God that was working together with his works (2:22), Abraham provides the audience with a model of one of those who "love" God by a faith combined with the doing of works. The audience, as brothers "beloved" by God (1:16, 19; 2:5), are to imitate Abraham by being rich in the faith that is combined with the doing of works and thereby become heirs of the heavenly kingdom and recipients of the crown of eternal life that God promised to those who "love" him (2:5; 1:12).

The example of Rahab the prostitute, who was "justified" from works (2:25), complements the example of Abraham our father, who was likewise "justified" from works (2:21). Together they provide the audience with a complete and convincing scriptural authorization that every person is "justified" from works and not from faith alone (2:24). The audience are likewise to combine their faith with their doing of works in order to be justified by God and made righteous for a proper and complete worship of God.

The comparison of the body without a spirit being "dead" to faith without works being "dead" (2:26) emphatically restates the assertion that faith, if it does not have works, is "dead" by itself (2:17). The audience are thus exhorted to combine the faith they profess during their liturgical worship with their doing of good works, especially in the assisting of the poor and needy among them (1:26-27; 2:15-16), as part of their ethical worship. This combination will make their worship complete, as it will be immediately life-giving to those in need and ultimately life-giving to those who help them. By combining the faith professed in their liturgical worship with the doing of works in their ethical worship for the complete worship that demonstrates the love of God, the audience may become heirs of the heavenly kingdom and recipients of the crown of eternal life that God promised to those who love him (2:5; 1:12).

James 3:1–10

The Tongue Is Constituted a World of Unrighteousness within Our Members (E)

The tongue is full of death-bringing poison

A ^{3:1} Not many of you should *become* teachers, *my brothers*, knowing that we will receive a greater judgment.

    B ^{2a} *For* we all stumble in many ways. If anyone does not stumble in word, this one is a perfect man *able* to bridle

        C ^{2b} even the *whole body*. ³ If we place bridles into the mouths of horses to persuade them toward us, even their *whole body* we guide. ⁴ Behold also ships, being so large and driven by rough winds, are guided by a tiny rudder wherever the inclination of the pilot decides.

            D ^{5a} So also the tongue is a small *member*, but boasts of great things.

                E ^{5b} Behold how small a *fire* so great a forest kindles.

                E′ ^{6a} And the tongue is a *fire*.

            D′ ^{6b} The tongue is constituted as the world of unrighteousness within our *members*,

        C′ ^{6c} defiling the *whole body* and setting fire to the course of the birth and being set on fire by Gehenna.

B' ⁷ *For* every species of animals and also of birds, of reptiles and also of sea creatures is tamed and has been tamed by the human species. ⁸ But the tongue no one among human beings is *able* to tame, an unstable evil, full of death-bringing poison.

A' ⁹ With it we bless the Lord and Father and with it we curse human beings who have *become* in accord with the likeness of God. ¹⁰ From the same mouth come out blessing and cursing. It is not necessary, *my brothers*, that these things *become* so.[1]

Audience Response to 3:1–10

3:1 (A): Not Many Should Become Teachers My Brothers

James once again exhorts his audience as his fellow "brothers" (cf. 1:2, 16, 19; 2:1, 5, 14): "Not many of you should become teachers, my brothers, knowing that we will receive a greater judgment" (3:1).[2] Not many in the audience should become teachers, that is, those who teach the word and law of God to others, knowing that "we," that is, James and any who would become a teacher like him, will be judged more strictly at the final judgment. Not many of you should "become" (γίνεσθε) teachers, because not only are you to "become" (γίνεσθε) doers of the word that is taught (1:22), but you must be careful, as teachers, to speak the word in a way that does not cause anger (1:19).

As those who speak the word to others, teachers will receive a greater "judgment [κρίμα]" (3:1), since not only doers but also speakers of the word are to be "judged" (κρίνεσθαι) through a law of freedom (2:12), the life-giving word of God that is able to save souls (1:21) from eternal death (1:15).[3] Teachers will receive a greater judgment as those

---

1. For the establishment of Jas 3:1–10 as a chiasm, see the Introduction.

2. "As is his custom in beginning a new section, James reminds his readers of their relationship to God and to himself by addressing them as 'my brothers'" (McCartney, *James*, 179).

3. "The appearance of κρίμα in this verse probably relies upon 2:12 for clarification. Since judgment involves deeds and words, those such as teachers who deal principally with words in their vocation should expect a more difficult time in eschatological judgment" (Baker, *Personal Speech-Ethics*, 123). "It is highly unlikely that

responsible not only for doing mercy but for teaching others the doing of mercy, for the "judgment" (κρίσις) is merciless for the one not doing mercy, but mercy triumphs over "judgment [κρίσεως]" (2:13).[4] That, as those who become teachers, "we will receive" (λημψόμεθα) a greater judgment reinforces the exhortation for everyone in the audience to become tested by enduring temptation, so that "he will receive" (λήμψεται) at the judgment the crown of eternal life that God promised to those who love him (1:12).

3:2a (B): A Perfect Man Is Able to Bridle

The focus of the audience continues to be directed to the issue of speaking the word: "For we all stumble in many ways. If anyone does not stumble in word, this one is a perfect man able to bridle" (3:2a). The audience have heard that whoever keeps the whole law, but "stumbles" (πταίσῃ) in one point, has become guilty of the whole of it (2:10). Conversely, the audience are to realize that, even though we all "stumble" (πταίομεν) in many ways, if anyone does not "stumble" (πταίει) in word, this person is "perfect" in the sense of being whole or complete.[5]

For anyone in "word" (λόγῳ) not to stumble (3:2a), with the phrase "in word" in a grammatically emphatic position,[6] involves not just stumbling with regard to one's speech in general but, as the audience are to recall, not stumbling with regard to the "word" (λόγῳ) of truth by which God brought us to birth for a new and eternal life (1:18).

James means 'judgment as condemnation' with the word κρίμα; his concern at this point is to warn of future accountability before God" (McKnight, *James*, 271n34).

4. "James, however, is dealing with the specific issue that, since all verbal activity is potentially dangerous, teaching is especially so, for the teaching of error has the potential not only to destroy the teacher, but also to harm the students" (McCartney, *James*, 179). "Not only are teachers 'in the know,' but their knowledge leads to responsibility for both what they teach and how they live" (McKnight, *James*, 271–72).

5. "From the apt example of teachers who use their tongues so much, James moves to the universal problem of controlling the tongue. This shift of focus is brought to the fore emphatically by the otherwise unnecessary use of ἅπαντες, the strengthened form of πᾶς ['all'], to bolster the assumed first person plural subject of πταίομεν" (Baker, *Personal Speech-Ethics*, 124).

6. McCartney, *James*, 180.

And not stumbling in word involves being a doer and not just a hearer of the word, since "if anyone does not stumble in word" (εἴ τις ἐν λόγῳ οὐ πταίει) resonates with "if anyone is a hearer of the word but not a doer [εἴ τις ἀκροατὴς λόγου ἐστὶν καὶ οὐ ποιητής]" (1:23). Indeed, the audience are to become doers of the "word" (λόγου) and not only hearers (1:22). That the "word" makes anyone who does not stumble in it "able [δυνατός]" (3:2a) means that he has a power oriented to saving his soul from eternal death (1:15), since the implanted "word" (λόγον) the audience are to welcome is "able" (δυνάμενον) to save their souls (1:21). Not stumbling in word, then, is part of a faith accompanied by works, a faith that is "able" (δύναται) to save (2:14).[7]

Anyone in the audience who does not stumble in word is a "perfect" (τέλειος) person in the sense of being whole and complete (3:2a). This kind of "perfection" is the goal for the whole audience. They have heard the exhortation for them to let endurance have its "perfect" (τέλειον) work, so that they may be "perfect" (τέλειοι) and complete, lacking in nothing (1:4), that is, completely qualified for the proper worship of God.[8] And such proper worship is part of a religion that includes bridling one's tongue. The assertion that if anyone does not stumble in word, this one is a perfect man able to "bridle [χαλιναγωγῆσαι]" (3:2a) resonates with the assertion that if anyone thinks he is religious, not "bridling" (χαλιναγωγῶν) his tongue but deceiving his heart, the religion, which includes worship, of this one is useless (1:26).

3:2b-4 (C): Even the Whole Body

The audience then hear what the "perfect" person who does not stumble in word is able to bridle: "even the whole body. If we place bridles into the mouths of horses to persuade them toward us, even their whole

---

7. "Further, the 'word' that teachers ought to bring is the word of truth that gives new birth and brings salvation (1:18, 21); it is the word that people are to do, not just hear (1:22). Therefore, it is all the more incumbent on teachers that their own lives exhibit the wholeness and integrity that the word they teach is expected to engender" (ibid.).

8. With regard to the term "perfect" here, McKnight (*James*, 275) notes that "the term speaks of maturity and completeness or, even better, of having arrived at the destined goal designed by God."

body we guide. Behold, also ships, being so large and driven by rough winds, are guided by a tiny rudder wherever the inclination of the pilot decides" (3:2b-4). With the term "body [σῶμα]" (3:2b) the audience hear the transitional term that links this unit (3:1–10) with the preceding unit (2:14–26), which concludes with a reference to the "body" (σῶμα) being dead without a spirit (2:26).

A couple of comparisons deepen the audience's appreciation for the power that the word of truth regarding our new birth to eternal life gives to bridle even the "whole body" (ὅλον τὸ σῶμα) of our persons (3:2b). The audience must admit that if we place "bridles" (χαλινούς), the means by which to "bridle [χαλιναγωγῆσαι]" (3:2a), into the mouths of horses to persuade them toward us, even their "whole body" (ὅλον τὸ σῶμα) we guide (3:3). And just as we "guide" (μετάγομεν) horses with the bridles we place in their mouths, so also even large ships driven by rough winds are "guided" (μετάγεται) by a tiny rudder, analogous to the bridle, wherever the inclination of the pilot of the ship decides (3:4).[9]

3:5a (D): The Tongue Is a Small Member but Boasts of Great Things

The small bridles placed into the mouths of horses to guide their whole body (3:3) and the tiny rudder that guides large ships (3:4) are then compared to the human tongue: "So also the tongue is a small member, but boasts of great things" (3:5a). That the tongue is a small member of the body like the tiny rudder and like the small bridles implies that it can guide or bridle one's whole body (3:2–4). But that is not what the

---

9. After thoroughly discussing the pros and cons of interpretations that view the "whole body" as a metaphor for the church, McCartney (*James*, 182–83) concludes "that James is simply making comparisons to the outsized power of speech and warning of its susceptibility to wickedness and the consequent necessity of guarding it closely. Teachers must be especially careful because their speech is especially important, but such advice is applicable not just to teachers. The horse and ships are only illustrations; they are not intended to be metaphors for the church." See also Moo, *James*, 152; Davids, *James*, 139. "The horse example is interesting because the literal mouth is the means of control; the ship is interesting because it harnesses great powers outside of itself that are then directed by means of the small rudder. Both examples emphatically illustrate the power of speech" (McCartney, *James*, 183).

audience now hear. Instead, they hear that the tongue, although it is a "small" (μικρόν) member, boasts of "great" (μεγάλα) things.[10] Rather than guiding or bridling the whole body, the tongue engages in "boasting" (αὐχεῖ), a type of uncontrolled behavior. This alerts the audience to a negative contrast between guidance by the bridles and rudder on the one hand and boasting by the tongue on the other. That the "tongue" (γλῶσσα) is a small member but boasts of great things reinforces the exhortation for anyone in the audience who thinks he is religious to bridle his "tongue" (γλῶσσαν) in order to offer effective worship to God (1:26).[11]

3:5b (E): How Small a Fire So Great a Forest Kindles

The attention of the audience is then directed to the destructive power of something small: "Behold how small a fire so great a forest kindles" (3:5b). In contrast to the "behold" (ἰδού) that directs the audience to the constructive impact of ships that are so "large" (τηλικαῦτα) being guided by a tiny rudder (3:4), "behold" (ἰδού) now directs the audience to the destructive impact of how a "small" (ἡλίκον) fire kindles a "great" (ἡλίκην) forest.[12]

---

10. The alliteration between "small member" (μικρὸν μέλος) and "great things" (μεγάλα) underlines the ability of such a diminutive part of the body to produce such grandiose effects.

11. "By promptly pairing the human tongue with a well-known form of uncontrolled speech like boasting, the author gently prepares the reader for the upcoming lesson of the vast differences between the human tongue and the horse's tongue or the ship's rudder. These can be perfectly controlled. The human tongue cannot be" (Baker, *Personal Speech-Ethics*, 126). "In the New Testament boasting was seen as a vice because it replaces trust in God with trust in one's own abilities" (Hartin, *James*, 175). "The negative tone is evident . . . a slow shift in thought from the power of the tongue to the evil of the tongue to the need for proper control" (Davids, *James*, 140).

12. "James puts the little-large contrast to work in negative imagery. He does this by cleverly employing the adjective ἡλίκος twice, this being a word which comments on the relative size of something, either big or small. Here, it accents the smallness of πῦρ ['fire'] in contrast to the largeness of ὕλην ['forest'], which the former can set to flames and thus destroy. Unlike the horse's tongue and the ship's rudder which are carefully monitored, the fire in the forest is totally out of control" (Baker, *Personal Speech-Ethics*, 126).

3:6a (E'): The Tongue Is a Fire

The implied connection between a fire and the tongue is made bluntly and emphatically explicit for the audience: "And the tongue is a fire" (3:6a). At this point the audience experience the pivotal progression of parallels at the center of this chiastic unit. They hear a progression from "how small a fire [πῦρ]" (3:5b) in the E element to "the tongue is a fire [πῦρ]" in this E' element. The audience are to appreciate that the tongue, as a "small" (μικρόν) member of the body that boasts of great things (3:5a), is not only like a "small" (ἡλίκον) fire that kindles a great forest (3:5b), but the tongue actually *is* a fire, with the implication that the tongue in itself can ignite tremendous destruction.[13]

3:6b (D'): The Tongue Is the World of Unrighteousness within Our Members

How the tongue itself is a fire begins to be elaborated for the audience: "The tongue is constituted as the world of unrighteousness within our members" (3:6b). At this point the audience hear a progression, via the chiastic parallels, from the D to the D' element of this chiastic unit. The focus on the tongue as a small "member" (μέλος) of the human body (3:5a) progresses to a focus on the tongue as the world of unrighteousness within the "members" (μέλεσιν) of the human body (3:6b).

That the "tongue," the "tongue" that is actually a fire (3:6a) and the "tongue" that is a small member of our body but boasts of great things (3:5a), is constituted as the "world" (κόσμος) of unrighteousness within our body's members develops the negative connotations the audience have heard for the term "world." They have heard that God chose the poor in this earthly "world" (κόσμῳ) dominated by the rich to be heirs of God's heavenly kingdom (2:5). And they were exhorted to keep themselves spotless from this "world" (κόσμου) of wealth by their ethi-

---

13. "The imagery is vigorous and hyperbolic in order to make the warning against the undisciplined tongue as sharp as possible. Flames are called 'tongues' in many languages because they resemble tongues; they flicker and make noise, and above all they do damage. The tongue, as the instrument of speech, can set the heart aflame with fury, or patriotic fervor, or courage, or love, or hate, and it can inflict damage that goes on for generations" (McCartney, *James*, 184–85).

cal worship of caring for orphans and widows in their affliction (1:27). The audience, then, are to be aware of and separate themselves from not only the external world around them but from the internal world of unrighteousness that the tongue, as a small member (3:5a), constitutes within the members of their physical bodies as well as within the communal body of their worshiping assembly.[14]

3:6c (C'): Defiling the Whole Body

The tongue, which is itself a fire (3:6a), and is constituted as the world of unrighteousness within the members of our bodies (3:6b) continues to be described: "defiling the whole body and setting fire to the course of the birth and being set on fire by Gehenna" (3:6c). At this point the audience hear a progression, via the chiastic parallels, from the C to the C' element of this chiastic unit. "Even the whole body [ὅλον τὸ σῶμα]" (3:2b) and "even their whole body [ὅλον τὸ σῶμα] we guide" (3:3) progress to "defiling the whole body [ὅλον τὸ σῶμα]" (3:6c).

That the tongue "defiles" (σπιλοῦσα) the whole body, the physical body of the individual person as well as the communal body of the worshiping assembly (3:6c), reinforces the exhortation for everyone in the audience to bridle his tongue (1:26). They are to become truly religious, practicing a religion that is "pure and undefiled," by performing the ethical worship of caring for orphans and widows in their affliction, in order to keep oneself "spotless" or "undefiled" (ἄσπιλον) from the world (1:27).[15] That the tongue sets fire to and thus harms the

14. "James's meaning is only to be grasped in the light of 1:27 and 2:5, where κόσμος and God are opposed . . . The expression 'among our members' means our physical bodies, but the metaphor extends naturally to the power of speech in the assembly of believers" (Johnson, *James*, 259). "The somewhat surprising use of the ὁ with κόσμος must be there in order to add to the emphasis that the world of wickedness centers on the tongue unlike anywhere else in the human body" (Baker, *Personal Speech-Ethics*, 127). "[T]he presence of the article specifies that the tongue is not simply 'a whole wicked world,' but '*the* whole wicked world'" (McCartney, *James*, 187). "The grammar suggests that the tongue is divinely appointed among the members of the body and that its placement as the speaking instrument gives it potency for abuse when humans choose to use it for what it was not intended to accomplish" (McKnight, *James*, 283).

15. "The use of the verb σπιλοῦν ('pollute/stain') is particularly appropriate here,

course of the "birth [γενέσεως]" (3:6c), that is, our divine birth to a new and eternal life (1:18), reinforces the exhortation for the audience to become doers of the word, especially through a bridled use of the tongue, rather than being like one who observes the appearance of his "birth" (γενέσεως) to eternal life in a mirror but promptly forgets his new identity (1:23).

And that the tongue is set on fire by Gehenna (3:6c), the place of eternal punishment and death, with its threat to destroy our new birth, our birth to eternal life by a word of truth (1:18), is underscored by the alliteration between "Gehenna" (γεέννης) and "birth" (γενέσεως). This reinforces the exhortation for the audience not to stumble in word through an unbridled use of the tongue (3:2).[16]

3:7–8 (B'): The Tongue of Human Beings No One Is Able to Tame

The audience are made aware of how difficult it is for human beings to control the extremely dangerous and destructive tongue: "For every species of animals and also of birds, of reptiles and also of sea creatures is tamed and has been tamed by the human species. But the tongue no one among human beings is able to tame, an unstable evil, full of death-bringing poison" (3:7–8). At this point the audience hear a progression, via the chiastic parallels, from the B to the B' element of this chiastic unit. A general explanation regarding all human beings, "for [γάρ] we all stumble in many ways" (3:2a), progresses to a general explanation regarding all animals, "for [γάρ] every species of animals . . . is tamed"

---

for it corresponds to the directive in 1:27 to 'Keep oneself unstained (ἄσπιλον) from the world (ἀπὸ τοῦ κόσμου).' But now the 'world of wickedness' dwells in the very body! Once more, the term σῶμα here means first the individual's body, but it can be extended—especially in the light of James' covenantal interest—to the communal body as well" (Johnson, *James*, 259). "The participle ἡ σπιλοῦσα is yet another word which elicits a cultic motif reminiscent of 1:27" (Baker, *Personal Speech-Ethics*, 127).

16. McCartney, *James*, 190n20. "The tongue is a world of injustice in that it is stoked by hell. The word 'hell' translates the Greek word *gehenna* (from 'valley of Hinnom,' 2 Kgs 23:10; Jer 7:31), the fire pit where rubbish was burned outside Jerusalem. The term became an idiom, not for the dwelling place of Satan or demons, but for the place of condemnation because it was an everlasting fire (Matt 5:22; 18:9)" (McKnight, *James*, 285–86).

(3:7).¹⁷ And "this one is a perfect man able [δυνατός] to bridle" (3:2a) progresses to "the tongue no one among human beings is able [δύναται] to tame" (3:8).

Although from the very beginning the human species has tamed every species within the animal world (3:7; cf. Gen 1:26, 28),¹⁸ no one among human beings is able to tame the "tongue [γλῶσσαν]" (3:8)—the "tongue" (γλῶσσα) that is constituted as the world of unrighteousness within our members (3:6b), the "tongue" (γλῶσσα) that is itself a destructive fire (3:6a), the "tongue" (γλῶσσα) that is a small member, but boasts of great things (3:5a), and the "tongue" (γλῶσσαν) that must be bridled (1:26) for one to properly perform the worship that is part of a pure and undefiled religion (1:27).¹⁹

That no one among human beings is "able" (δύναται) to tame the tongue (3:8) reinforces the exhortation for no one in the audience to use his tongue in a way that causes him to stumble in word, so that he may be a perfect man "able" (δυνατός) to bridle even the whole body (3:2).²⁰ This reminds the audience that not stumbling in word through the tongue is part of a faith accompanied by works that is "able" (δύναται)

17. "The γάρ of Jas 3:7 is explanatory, but in a more general sense instead of a precisely rational reason for 3:6. Jas 3:7–8 is connected to 'the tongue is a fire' in 3:6a and to the general thrust of 3:3–6" (McKnight, *James*, 286n91).

18. "The clever use of τῇ φύσει in connection with τῇ ἀνθρωπίνῃ puts man at the same level with the creatures and further alludes to man's dependence on God for his authority over the animals" (Baker, *Personal Speech-Ethics*, 129). "James creates a play on the word δαμάζω ('to tame') by using the present and perfect tenses. While this is a redundancy, the effect is to stress the control human beings have exercised on the animal world from the very beginning" (Hartin, *James*, 179). "James uses the verb 'tame' twice: once in the present tense to stress the continuing process by which human beings are subduing creatures, and again in the perfect tense—*have been tamed*—to show that this process is rooted in the state of affairs created by the divine mandate" (Moo, *James*, 161).

19. "James' point here is that there is an incontrovertible paradox in the created world in that mankind can and does subdue the wildest and most powerful animals, but the individual cannot do anything to deter the wanton destructiveness of his own tongue, a relatively small and seemingly unpretentious part of his body" (Baker, *Personal Speech-Ethics*, 129).

20. "James creates a deliberate alliteration with the phrase δαμάσαι δύναται ('can tame'). He demonstrates a pessimistic attitude: the tongue alone among all created things is impossible to control" (Hartin, *James*, 179).

to save one (2:14). The "word" regarding which they are not to stumble through their use of the untamable tongue includes the implanted "word" they are to welcome, which is "able" (δυνάμενον) to save their souls from eternal death (1:21). It thus includes the "word" of truth by which we were brought to birth for eternal life (1:18).

That the untamable tongue is an unstable "evil [κακόν]" (3:8) reminds the audience that it is one of the "evil things" (κακῶν) of which God tempts no one (1:13). And that the tongue is an "unstable" (ἀκατάστατον) evil reinforces the warning for no one in the audience to use the tongue for disputing (1:6), since such a person is "unstable" (ἀκατάστατος) in all this ways (1:8) and must not suppose that he will receive anything from the Lord through his use of the tongue in prayer (1:7).[21] Finally, that the untamable tongue of human beings is full of "death-bringing" (θανατηφόρου) poison (3:8; cf. Sir 28:17-23) associates it with the human desire, especially the desire for wealth, that gives birth to sin, which brings birth to the "death [θάνατον]" (1:15) that contradicts and destroys our new birth to eternal life (1:18).[22] The audience, then, are to heed the warning that the untamable, unstable evil that is the human tongue possesses the deadly destructive poisonous power to deprive them of the new and eternal life for which God brought them to birth.

3:9–10 (A'): It Is Not Necessary My Brothers That These Things Become So

The audience are then presented with our contradictory, incongruous, and inconsistent uses of the tongue: "With it we bless the Lord and Father and with it we curse human beings who have become in accord with the likeness of God. From the same mouth come out blessing and cursing. It is not necessary, my brothers, that these things become so"

---

21. "The tongue's instability recalls the double-minded person who is unstable in all his paths (1:8), and it anticipates the instability generated by jealousy and striving (3:16)" (McCartney, *James*, 192).

22. The phrase "full of death-bringing poison" "accents the utter potency of the tongue's evil to spread and cause death. In one sense, it may be related to the poisonous tongue of a snake" (Baker, *Personal Speech-Ethics*, 130).

(3:9-10). At this point the audience experience a progression, via the chiastic parallels, from the A to the A' element of this chiastic unit. "Not many of you should become [γίνεσθε] teachers, my brothers [ἀδελφοί μου]" (3:1) progresses to "human beings who have become (γεγονότας) in accord with the likeness of God" (3:9) and "it is not necessary, my brothers [ἀδελφοί μου], that these things become [γίνεσθαι] so" (3:10).

With the tongue we bless the "Lord and Father" (κύριον καὶ πατέρα) in our liturgical worship (3:9),[23] the worship that is part of a religion pure and undefiled before the "God and Father [θεῷ καὶ πατρί]," that is, to care for orphans and widows in their affliction, to keep oneself spotless from the world (1:27).[24] But with the same tongue we curse "human beings" (ἀνθρώπους),[25] ironically the "human beings" (ἀνθρώπων) among whom no one can tame the tongue (3:8), who have "become" (γεγονότας, perfect tense), that is, who were originally created to be and who still are, in accord with the likeness of the God (Gen

---

23. "Blessing, or praising, God is one of the most important and positive forms of human speech. James might be thinking specifically of the worship of the community, in which believers united their voices in singing and asserting the praise of God" (Moo, *James*, 163). "[T]he use (and misuse) of the tongue is related primarily to the worship setting of the church as a body . . . it makes what follows even more blameworthy. From one side of the worshiper's mouth comes praise to God; from the other side of the same mouth come curses aimed at another fellow worshiper" (Martin, *James*, 118). "[T]his blessing is undoubtedly a liturgical blessing of God" (Davids, *James*, 146).

24. "The addition of πατέρα to τὸν κύριον may be to make sure the reader understands that he means God here rather than Christ. As in 1:27, it probably also functions as a reminder of the brotherhood of man which derives from God's creatorhood and fatherhood of all men . . . cursing one's fellow man amounts to cursing God. This being the case, it casts doubt on the genuineness presumed by the author of James of the praise being offered to God, especially in light of 1:26-27" (Baker, *Personal Speech-Ethics*, 131).

25. "To use an imprecatory *curse* on someone, stemming as it did from an ancient perlocutionary understanding of how language works, both labels a person socially but also renders that person's standing before God as one condemned" (McKnight, *James*, 293). "The ancient curse was far more than abusive language; it called on God, in effect, to cut a person off from any possible blessing and to consign that person to Hell . . . As James emphasizes, what makes cursing especially evil is that the one whom we pronounce damned has been made *in God's likeness* (emphasis original)" (Moo, *James*, 163).

1:26–28) we worship.²⁶ These are the human beings we believers should be caring for as the ethical worship that is part of a religion pure and undefiled before God.

That out of the same human "mouth" (στόματος), in ironic contrast to the "mouths" (στόματα) of horses which can be properly guided (3:3), come blessing and cursing (3:10) exemplifies the unbridled tongue that prevents proper worship by religious persons (1:26). Just as not many of the audience, addressed as "my brothers," should "become" (γίνεσθε) teachers, knowing that we will receive a greater judgment (3:1), so it is not necessary for the audience, again addressed as "my brothers," to allow that these things—these contradictory and inconsistent uses of the tongue—to "become" (γίνεσθαι) so (3:10).²⁷ The audience are thus exhorted to complement their liturgical worship of blessing God with their tongues by including with it their ethical worship that, rather than cursing human beings with their tongues, cares for them as persons created in the very likeness of the God they worship (3:9). The audience will thereby become truly a religious people who offer a complete liturgical and ethical worship, which comprises a religion pure and undefiled before the God and Father (1:26–27).²⁸

Summary on 3:1–10

Not many in the audience should become teachers, since teachers will receive a greater judgment (3:1) as those responsible not only for doing mercy but for teaching others the doing of mercy, for the judgment is merciless for the one not doing mercy, but mercy triumphs over judgment (2:13). That, as those who become teachers, "we will receive" a greater judgment reinforces the exhortation for everyone in the audience to become tested by enduring temptation, so that "he will receive"

---

26. "James uses the perfect here to depict completed, or perfected, action. Image of God, then, is the condition of humans" (McKnight, *James*, 293n121).

27. "James does not claim that such inconsistent speech is impossible, but declares vigorously that it ought not to happen, it must not happen" (McCartney, *James*, 192).

28. For the anthropological presuppositions regarding the use of the tongue in Jas 3:1–10, see Wolmarans, "Tongue," 523–30.

at the judgment the crown of eternal life that God promised to those who love him (1:12).

For anyone in "word" not to stumble (3:2a) involves not just stumbling with regard to one's speech in general but not stumbling with regard to the "word" of truth by which God brought us to birth for a new and eternal life (1:18). And not stumbling in word involves being a doer and not just a hearer of the word (1:23). Indeed, the audience are to become doers of the "word" and not only hearers (1:22). That the "word" makes anyone who does not stumble in it "able" (3:2a) means that he has a power oriented to saving his soul from eternal death (1:15), since the implanted "word" the audience are to welcome is "able" to save their souls (1:21). Not stumbling in word, then, is part of a faith accompanied by works, a faith that is "able" to save (2:14).

Anyone who does not stumble in word is "perfect" in the sense of being whole and complete (3:2a). This kind of "perfection" is the goal for the whole audience. They have heard the exhortation for them to let endurance have its "perfect" work, so that they may be "perfect" and complete, lacking in nothing (1:4), that is, completely qualified for the proper worship of God. And such proper worship is part of a religion that includes bridling one's tongue. The assertion that if anyone does not stumble in word, this one is a perfect man able to "bridle" (3:2a) resonates with the assertion that if anyone thinks he is religious, not "bridling" his tongue but deceiving his heart, the religion, which includes worship, of this one is utterly useless (1:26).

That the tongue is a small member of the body like the tiny rudder of a large ship and like the small bridles in the mouths of horses implies that it can guide or bridle one's whole body (3:2–4). But rather than guiding or bridling the whole body, the tongue engages in "boasting" (3:5a), a type of uncontrolled behavior. That the "tongue" is a small member but boasts of great things reinforces the exhortation for anyone in the audience who thinks he is religious to bridle his "tongue" in order to offer effective worship to God (1:26).

The audience are to appreciate that the tongue, as a "small" member of the body that boasts of great things (3:5a), is not only like a "small" fire that kindles a great forest (3:5b), but the tongue actually *is* a fire (3:6a), with the implication that the tongue in itself can ignite tremendous destruction. That the tongue is constituted as the "world" of unrighteousness within our body's members (3:6b) develops the negative connotations the audience have heard for the term "world." They have heard that God chose the poor in this earthly "world" dominated by the rich to be heirs of God's heavenly kingdom (2:5). And they were exhorted to keep themselves spotless from this "world" of wealth by their ethical worship of caring for orphans and widows in their affliction (1:27). The audience, then, are to be aware of and separate themselves from not only the external world around them but from the internal world of unrighteousness that the tongue, as a small member (3:5a), constitutes within the members of their physical bodies as well as within the communal body of their worshiping assembly.

That the tongue "defiles" the whole body, the physical body of the individual person as well as the communal body of the worshiping assembly (3:6c), reinforces the exhortation for everyone in the audience to bridle his tongue (1:26). They are to become truly religious, practicing a religion that is "pure and undefiled," by performing the ethical worship of caring for orphans and widows in their affliction, in order to keep oneself "spotless" or "undefiled" from the world (1:27). That the tongue sets fire to and thus harms the course of the "birth" (3:6c), that is, our divine birth to a new and eternal life (1:18), reinforces the exhortation for the audience to become doers of the word, especially through a bridled use of the tongue, rather than being like one who observes the appearance of his "birth" to eternal life in a mirror but promptly forgets his new identity (1:23). And that the tongue is set on fire by Gehenna (3:6c), the place of eternal punishment and death, with its threat to destroy our new birth to eternal life, reinforces the exhortation for the audience not to stumble in word through an unbridled use of the tongue (3:2).

Although from the very beginning the human species has tamed every species within the animal world (3:7), that no one among human beings is "able" to tame the tongue (3:8) reinforces the exhortation for no one in the audience to use his tongue in a way that causes him to stumble in word, so that he may be a perfect man "able" to bridle even the whole body (3:2). This reminds the audience that not stumbling in word through the tongue is part of a faith accompanied by works that is "able" to save one (2:14). The "word" regarding which they are not to stumble through their use of the untamable tongue includes the implanted "word" they are to welcome, which is "able" to save their souls from eternal death (1:21). It thus includes the "word" of truth by which we were brought to birth for eternal life (1:18).

That the untamable tongue is an unstable "evil" (3:8) reminds the audience that it is one of the "evil things" of which God tempts no one (1:13). And that the tongue is an "unstable" evil reinforces the warning for no one in the audience to use the tongue for disputing (1:6), since such a person is "unstable" in all this ways (1:8) and must not suppose that he will receive anything from the Lord through his use of the tongue in prayer (1:7). And that the untamable tongue of human beings is full of "death-bringing" poison (3:8) associates it with the human desire, especially the desire for wealth, that gives birth to sin, which brings birth to the "death" (1:15) that contradicts and destroys our new birth to eternal life (1:18). The audience, then, are to heed the warning that the untamable, unstable evil that is the human tongue possesses the deadly destructive poisonous power to deprive them of the new and eternal life for which God brought them to birth.

With the tongue we bless the "Lord and Father" in our liturgical worship (3:9), the worship that is part of a religion pure and undefiled before the "God and Father," that is, to care for orphans and widows in their affliction, to keep oneself spotless from the world (1:27). That out of the same human mouth come blessing and cursing (3:10) exemplifies the unbridled tongue that prevents proper worship by religious persons (1:26). Just as not many in the audience should "become" teachers (3:1), so it is not necessary for the audience to allow that these things—these contradictory and inconsistent uses of the tongue—to "become" so (3:10). The audience are thus exhorted to complement their liturgical worship of blessing God with their tongues by including with it their ethical worship that, rather than cursing human beings with their tongues, cares for them as persons created in the very likeness of the God they worship (3:9). The audience will thereby become truly a religious people who offer a complete liturgical and ethical worship, which comprises a religion pure and undefiled before the God and Father.

James 3:11–18

Worship in the Humility of Wisdom That Is from Above (F)

A fruit of righteousness in peace is sown
among those who make peace to live by

A ¹¹ A spring from the same opening does not pour forth the sweet and the bitter, does it? ¹² My brothers, a fig tree is not able to *make* olives or a vine figs, is it? Neither is salty able to *make* sweet water.

    B ¹³ Who is *wise* and understanding among you? Let him show from praiseworthy conduct his works in humility of *wisdom*. ¹⁴ But if you have bitter *envy* and *selfishness* in your heart, do not boast against and lie against the truth. ¹⁵ᵃ This is not the *wisdom from above* coming down

        C ¹⁵ᵇ but earthly, this-worldly, demonic.

    B' ¹⁶ For where there is *envy* and *selfishness*, there is disorder and every foul practice. ¹⁷ᵃ But the *from above wisdom* is first of all pure,

A' ¹⁷ᵇ then peaceable, gentle, compliant, full of mercy and good fruits, nondisputive, nonpretentious. ¹⁸ And a fruit of righteousness in peace is sown among those who *make* peace.[1]

---

1. For the establishment of Jas 3:11–18 as a chiasm, see the Introduction.

James 3:11-18

Audience Response to 3:11-18

3:11-12 (A): A Fig Tree Unable To Make Olives and Salty Unable To Make Sweet

The audience hear the A element (3:11-12) of this chiastic unit as a chiastic pattern in itself:

a) A spring from the same opening does not pour forth the *sweet* and the bitter, does it (3:11)?

    b) My brothers, a *fig tree* is not able to make olives (3:12a)

    b′) or a vine *figs*, is it (3:12b)?

a′) Neither is salty able to make *sweet* water (3:12c).

At the center of this chiastic sub-unit the audience experience a pivot of parallels involving the only occurrences in James of terms referring to figs. They hear a progression from a "fig tree" (συκῆ) in the b) sub-element (3:12a) to the "figs" (σῦκα) themselves in the b′) sub-element (3:12b). They then experience a progression of parallels involving the only occurrences in James of the term "sweet." "Pour forth the sweet [γλυκύ]" in the a) sub-element (3:11) progresses to "able to make sweet [γλυκύ]" in the a′) sub-element (3:12c).

When the audience hear the phrase "from the same [ἐκ τῆς αὐτῆς] opening" at the beginning of this unit (3:11), they hear the transitional words that link this unit (3:11-18) with the preceding unit (3:1-10), which contains a reference to "from the same [ἐκ τοῦ αὐτοῦ] mouth" at its conclusion (3:10).[2] In contrast to the "same mouth" out of which come both a blessing of God and a cursing of human beings created in the likeness of God (3:9), and as a further reason why the audience should not allow this to happen (3:10), the audience must admit that a spring from the "same opening" does not pour forth the sweet and the bitter (3:11).[3]

---

2. "The fact that ἐκ τῆς αὐτῆς ὀπῆς is unnecessary to the sense of the question gives credence to the view that there is correspondence in terms of structure and imagery with ἐκ τοῦ αὐτοῦ στόματος and all the other elements of 3:10a" (Baker, *Personal Speech-Ethics*, 133-34).

3. "[I]t may be that James has chosen πικρός ['bitter'] in order to describe the cursing that issues from the tongue in a metaphorical sense" (Martin, *James*, 120).

Again addressed affectionately as "my brothers" (cf. 1:2, 16, 19; 2:1, 5, 14; 3:1, 10), the audience must agree that just as a fig tree is "not able" (μὴ δύναται) to make olives or a vine figs, so neither is salty able to make "sweet" water (3:12), reinforcing the fact that the same opening does not pour forth both the "sweet" and the bitter (3:11). This recalls and resonates with the assertion that "no one" (οὐδείς) among human beings is "able" (δύναται) to tame the tongue (3:8). The audience are to make the connection between not being able to tame the tongue and having a faith without works which is "not able" (μὴ δύναται) to save one (2:14). The audience then are to appreciate that just as it is incongruous for fig trees to be able to produce olives, vines to be able to produce figs, and salty to be able to produce sweet water, so it is incongruous for the same mouth to be able to produce both blessing and cursing, as this contradicts their welcoming the implanted word that truly is "able" (δυνάμενον) to save their souls (1:21).[4]

3:13–15a (B): Envy and Selfishness Are Not the Wisdom from Above

The audience hear the B element (3:13–15a) of this chiastic unit as a chiastic pattern in itself:

a) Who is *wise* and understanding among you? Let him show from praiseworthy conduct his works in humility of *wisdom* (3:13).

  b) But if you have bitter envy and selfishness in your heart, do not boast *against* (3:14a)

  b′) and lie *against* the truth (3:14b).

a′) This is not the *wisdom* from above coming down (3:15a).

At the center of this chiastic sub-unit the audience experience a pivot of parallels involving the only occurrences in this sub-unit of terms expressing "against." They hear a progression from "do not boast against [κατακαυχᾶσθε]" in the b) sub-element (3:14a) to "lie against

---

4. "James borrows these metaphors from the world with which he is familiar to express the idea that inconsistency in human speech should be just as inconceivable for a believer as it is for a tree to produce a fruit different from its type or species" (Hartin, *James*, 180–81).

[κατά] the truth" in the b') sub-element (3:14b). They then experience a progression of parallels involving the only occurrences in this sub-unit of terms expressing "wise/wisdom." "Who is wise [σοφός]" and "in humility of wisdom [σοφίας]" in the a) sub-element (3:13) progress to "not the wisdom [σοφία] from above" in the a') sub-element (3:15a).

The question of "who" (τίς) is "wise" (σοφός) and understanding among "you [ὑμῖν]" (3:13), that is, among the members of the audience, implies that such an individual possesses the faith necessary to receive the gift of wisdom from God. It recalls the statement that if "anyone" (τις) of "you" (ὑμῶν) is lacking "wisdom" (σοφίας), he should prayerfully ask for it from God (1:5) in faith (1:6). Such a wise and understanding one is to "show" (δειξάτω) from "praiseworthy" (καλῆς) conduct, that is, conduct that leads to the praise of God in worship, like the "praiseworthy" (καλόν) divine name invoked in worship (2:7), his "works [ἔργα]" (3:13). These are the works that demonstrate faith, as this exhortation reminds the audience of the assertion, "show [δεῖξόν] me your faith without works [ἔργων], and I will show [δείξω] you, from my works [ἔργων], faith" (2:18).[5]

That every wise and understanding member of the audience is to show from praiseworthy conduct his works that demonstrate his faith "in humility" (ἐν πραΰτητι) of wisdom (3:13) resonates with the exhortation for the audience to welcome "in humility" (ἐν πραΰτητι) the implanted word that is able to save their souls (1:21). This is the word of truth by which God brought us to new birth for eternal life (1:18). As among those individuals who aspire to be one who is "wise," the audience are thus to realize that the humility of "wisdom" in which they are to show their works of faith involves an understanding that God has brought them to birth for eternal life. This is the "wisdom" that comes from God (1:5) and by which they are to understand that the desire to be wealthy brings birth to death (1:15), which contradicts their birth to eternal life. That they are to show the "works" (ἔργα) of faith in this humility of wisdom reminds the audience that each of them is to be a

---

5. "[The] description of 'wise and understanding' is not exclusively applicable to teachers, but may include the community . . . What James has in mind here is a wisdom that results not so much in what one thinks or says as in what one does ('practical wisdom')" (Martin, *James*, 128–29).

doer of "work [ἔργου]" (1:25), the work that includes caring for poor widows and orphans as the ethical worship that is part of authentic religion (1:27).[6]

The warning that if the audience have "bitter" (πικρόν) envy and selfishness in their heart (3:14) resonates with the assertion that a spring from the same opening does not pour forth the sweet and the "bitter [πικρόν]" (3:11), with the "bitter" corresponding to the cursing that, along with blessing, comes out of the same mouth (3:10).[7] The audience are to appreciate the implication that the "bitter" cursing of a fellow human being created in the likeness of God (3:9) may stem from their envy of the wealth that person possesses.[8] The audience's having selfishness in their "heart" (καρδίᾳ) resonates with the notice that if anyone thinks he is religious, not bridling his tongue, as exemplified in the bitter cursing caused by envy, but deceiving his "heart" (καρδίαν), the religion of this one is useless (1:26). The audience are to realize that having such bitter envy and selfishness in their heart would exemplify a deceived heart that would prevent them from performing the unselfish ethical worship of caring for poor widows and orphans in order to be truly religious (1:27).

If the audience have bitter envy and selfishness in their heart, they are to be careful that this does not cause them to boast against or lie against the "truth [ἀληθείας]" (3:14), that is, the word of "truth" (ἀληθείας) by which God brought us to a new birth for eternal life (1:18).[9] The exhortation to beware that "you do not boast against

---

6. On the eschatological perspective of wisdom in James, see Hartin, "Who Is Wise," 969–99. "James is clearly trying to say two things here: true wisdom produces good works and true wisdom produces humility" (Moo, *James*, 170).

7. "The adjective πικρόν connects this verse to 3:11, identifying the jealousy as 'bitter.' Just as evils perpetrated by speech leave, as it were, a harsh taste in the mouth, so too does jealousy" (Hartin, *James*, 192).

8. The term ζῆλος, often translated as "jealousy," "denotes the desire to acquire by taking something away from another. In this sense, 'jealousy' is equivalent to envy (φθόνος), and Hellenistic moralists tend to use the terms interchangeably, as James does [cf. 4:5]" (Johnson, *James*, 271).

9. "In the present case, then, 'lying against the truth' must mean living in a manner contrary to the 'word of truth' (1:18) that was implanted in them and that they were to receive 'with meekness' (1:21). Such an existential, rather than conceptual,

[κατακαυχᾶσθε]" the truth recalls the need for the audience to have the mercy appropriate to living this eternal life, the mercy that does not impose judgment against the poor (2:2–4), but rather "boasts over" (κατακαυχᾶται) judgment (2:13). It reinforces the exhortation that each member of the audience should be a humble brother who is to "boast" (καυχάσθω) in his exaltedness (1:9), that is, as one exalted by God to a new birth for eternal life.

The audience are to realize that their bitter envy of those who are wealthy and the selfishness (3:14) that prevents their caring for the poor may lead to a boasting against the truth of our birth for eternal life which does not accord with the "wisdom coming down from above [σοφία ἄνωθεν κατερχομένη]" (3:15a). This is the "wisdom" (σοφίας) that is a gift of God (1:5), a perfect gift "from above" (ἄνωθέν) "descending" (καταβαῖνον) from the Father of lights (1:17).[10] This wisdom enables the audience to understand that the desire for wealth ultimately brings birth to the death (1:15) that contradicts our birth to eternal life (1:18). It is in the humility of this "wisdom" (σοφίας) that anyone in the audience who would be "wise" (σοφός) and understanding is to show from praiseworthy conduct his works (3:13) of faith. These works preeminently entail caring for those who are materially poor among them. And thus it is in this humility that the audience are to welcome the implanted word (1:21), the word of the truth of our new birth for eternal life (1:18).

3:15b (C): But Earthly, This-Worldly, Demonic

Having bitter envy and selfishness in the heart and boasting against and lying against the truth (3:14) is not the wisdom from above coming down (3:15a), "but earthly, this-worldly, demonic" (3:15b). The audience are to appreciate that having bitter envy for the wealth of others and selfishness that prevents their caring for the poor amounts to conduct which, being earthly, this-worldly, and demonic, accords more

---

understanding of truth is supported as well by James' last use of the term in 5:19" (ibid., 271–72).

10. "By this gift one shares in God's wisdom and is shown how to act" (Hartin, *James*, 192).

The Letter of James

with the desire that ultimately brings birth to death (1:15) than with the word of truth by which God brought us to birth for eternal life (1:18).

Envy and selfishness represent conduct that is "earthly" as opposed to the conduct of one brought to birth to live already the eternal life that is heavenly.[11] Its focus is limited to what is merely "this-worldly" and mortal without a vision for the other-worldly, divine, and eternal life that transcends this world.[12] And its origin is the "demonic" realm of evil rather than the divine realm, from which descend every good giving and perfect gift from above (1:17). That it is "demonic" (δαιμονιώδης) reminds the audience that although the "demons" (δαιμόνια) believe that God is one, their behavior does not accord with this belief (2:19).[13] Thus, this emphatic rhetorical triplet of similar negative descriptions (3:15b) persuades the audience to avoid the false wisdom of jealous and selfish behavior not in accord with our new birth for eternal life.[14]

3:16–17a (B'): Envy and Selfishness and the from-Above Wisdom

The audience then hear further elaboration of the wisdom that is not from above, but earthly, this-worldly, demonic (3:15): "For where there is envy and selfishness, there is disorder and every foul practice. But the from-above wisdom is first of all pure" (3:16–17a). After the central and unparalleled C element, "but earthly, this-worldly, demonic" (3:15b), the audience experience a pivot of parallels from the B (3:13–15a) to the B' element (3:16–17a) of this chiastic unit. "If you have bitter envy [ζῆλον] and selfishness [ἐριθείαν] in your heart" (3:14) progresses to

---

11. "[W]hen used in the sense of thinking or behavior, 'earthly' [ἐπίγειος] has a negative nuance, suggesting a narrow perspective that fails to consider God's realm and will" (Moo, *James*, 173).

12. The term translated as "this-worldly" is ψυχική, which pertains "to the life of the natural world and whatever belongs to it" (BDAG, 1100).

13. "The behavior of those in question is thought to be instigated by the demons themselves. Demonic forces are viewed in the NT as responsible for thoughts and actions in opposition to God" (Martin, *James*, 132).

14. "James uses three adjectives that are relatively rare and that gain their specific sense from the context in which he uses them. They move in a negative progression" (Johnson, *James*, 272). "The terms . . . describe in differing ways a life that is shaped by something other than God" (McKnight, *James*, 306).

"for where there is envy [ζῆλος] and selfishness [ἐριθεία]" (3:16). And "who is wise [σοφός]" (3:13), "in humility of wisdom [σοφίας]" (3:13), and "the wisdom from above [σοφία ἄνωθεν]" (3:15a) progress to "the from-above wisdom [ἄνωθεν σοφία]" (3:17a).

The audience are to realize that where there is envy for wealth and selfishness that prevents their giving to the poor, there is "disorder [ἀκαταστασία]" (3:16), the disorder caused by the "unstable" (ἀκατάστατον) evil of the tongue (3:8), and that resonates with one being "unstable" (ἀκατάστατος) in all his ways (1:8), preventing his receiving anything from the Lord (1:7).[15] And where there is envy and selfishness there is "every" (πᾶν) foul practice (3:16), in contrast to "every" (πᾶν) perfect gift that comes from God (1:17).[16]

On the other hand, the *from-above* wisdom [ἄνωθεν σοφία] (3:17a), emphasizing that this is the "wisdom from above" (σοφία ἄνωθεν) coming down from God (3:15a), in contrast to what is "earthly, this-worldly, demonic" (3:15b), is indeed a perfect gift "from above" (ἄνωθεν) descending from the Father of lights (1:17).[17] The audience are to appreciate that this "from-above" divine wisdom is first of all "pure [ἁγνή]" (3:17a), a term with ritualistic and cultic connotations indicating that this wisdom qualifies one to offer proper worship to God, including preeminently the ethical worship of caring for the poor.[18]

---

15. "Earthly wisdom traffics in jealousy and ambition, the external qualities indicative of one motivated by self-interest viewing others as rivals because they possess what he himself lacks. James has already noted that the 'double-minded' man is ἀκατάστατος ('unstable'; 1.8) in all his ways, which is thematically and lexically similar to the idea here that 'earthly' wisdom produces social 'disorder' (ἀκαταστασία) by means of jealousy and ambition . . . Here the term specifically refers to social strife that threatens cohesion" (Lockett, *Purity*, 127). "The Greek word translated 'disorder' (ἀκαταστασία) is another form of a word that James has used in 1:8 and 3:8 to describe the 'double-minded' person and the 'double-speaking' tongue" (Moo, *James*, 174).

16. That these are the only occurrences in James of the nominative neuter singular adjective "every" (πᾶν) enhances this connection.

17. "In contrast to earthly wisdom, wisdom 'from above' (3:17), a wisdom implied already in 1:5, is one of the gifts, perhaps the principal one, that come 'from above' (cf. 1:17)" (McCartney, *James*, 201).

18. "The term ἁγνός is surprisingly infrequent in the LXX (11x) where it is associated with the more common term for ritual purity (καθαρός) . . . ἁγνός denotes that

3:17b–18 (A'): Those Who Make Peace

The audience hear the A' element (3:17b–18) of this chiastic unit as a chiastic pattern in itself:

a) then *peaceable*, gentle, compliant (3:17b),

    b) full of mercy and good *fruits* (3:17c),

        c) *nondisputive* (3:17d),

        c') *nonpretentious* (3:17e),

    b') And a *fruit* of righteousness (3:18a)

a') in *peace* is sown among those who make *peace* (3:18b).

At the center of this chiastic sub-unit the audience experience a pivot of alliterative, more or less synonymous terms—from "nondisputive" (ἀδιάκριτος) in the c) sub-element (3:17d) to "nonpretentious" (ἀνυπόκριτος) in the c') sub-element (3:17e). The audience then hear a progression of parallels involving the only occurrences in this unit of the term "fruit." "Good fruits [καρπῶν]" in the b) sub-element (3:17c) progresses to "fruit [καρπός] of righteousness" in the b') sub-element (3:18a). Finally, they hear a progression of parallels involving the only occurrences in this unit of terms referring to "peace." "Peaceable" (εἰρηνική) in the a) sub-element (3:17b) progresses to "in peace [εἰρήνῃ]" and "those who make peace [εἰρήνην]" in the a') sub-element (3:18b).[19]

At this point the audience hear a progression, via the chiastic parallels, from the A (3:11–12) to the A' (3:17b–18) element of this chiastic unit. "A fig tree is not able to make [ποιῆσαι] olives" (3:12) and "neither

---

'wisdom from above' is free from moral pollution and, therefore, entails total sincerity or devotion" (Lockett, *Purity*, 128). "James places this term [ἁγνή] first because of the thematic importance of being 'unstained from the world' for what he calls 'pure (καθαρός) religion before God' (1:27)" (Johnson, *James*, 273). "This purity, then, means that the person partakes of a characteristic of God: he follows God's moral directives with unmixed motives. This person serves God alone" (Davids, *James*, 154).

19. "In this list of adjectives James exhibits his considerable skill as a writer, as was observed earlier. The four adjectives following ἁγνή ['pure'] begin with the same letter, ε, in order to produce an alliteration. Also we see that the second pair of these four have the same ending (-ης). The last two of the series begin with the letter α and exhibit rhythmical endings (-κριτος)" (Martin, *James*, 133).

is salty able to make [ποιῆσαι] sweet water" (3:12) progress to "those who make [ποιοῦσιν] peace" (3:18).

The divine wisdom from above that is first of all "pure" (3:17a), with its cultic, worshiping connotations, is then further described with an alliterative triplet of similar qualities. Such wisdom is then also "peaceable" (εἰρηνική), "gentle" (ἐπιεικής), "compliant [εὐπειθής]" (3:17b). That it is "peaceable" reminds the audience that it is not enough for any of them to simply say to a brother or sister without clothing and lacking daily food (2:15), "Go in peace [εἰρήνῃ]" (2:16). To be truly "peaceable," they must give them what is necessary for the body (2:16), and so demonstrate their faith with works (2:17-18), performing the ethical worship of caring for those who are poor as part of a pure and undefiled religion (1:27).[20]

In contrast to the tongue as "full" (μεστή) of death-bringing poison (3:8), the wisdom from above is "full" (μεστή) of life-giving "mercy [ἐλέους]" (3:17c), reminding the audience that the judgment is merciless for the one not doing "mercy" (ἔλεος), but "mercy" (ἔλεος), particularly mercy toward the poor (2:2-4), boasts over judgment (2:13).[21] And that the wisdom "from above" (ἄνωθεν) is also full of "good" (ἀγαθῶν) fruits (3:17c) implies the audience's "good" giving to the poor in response to and as part of the wisdom God has given to the audience, as it resonates with the assertion that every "good" (ἀγαθή) giving and every perfect gift "from above" (ἄνωθέν) is descending from the Father of lights (1:17).[22] That the wisdom from above is full of good "fruits" thus means that it is full of the good results, outcomes, or benefits produced by the audience's giving to the poor in accord with their reception of the divine gift of this wisdom.

The description of the wisdom from above concludes with an alliterative couplet of closely related qualities. It is "nondisputive

---

20. "The 'peaceable' person, then is not simply the tranquil person at rest with himself or herself, but the person who ... uses the tongue and gifts and behaviors to foster peace with God, self, others, and the world" (McKnight, *James*, 313).

21. That these are the only occurrences in James of the terms "full" (μεστός) and "mercy" (ἔλεος) enhances these connections.

22. That these are the only two occurrences in James of the adjective "good" (ἀγαθός) enhances this connection.

[ἀδιάκριτος]" (3:17d), "nonpretentious (ἀνυπόκριτος)" (3:17e).²³ That it is "nondisputive" reinforces the exhortation for the audience to extend mercy toward the poor as part of their ethical worship, so that they are not "divided" (διεκρίθητε) or in dispute among themselves, becoming judges with evil designs (2:4). It also reminds the audience that none of them is to be "disputing" (διακρινόμενος) anything, for the one who "disputes" (διακρινόμενος) is like a wave of the sea blown and driven about by the wind (1:6). That person cannot expect to receive anything from the Lord in prayer (1:7).

The wisdom from above is not only full of mercy and good "fruits [καρπῶν]" (3:17c), implying the audience's merciful and good giving to the poor, but one of its results or outcomes is a "fruit" (καρπός) of righteousness (3:18a).²⁴ The reference to a fruit of "righteousness" (δικαιοσύνης) reminds the audience that Abraham believed God, and it was reckoned to him as "righteousness [δικαιοσύνην]" (2:23; cf. Gen 15:6). This righteousness resulted from Abraham's faith, working together with his works, and from the works the faith was perfected (2:22). It also reminds the audience that the anger of a man does not work the "righteousness" (δικαιοσύνην) of God (1:20). These reminders reinforce the exhortation for the audience to demonstrate their faith with works (2:18), especially the works of mercifully helping the poor (2:15–16), rather than being angry toward them (cf. 2:2–4).

Further developing how the wisdom from above is "peaceable [εἰρηνική]" (3:17b), James asserts that a fruit of righteousness in "peace" (εἰρήνη) is sown among those who make "peace [εἰρήνην]" (3:18).²⁵ That a fruit of righteousness "in peace" (ἐν εἰρήνῃ) is sown among those

---

23. "James places ἀδιάκριτος between statements about 'peace' (εἰρηνικος, εἰρήνη [3:17. 18]) and 'good fruits' (καρπός [3:17, 18]) and adjacent to the adjective 'nonpretentious' (ἀνυπόκριτος). As ἀνυπόκριτος marks the opposite of a particular social behavior, *hypokrisis*; ἀδιάκριτος can be understood to be the opposite of *diakrisis*, which, according to 1:6, is characteristic of the disputer. Neither *hypokrisis* nor *diakrisis* is a quality that nurtures 'peace' or 'good fruits'" (Spitaler, "Dispute with God," 573).

24. "What James has in mind in this metaphorical expression is the yield of acting rightly, namely concrete acts of justice" (McKnight, *James*, 318).

25. "Certainly there is tautology here, but it is that type of emphatic tautology which is used for rhetorical effect" (Davids, *James*, 155).

who make peace reinforces the exhortation for the audience not merely to say to those in need, "Go in peace [ἐν εἰρήνῃ]," but to make peace for them by giving them what is necessary for the body (2:16). In contrast to the fact that a fig tree is not able to "make" (ποιῆσαι) olives, and salty is not able to "make" (ποιῆσαι) sweet water (3:12), the audience, as those who sow peace by being those who "make" (ποιοῦσιν) peace by helping the poor, may produce a fruit of the righteousness that pleases God (1:20). This is the ethical worship of a religion pure and undefiled before God (1:27) in accord with the word of truth by which God brought us to new birth for eternal life (1:18).[26]

Summary on 3:11–18

In contrast to the "same mouth" out of which come both a blessing of God and a cursing of human beings created in the likeness of God (3:9), and as a further reason why the audience should not allow this to happen (3:10), the audience must admit that a spring from the "same opening" does not pour forth the sweet and the bitter (3:11). The audience then are to appreciate that just as it is incongruous for fig trees to be able to produce olives, vines to be able to produce figs, and salty to be able to produce sweet water (3:12), so it is incongruous for the same mouth to be able to produce both blessing and cursing, as this contradicts their welcoming the implanted word that truly is able to save their souls (1:21).

The audience are to realize that their bitter envy of those who are wealthy and the selfishness (3:14) that prevents their caring for the

---

26. "Although jealousy and striving produce instability and every evil thing (3:16), those who are peace-doers sow seed that results in righteousness. The verse also reiterates what James declared in 1:20: human anger does not accomplish God's righteousness ... James's point is that those who do deeds of peace and promote peace thereby plant seeds and create an environment that eventually yields righteousness, not only for the sower, but also for the whole community to whom peace comes" (McCartney, *James*, 203). "*Righteousness* in Jas. 1:20 meant that conduct which is pleasing to God, and this is the 'fruit' intended here also. It includes all the virtues listed in v. 17 and is the opposite, as we have suggested, of 'every evil practice' (v. 16). This righteousness cannot be produced in the context of human anger (1:20); but it *can* grow and flourish in the atmosphere of peace (emphases original)" (Moo, *James*, 178).

poor may lead to a boasting against the truth of our birth for eternal life which does not accord with the wisdom coming down from above (3:15a). This is the wisdom that is a gift of God (1:5), a perfect gift from above descending from the Father of lights (1:17), not the false wisdom that is earthly, this-worldly, demonic (3:15b). This wisdom enables the audience to understand that the desire for wealth ultimately brings birth to the death (1:15) that contradicts our birth to eternal life (1:18). It is in the humility of this wisdom that anyone in the audience who would be wise and understanding is to show from praiseworthy conduct his works (3:13) of faith. These works preeminently entail caring for those who are materially poor among them. And thus it is in this humility that the audience are to welcome the implanted word (1:21), the word of the truth of our new birth for eternal life (1:18).

The audience are to realize that where there is envy for wealth and selfishness that prevents their giving to the poor, there is disorder (3:16), the disorder that is caused by the unstable evil of the tongue (3:8), and that resonates with one being unstable in all his ways (1:8), preventing his receiving anything from the Lord (1:7). The audience are to appreciate that this "from-above" divine wisdom is first of all "pure" (3:17), a term with ritualistic and cultic connotations indicating that this wisdom qualifies one to offer proper worship to God, including preeminently the ethical worship of caring for the poor.

In contrast to the tongue as "full" of death-bringing poison (3:8), the wisdom from above is "full" of life-giving "mercy" (3:17), reminding the audience that the judgment is merciless for the one not doing "mercy," but "mercy," particularly mercy toward the poor (2:2–4), boasts over judgment (2:13). And that the wisdom "from above" is also full of "good" fruits (3:17) implies the audience's "good" giving to the poor in response to and as part of the wisdom God has given to the audience, as it resonates with the assertion that every "good" giving and every perfect gift "from above" is descending from the Father of lights (1:17). That the wisdom from above is full of good "fruits" thus means that it is full of the good results, outcomes, or benefits produced by the audience's giving to the poor in accord with their reception of the divine gift of this wisdom.

James 3:11–18

That a fruit of righteousness "in peace" is sown among those who make peace (3:18) reinforces the exhortation for the audience not merely to say to those in need, "Go in peace," but to make peace for them by giving them what is necessary for the body (2:16). In contrast to the fact that a fig tree is not able to "make" olives, and salty is not able to "make" sweet water (3:12), the audience, as those who sow peace by being those who "make" peace by helping the poor, may produce a fruit of the righteousness that pleases God (1:20). This is the ethical worship of a religion pure and undefiled before God (1:27) in accord with the word of truth by which God brought us to new birth for eternal life (1:18).

James 4:1–10

Passions Battle within Your Members and an Enemy of God Is Constituted (E′)

Be humbled before the Lord and he will exalt you with life

A ⁴:¹ Whence are the wars and whence are the fights among *you*? Is it not from this, from *your* passions battling within *your* members? ² You desire but you do not have; you murder and envy but you are not able to obtain; you fight and wage war; you do not have because *you* do not ask; ³ you ask but you do not receive because you ask wrongly, so that you may spend on *your* passions.

    B ⁴ Adulteresses! Do you not know that friendship with the world is enmity with God? Whoever *then* decides to be a friend with the world, an enemy of God is constituted.

        C ⁵ Or do you think in vain the scripture *says*, "Toward envy longs the spirit that he caused to dwell in us"? ⁶ᵃ But he *gives* greater *grace*.

        C′ ⁶ᵇ Therefore it *says*, "God opposes the haughty, but to the humble he *gives grace*" (Prov 3:34).

    B′ ⁷ᵃ Submit *then* to God, but resist the devil

A′ ⁷ᵇ and he will flee from *you*. ⁸ Draw near to God and he will draw near to *you*. Cleanse hands, sinful ones, and purify hearts, double-minded ones. ⁹ Be miserable and mourn and weep. Let *your* laughter to mourning be turned and the joy to dejection. ¹⁰ Be humbled before the Lord and he will exalt *you*.[1]

Audience Response to 4:1–10

Having heard the unparalleled and central F unit (3:11–18), the audience now begin to experience the progression of macrochiastic parallels from the E (3:1–10) to the E′ (4:1–10) unit. That the tongue "is constituted" (καθίσταται) as the world of unrighteousness "within our members [ἐν τοῖς μέλεσιν ἡμῶν]" (3:6) progresses to your passions battling "within your members [ἐν τοῖς μέλεσιν ὑμῶν]" (4:1) and an enemy of God "is constituted [καθίσταται]" (4:4). In addition, when the audience hear the adverb "whence [πόθεν]" (4:1) at the beginning of this unit, they hear the transitional word that links this unit to the preceding unit, which has the alliteratively similar adverb "from above [ἄνωθεν]" (3:17), the next occurrence of a word ending with the Greek syllable –θεν, near its conclusion.

4:1–3 (A): Your Passions Battling within Your Members

The audience hear the A element (4:1–3) of this chiastic unit as a chiastic pattern in itself:

a) Whence are the wars and whence are the fights among you? Is it not from this, from your *passions* battling within your members? You desire but you do not have; you murder and envy but you are not able to obtain; you fight and wage war (4:1–2a);

  b) you do not have because you do not *ask* (4:2b);

  b′) you *ask* but you do not receive because you *ask* wrongly (4:3a),

a′) so that you may spend on your *passions* (4:3b).

At the center of this chiastic sub-unit the audience experience a pivot of parallels involving the only occurrences in this unit of the verb "ask." They hear a progression from "you do not have because you do not ask [αἰτεῖσθαι]" in the b) sub-element (4:2b) to "you ask [αἰτεῖτε]

1. For the establishment of Jas 4:1–10 as a chiasm, see the Introduction.

but you do not receive because you ask [αἰτεῖσθε] wrongly" in the b') sub-element (4:3a). They then experience a progression of parallels involving the only occurrences in James of the term for "passions." "Your passions [ἡδονῶν] battling within your members" in the a) sub-element (4:1–2a) progresses to "you may spend on your passions [ἡδοναῖς]" in the a') sub-element (4:3b).

In addition, the audience hear the a) sub-element (4:1–2a) of this chiastic sub-unit as another chiastic pattern in itself:

(a) Whence are the *wars* and whence are the *fights* among you (4:1a)?

> **(b)** Is it *not* from this, from your passions battling within your members? You desire but you do *not* have (4:1b–2a);
>
>> **(c)** you murder and envy (4:2b)
>
> **(b′)** but you are *not* able to obtain (4:2c);

(a′) you *fight* and *wage war* (4:2d).

After the central and unparalleled (c) sub-element (4:2b), "you murder and envy," the only occurrence of these verbs in this unit, the audience experience a chiastic progression of parallels involving the only occurrences in this chiastic pattern of the adverb "not." They hear a progression from "not [οὐκ] from this" (4:1b) and "you do not [οὐκ] have" (4:2a) in the (b) sub-element to "you are not [οὐ] able to attain" (4:2c) in the (b′) sub-element. They then hear a chiastic progression of parallels involving the only occurrences in James of terms referring to "war" and "fighting." "Whence are the wars [πόλεμοι] and whence are the fights [μάχαι]" (4:1a) in the (a) sub-element progresses to "you fight [μάχεσθε] and wage war [πολεμεῖτε]" in the (a′) sub-element.

After being informed regarding the divine wisdom "from above" (ἄνωθεν) coming down (3:15) and the "from-above" (ἄνωθεν) wisdom (3:17), the question of "whence" (πόθεν) are the wars and "whence" (πόθεν) are the fights among the audience (4:1a) implies that such wars and fights are not in accord with the wisdom of God by which the audience are to live. The wars and fights "among you [ἐν ὑμῖν]" (4:1a), the audience, thus contradict the wisdom and understanding to which the members of the audience should aspire, as indicated by the question, "Who is wise and understanding among you [ἐν ὑμῖν]?" (3:13).[2]

The audience must admit that these wars and fights come from their passions battling "within your members [ἐν τοῖς μέλεσιν ὑμῶν]" (4:1). The audience are to deduce that their passions which cause wars and fights among them are related to a wrong use of the tongue, as they hear a resonance with the assertion that the tongue is constituted as the world of unrighteousness "within our members" (ἐν τοῖς μέλεσιν ἡμῶν), defiling the whole body and setting fire to the course of our "birth" (3:6) for eternal life (cf. 1:18).[3] They are to appreciate the double meaning implied by the phrase "within your/our members" as referring not only to the members within their individual physical bodies but also to the members within their communal body. Passions, especially for wealth, cause wars and fights associated with the tongue, not only within the personal body but within the communal body as a worshiping assembly.[4]

The accusation that "you desire" (ἐπιθυμεῖτε) but you do not have (4:2a) reinforces the warning for the audience not to be led astray (1:16) from their birth for eternal life (1:18) by the desire for wealth. It reminds the audience that each person is tempted by his own "desire" (ἐπιθυμίας), being dragged away and enticed (1:14) by the desire especially for wealth. When the "desire" (ἐπιθυμία) conceives, it gives birth to sin, and the sin having been brought to completion, brings birth to the death (1:15) that contradicts our birth for eternal life. That "you do not have [ἔχετε]" what is desired (4:2a) ironically implies that this is because "you have" (ἔχετε) bitter envy and selfishness in your heart (3:14). This reinforces the exhortation for the audience that "you have"

2. That these are successive occurrences of the phrase "among you" within successive questions in James enhances this connection.

3. "The locative prepositional phrase recalls the negative picture of the evil tongue infecting all the members of the body with its evil in 3:6" (Baker, *Personal Speech-Ethics*, 135).

4. "These pleasures, or the desire for them, wage war 'in' your members, which may be understood as internal (within a person) or external (among members of the community) . . . In any case, it certainly is true that the faithless/unbelieving internal war of covetousness and frustrated desires generate faithless/unbelieving outward conflict, jealousy, and even murder among people" (McCartney, *James*, 207).

(ἔχετε) the faith in our Lord Jesus Christ of glory without partiality (2:1) for the rich over the poor (2:2–4).

The further accusation that "you murder [φονεύετε] and envy" (4:2b) reminds the audience of the warning that whoever keeps the whole law, but stumbles in one point, has become guilty of all of it (2:10). The one who said, "Do not commit adultery," said also, "Do not murder [φονεύσῃς]." If "you murder" (φονεύεις), you have become a transgressor of the law (2:11), the law of freedom (1:25; 2:12). This law of freedom is included within and embraced by the word of truth by which God brought us to birth for eternal life (1:18). For the audience to commit murder would thus contradict the eternal life for which they have been brought to a new birth. And that "you murder and envy [ζηλοῦτε]" reinforces the exhortation for the audience not to have bitter "envy" (ζῆλον) and selfishness in their heart (3:14), as this contradicts the divine wisdom from above (3:15). Their envy, especially for wealth, that can lead to murder confirms the assertion that where there is "envy" (ζῆλος) and selfishness, there is disorder and every foul practice (3:16). Murder does not eliminate but rather promotes more envy.[5]

Although their desire for the wealth they do "not" (οὐκ) have (4:2a) leads the audience to murder and envy (4:2b), they still are "not" (οὐ) able to obtain (4:2c). The impossibility that "you are not able [δύνασθε]" to obtain resonates with the impossibility for a fig tree to be "able" (δύναται) to make olives (3:12), for anyone to be "able" (δύναται) to tame the tongue (3:8), and for a faith without works to be "able" (δύναται) to save a person (2:14). The audience's not being "able" to obtain from others the wealth they desire even if they murder and envy reinforces the exhortation for them to put away all filthiness and excess of evil and in humility welcome the implanted word that is "able"

---

5. According to Moo (*James*, 184), we should "take 'you kill' in its normal, literal sense, but as a hypothetical eventuality rather than as an actual occurrence. As we have seen, the tradition to which James is indebted often portrayed murder as the end product of envy. James is warning his readers about just where their envious desires might lead them if not checked in time." "[I]n the *topos* on envy, murder is regarded as a logical concomitant of envy" (Johnson, *James*, 277). "While James' community may have not yet experienced and engaged in literal murder on a mass scale, the contingency is a very real one and must be warned against" (Martin, *James*, 144).

(δυνάμενον) to save their souls (1:21) by bringing them to a new birth for eternal life (1:18).

That "you fight [μάχεσθε] and wage war [πολεμεῖτε]" (4:2d) because you do not obtain (4:2c) through murder and envy (4:2b) what you do not have (4:2a) confirms the answer to the question of whence are the "wars" (πόλεμοι) and whence are the "fights" (μάχαι) among you (4:1a). The audience are to appreciate that their passions for the possession of wealth "battling" (στρατευομένων) within their members (4:1b) merely cause them to fight and wage war among themselves. Their wars and fights cause murder and ever more envy rather than promote their possession of the eternal life for which God has brought them to birth (1:18).

That "you do not have" (οὐκ ἔχετε) because you do not ask (4:2e) develops the accusation that you desire but "you do not have [οὐκ ἔχετε]" (4:2a). One of the reasons the audience do not have is that "you do not ask [αἰτεῖσθαι]." But even when "you ask" (αἰτεῖτε) you do not receive because "you ask" (αἰτεῖσθε) wrongly (4:3a), to spend on your passions (4:3b). That "you do not receive [λαμβάνετε]" implies that the audience do not receive from God what they ask for in prayer, as it resonates with the warning that not many of them should become teachers, knowing that "we will receive" (λημψόμεθα) from God a greater judgment (3:1). It also implies that they are asking wrongly by not asking in faith, as it confirms the exhortation for a person to "ask" (αἰτείτω) in faith (1:6), otherwise that person must not suppose that he "will receive" (λήμψεταί) anything from the Lord (1:7).[6] But blessed is a man who endures temptation, especially the temptation caused by passions for wealth, for having become tested, he "will receive" (λήμψεταί) the crown of eternal life (1:12).

Although "you ask" (αἰτεῖσθε) wrongly, to spend on passions (4:3), the audience instead are to ask God for the divine wisdom from above in order to understand that the desire for wealth not only leads to bitter envy and selfishness (3:13–16) but brings birth to eternal death (1:9–11, 15). This accords with the exhortation that if anyone in the audience is lacking wisdom, let him "ask" (αἰτείτω) from the God who gives to all

---

6. "Asking for personal gratification is not asking in faith (1:5–6), and so the one asking cannot expect to receive (1:7)" (McCartney, *James*, 209).

unreservedly, indeed not reproaching, and it will be given to him (1:5).[7] The audience are to realize that by asking wrongly, to spend on their "passions" (ἡδοναῖς), they are asking to spend on the very "passions" (ἡδονῶν) that are battling within their members, causing the wars and fights among them (4:1), which lead to the murder and envy (4:2b) that contradict their new birth for eternal life (1:18).[8]

4:4 (B): Whoever Then Decides to Be a Friend with the World

The audience then hear of the stern consequences of their battles to gain wealth: "Adulteresses! Do you not know that friendship with the world is enmity with God? Whoever then decides to be a friend with the world, an enemy of God is constituted" (4:4). The audience have heard that the one who said, "Do not commit adultery [μοιχεύσῃς]," said also, "Do not murder." If "you do not commit adultery [μοιχεύεις]" but you murder, you have become a transgressor of God's law (2:11). That the audience are now bluntly addressed as "adulteresses" (μοιχαλίδες) brings them to the realization that their passions for wealth lead them not only to the murder (4:2) but to the adultery that makes them transgressors of the law of freedom (1:25; 2:12), by which God brought us to birth for eternal life (1:18).

While the accusation that "you murder" (4:2) apparently refers to literal murder, the accusation that the audience are "adulteresses" (4:4) is clearly metaphorical, based on the biblical prophetic tradition of portraying the covenant between God and his chosen people as a nuptial

---

7. "The use of αἰτεῖν ('ask') here deliberately echoes 1:5. If persons do not already live within the 'wisdom from above,' however, they are not likely to turn to God with their requests" (Johnson, *James*, 277–78). "James is exhorting his readers to ask (lit. 'to pray to') God for their desires, but in the light of 3:13–17 the object is not gain or power, but wisdom. Peace will not come as a result of fighting and killing, but this fruit of the Spirit is promised to those who ask God for wisdom from above" (Martin, *James*, 147).

8. According to Johnson (*James*, 278), the verb "you may spend" (δαπανήσητε) "means simply to spend any resource but can also imply extravagance. Here the dative ἐν ἡδοναῖς is cryptic: they ask to acquire the resources to enable them to obtain the objects of their desire and craving . . . The gift-giving God is here manipulated as a kind of vending machine precisely for the purpose of self-gratification."

union, with God as the "bridegroom" and his people as his "bride." "Adultery" then metaphorically characterizes the abandonment of the worship of the true God for the worship of false gods. Addressed with the feminine vocative plural form, "adulteresses," in accord with the biblical imagery of their being the corporate "bride" of God, the audience are to realize how their passions for wealth lead them to become, in effect, adulterous idolaters, who stray from an authentic worship of God as their "bridegroom."⁹

As metaphorical "adulteresses" who foster a friendship with the world in order to become wealthy rather than with the God who promised his royal crown of eternal life to those who *love* him (2:5; 1:12), the audience must acknowledge that friendship with the world is enmity with God and that whoever decides to be a friend of the world, an enemy of God is constituted (4:4).¹⁰ Anyone in the audience who would

---

9. According to Schmitt ("You Adulteresses," 327–37), the address of the audience as "adulteresses" alludes to the way of an adulteress woman in Prov 30:20, who commits her evil deed yet feels no remorse. "Hosea was the first to speak of the covenant relationship of Israel with YHWH in terms of marital intimacy and marital fidelity (Hos 1–3; 9:1). His language was then picked up, like variations on a theme, by Isaiah (54:1–6; 57:3), Jeremiah (2:2; 3:6–14, 20), and Ezekiel (16:23–26, 38; 23:45). Both Jesus and the early Christians carried on this tradition by using marital imagery for God's people and referring to disobedience as relational, covenantal infidelity" (McKnight, *James*, 332). "In the OT idolatry sometimes was called 'adultery' because Israel was represented as God's bride, and, like marriage, Israel's covenant relationship with God demanded exclusive fealty. Although James does not spell it out, he no doubt shares the conviction of other NT writers (e.g., John 3:29; Eph. 5:28–32; Rev. 21:2) that the present-day community of faith, the people of God, is the bride of Christ, and hence idolatry or covenantal unfaithfulness of any kind is tantamount to adultery" (McCartney, *James*, 210). "In symbolic shorthand, James' epithet accuses the readers of idolatry, which is precisely what their manner of prayer (4:3) revealed" (Johnson, *James*, 278).

10. "[T]he use of 'friendship' in the first century was much more restrictive and had deeper connotations than today. One of the most common uses of friendship in ancient literature applied to alliances, cooperation or non-aggression treaties among peoples. The alliance between friends referred to the fact that friends shared similar vision and values" (Lockett, "*Purity*," 131–32). "The word for 'friendship' (φιλία) ordinarily means simply 'affectionate regard,' but it can slide over into the semantic range of sexual love (cf. Prov. 5:19 LXX). Hence, when James berates the world's would-be 'friends' as 'adulteresses,' he implies that flirting with the world is akin to spousal unfaithfulness" (McCartney, *James*, 209). "'Enemy,' especially in light of the

"decide" (βουληθῇ) to be a friend with the world is not properly guided by his tongue, in contrast to a pilot who guides his ship with a tiny rudder, comparable to the tongue, wherever he "decides [βούλεται]" (3:4). The audience are to realize that such a misguided decision contradicts the deliberate decision of God who "decided" (βουληθείς) to bring us to birth for eternal life (1:18), which friendship with the world cannot give. For any believing member of the audience to be a "friend" (φίλος) of the world means being constituted as an enemy of God, and this would not accord with the faith accompanied by works, by which one can, like Abraham, be called a "friend" (φίλος) of God (2:23).[11]

The audience are to appreciate that fostering friendship with the "world" (κόσμου) and being a friend with the "world [κόσμου]" (4:4) would make them adulterous idolaters rather than practitioners of a pure and undefiled religion that includes the ethical worship of caring for orphans and widows in their affliction, in order to keep themselves spotless from the "world [κόσμου]" (1:27).[12] The audience are not to become friends with the world for the purpose of becoming rich, because God chose the poor in this "world" (κόσμῳ) to be rich in faith and heirs of the kingdom that he promised to those who love him (2:5). The audience are to avoid being a friend with the world, one who "is constituted" (καθίσταται) an enemy of God (4:4), in accord with the passions for wealth battling "within your members [ἐν τοῖς μέλεσιν

OT background we have cited, must involve hostility of God toward the believer as well as that of the believer toward God. We have no evidence that James's readers were overtly disclaiming God and consciously deciding to follow the world instead. But their tendency to imitate the world by discriminating against people (2:1–13), by speaking negatively of others (3:1–12), by exhibiting 'bitter envy' and 'selfish ambition' (3:13–18), and by pursuing their own destructive pleasures (4:1–3) amounted to just that" (Moo, *James*, 187).

11. "The phrase 'friend of the world' (φίλος τοῦ κόσμου) exactly opposes the description of Abraham in 2:23 as 'friend of God' (φίλος θεοῦ)" (Johnson, *James*, 279). "Even the attempt to cultivate the world is disastrous, for that inner disposition constitutes (καθίσταται) one not just a compromiser or a poor Christian, but an enemy of God!" (Davids, *James*, 161). "The expression 'enemy of God' is extremely harsh" (Johnson, *James*, 280).

12. "The 'world' in 4:4, as in 1:27, refers to the 'system of human existence in its many aspects' (BDAG, 562), in particular to the sphere of desires, influences, and structures that draw a person's attention away from God" (McCartney, *James*, 209).

ὑμῶν]" (4:1). Such friendship would be fostered by a misguided use of the tongue that "is constituted" (καθίσταται) as the "world" (κόσμος) of unrighteousness "within our members" (ἐν τοῖς μέλεσιν ἡμῶν), defiling the whole body and setting fire to the course of our birth (3:6) for eternal life (1:18).[13]

4:5–6a (C): But He Gives Greater Grace

The audience continue to be addressed with regard to envy for the possession of riches: "Or do you think in vain the scripture says, 'Toward envy longs the spirit that he caused to dwell in us'? But he gives greater grace" (4:5–6a).[14] The question of whether the audience "think" (δοκεῖτε) that in vain the scripture warns against envy for wealth (4:5) resonates with the exhortation that if anyone "thinks" (δοκεῖ) he is religious (1:26), he should care for orphans and widows in their affliction (1:27), rather than being envious for the riches of the wealthy.[15]

The reference to what "the scripture says" (ἡ γραφὴ λέγει) about envy (4:5) reminds the audience of the fulfillment of what "the scripture says" (ἡ γραφὴ ἡ λέγουσα) regarding Abraham (2:23), namely, that his faith working together with his works (2:22) God reckoned to him as righteousness (Gen 15:6 in 2:23). Warned by the divine authority of the scripture regarding envy for wealth, the audience, instead of being envious for wealth, are to follow the scriptural example of Abraham by demonstrating a faith working together with works in providing a poor

---

13. van de Sandt, "James 4,1–4," 38–63. "James means friendship with the world to be equated with the desire for possessions" (Baker, *Personal Speech-Ethics*, 224).

14. For recent discussions of the many issues involved in determining the meaning and scriptural source of 4:5, see McKnight, *James*, 335–43; and McCartney, *James*, 210–17. They both conclude that "the scripture" in 4:5 refers to the quotation from Prov 3:34 in 4:6b. Similarly, see also Carpenter, "James 4.5," 189–205; and see Popkes, "James and Scripture," 224–27. However, somewhat analogously to John 7:38, "the scripture" in Jas 4:5 may refer to a scriptural text unknown to us or to an amalgamation of various texts whose source is "the scripture" in a general sense. "Whatever the solution, James considered this to be a quotation from Scripture and the audience would have heard it in a similar way. Consequently, we should take it as such" (Hartin, *James*, 199).

15. That these are the only occurrences in James of the verb "think" (δοκέω) enhances this connection.

brother or sister (2:15) what is necessary to keep warm and well fed (2:16). What the scripture says about envy also reminds the audience of the exhortation for them to complete the royal law according to "the scripture" (τὴν γραφήν), "You shall love your neighbor as yourself [Lev 19:18]" (2:8). In the context, the "neighbor" refers particularly to the poor whom the audience are to honor by welcoming them into their worshiping assembly without an envious partiality toward the rich over the poor (2:1–7).

The scriptural warning that toward envy, especially envy for wealth, longs the human "spirit" (πνεῦμα) that God caused to dwell in us (4:5) reminds the audience of the assertion that just as the body without a "spirit" (πνεύματος) is dead, so also faith without works is dead (2:26).[16] The audience, however, may be able to counter their "spirit" that "longs" (ἐπιποθεῖ) toward envy for riches, resonating with being dragged away and enticed by one's own "desire [ἐπιθυμίας]" (1:14), the "desire" (ἐπιθυμία) that ultimately results in eternal death (1:15), with the life-giving "spirit" represented by the works that accompany a faith which, without works, leads to eternal death. Although the body without a spirit is dead, with the works, the life-giving "spirit," of giving to the poor what is necessary for the body, the audience may offset their spirit that longs toward envy for wealth with the spirit of a faith whose works prevent death and promote life (2:15–17).[17]

Although the scripture says that toward envy, especially for wealth, longs the human spirit (4:5), the audience are to be encouraged that, nevertheless, God gives greater grace (4:6a), a divine grace "greater" (μείζονα) than the "great things" (μεγάλα) of which the tongue boasts (3:5), and the "greater" (μεῖζον) divine judgment those who become teachers, and who may use such a tongue, will receive (3:1). That God "gives" (δίδωσιν) greater grace reinforces the exhortation for the audi-

16. That these are the only occurrences in James of the term "spirit" (πνεῦμα) enhances this connection.

17. Regarding an alternative interpretation that construes God rather than the human spirit as the subject of the verb "longs" (ἐπιποθεῖ) here, Hartin (*James*, 200) notes: "The verb ἐπιποθεῖν is never used to refer to God. Further, the noun φθόνος is always used in reference to a vice. While ζῆλος has a positive ('zeal, ardor') and a negative meaning ('jealousy, envy'), φθόνος always has a negative connotation. This then argues for the spirit as being the subject of the verb, rather than God."

ence, inspired and empowered by divine grace, to "give" (δῶτε) the poor what is necessary for the body (2:16) to overcome the audience's envy for riches. And that God gives greater grace reinforces the exhortation for anyone in the audience who lacks wisdom to ask from the God who "gives" (διδόντος) to all unreservedly and it "will be given" (δοθήσεται) to him (1:5; cf. 1:17). The audience are to appreciate that this divine grace of the wisdom from above can enable them to overcome the bitter envy for wealth (3:13–18) that leads to eternal death (1:15) rather than to the eternal life for which God has brought us to birth (1:18).[18]

4:6b (C'): To the Humble God Gives Grace

The audience then hear another quotation with the divine authority of scripture: "Therefore it says, 'God opposes the haughty, but to the humble he gives grace' [Prov 3:34]" (4:6b). At this point the audience experience a pivot of parallels at the center of this chiastic unit. "The scripture says (λέγει)" (4:5) and "he gives [δίδωσιν] greater grace [χάριν]" (4:6a) in the C element progress to "therefore it says [λέγει]" and "to the humble he gives [δίδωσιν] grace [χάριν]" in this C' element (4:6b).

The implicit references to God as the subject who caused the spirit that longs toward envy to dwell in us (4:5) and who gives greater grace (4:6a) become emphatically explicit in the scriptural quotation from Prov 3:34, according to which "God" (ὁ θεός) opposes the haughty (4:6b).[19] That God opposes the haughty confirms for the audience, by means of the divine authority of scripture, that friendship with the world is enmity with "God" (τοῦ θεοῦ) and that whoever decides to be a friend of the world, an enemy of "God" (τοῦ θεοῦ) is constituted (4:4). The audience are to realize that being a friend of the world in order to gain wealth makes one a haughty enemy whom God opposes.

That to the "humble" (ταπεινοῖς) God gives grace (4:6b) reinforces the exhortation for every member of the audience to be a "humble"

18. "In contrast to the human envy, which seeks to compete with others in order to secure for oneself what they have, God's *aphthonia* ['lack of envy'] is demonstrated by his abundant giving" (Johnson, *James*, 282).

19. The LXX text of Prov 3:34 has "Lord" (κύριος) rather than "God" (ὁ θεός) as the subject.

(ταπεινός) brother who boasts in his exaltedness from God (1:9), rather than a rich person who can only boast in his lowliness (1:10), as one destined for destruction and death (1:11). Rather than aspiring to be materially wealthy, the audience are not only to care for the materially poor (1:27; 2:16) but to be humble poor ones spiritually themselves, since God chose the humble poor in this world to be rich in faith and heirs of the kingdom, as well as recipients of the crown of eternal life, that he promised to those who love him (2:5; 1:12). The audience are to be humble poor ones, because to the humble God gives grace, the greater grace (4:6a) by which they can overcome their propensity toward envy of those who are wealthy in the world (4:5), but who are haughty enemies opposed by God.[20]

4:7a (B'): Submit Then to God

A conclusion is drawn for the audience from the previous quotations of scripture (4:5–6): "Submit then to God, but resist the devil" (4:7a). At this point the audience hear a progression, via the chiastic parallels, from the B (4:4) to the B' (4:7a) element of this chiastic unit. "Whoever then [οὖν] decides to be a friend with the world, an enemy of God is constituted" (4:4b) progresses to "submit then [οὖν] to God" (4:7a).

Rather than fostering friendship with the world, which is enmity with "God" (τοῦ θεοῦ) and constitutes one as an enemy of "God [τοῦ θεοῦ]" (4:4), the audience are to humbly submit to "God [τῷ θεῷ]" (4:7a), in order thereby to be a friend of "God [θεοῦ]" (2:23). By submitting to God, the audience become part of the humble to whom God gives grace, the greater grace (4:6) that inspires and empowers one to overcome the tendency toward envy for wealth (4:5).[21] And by submitting to God to

---

20. "The 'humble' may refer either to those who already practice what God desires or those who, when convicted of sin, will humble themselves, repent, and submit to God. More specifically the term refers to the pious poor (1:6) who await God's deliverance from trials (1:12) and will enter his kingdom (2:5) as they are patient to trust him (5:8) to the end" (Martin, *James*, 151). "The exhortation of 1.9 is thus given an ongoing and present grounding; the lowly are reminded that God provides for them; thus, they do not need to engage in jealous striving according to the standards of the world, as depicted in 4.1–5" (Hutchinson Edgar, *Has God Not Chosen*, 194n29).

21. "This is not simply a call to a general disposition of living under the lordship

receive grace from the God who "opposes" (ἀντιτάσσεται) the haughty (4:6b), the audience then are to "resist" (ἀντίστητε) the devil (4:7a), the origin of the "demonic" wisdom that is not from above (3:15), and of the envious desire for wealth that brings birth to eternal death (1:15) rather than promoting our birth for eternal life (1:18).[22]

4:7b–10 (A'): God Will Draw Near to You and Will Exalt You

The audience hear the A' element (4:7b–10) of this chiastic unit, consequences of their resisting the devil (4:7a), and further imperatives, as a chiastic pattern in itself:

a) and he will flee from *you*. Draw near to God and he will draw near to *you* (4:7b–8a).

    b) *Cleanse hands, sinful ones* (4:8b),

    b') and *purify hearts, double-minded ones* (4:8c).

a') Be miserable and mourn and weep. Let *your* laughter to mourning be turned and the joy to dejection. Be humbled before the Lord and he will exalt *you* (4:9–10).

At the center of this chiastic sub-unit the audience experience a pivot of parallels involving a threefold complementary correspondence of synonymous and alliterative terms. The imperative verb "cleanse" (καθαρίσατε), the reference to "hands" (χεῖρας) as part of one's person, and the address to "sinful ones" (ἁμαρτωλοί) in the b) sub-element

---

of God but also a summons to submit to God for the grace of forgiveness that is granted to those who repent" (McKnight, *James*, 346).

22. "The devil personifies the negative side of James' cosmic dualism, the force that influences the κόσμος resistant to God's kingdom. In particular the mention of the διάβολος here corresponds to the characterization of earthbound wisdom as δαιμονιώδης in 3:15" (Johnson, *James*, 283–84). "As God resists the proud, so believers are to resist the devil (cf. 1 Pet. 5:8–9), the quintessential architect and archetype of pride. It is the devil who fosters jealousy and ambition, offers a fake wisdom and a false faith, and brews a broth of discord and contention and murderous envy to sap the church's vitality and undermine its integrity" (McCartney, *James*, 217). "The desires that yearn toward envy are animated, at least in part, by 'the devil.' It is reasonable to think that the desires of 1:13–15 are also partly inspired by the devil" (McKnight, *James*, 348).

(4:8b) progress to the imperative verb "purify" (ἁγνίσατε), the reference to "hearts" (καρδίας) as part of one's person, and the address to "double-minded ones" (δίψυχοι) in the b') sub-element (4:8c). The audience then hear a progression of parallels involving the only occurrences in this sub-unit of the second person plural pronoun. "He will flee from you (ὑμῶν)" and "he will draw near to you [ὑμῖν]" in the a) sub-element (4:7b–8a) progress to "let your [ὑμῶν] laughter" and "he will exalt you [ὑμᾶς]" in the a') sub-element (4:9–10).

In addition, at this point the audience also experience a progression, via the chiastic parallels, from the A (4:1–3) to the A' (4:7b–10) element of this chiastic unit. "Among you [ὑμῖν]" (4:1), "your [ὑμῶν] passions" (4:1, 3), "your [ὑμῶν] members" (4:1), and "because you [ὑμᾶς] do not ask" (4:2) progress to "from you [ὑμῶν]" (4:7b), "near to you [ὑμῖν]" (4:8), "your [ὑμῶν] laughter" (4:9), and "he will exalt you [ὑμᾶς]" (4:10).

If the audience resist the devil (4:7a), they are promised that then he will flee from "you [ὑμῶν]" (4:7b), with the implication that then "your" (ὑμῶν) passions (4:1, 3) for the possession of wealth that are battling within "your" (ὑμῶν) members (4:1) will be quelled. The exhortation for the audience to draw near to "God [τῷ θεῷ]" (4:8a) reinforces and elaborates the previous exhortation for them to submit to "God [τῷ θεῷ]" (4:7a). If they draw near to God, with the cultic connotation of drawing near in worship, they are promised that then God, in contrast to his opposing the haughty (4:6b), will draw near to "you [ὑμῖν]" (4:8a), with the implication that then the wars and fights, caused by envious passions for wealth (4:1b–3), among "you [ὑμῖν]" (4:1a) will cease.[23]

The command for the audience that you "cleanse" (καθαρίσατε) hands (4:8b) reinforces the exhortation for them to practice a religion that is "pure" or "clean" (καθαρά) and undefiled before the God and

23. "Significantly the author describes drawing near to God and resisting the devil in terms of purification. The verb ἐγγίζω is often used in the LXX to refer to the priest 'drawing near' to God in cultic worship. And this image is reinforced by the parallel command. 'Cleanse your hands, you sinners, and purify your hearts, you double-minded' (4.8b)" (Lockett, *Purity*, 134). "Opposition to the proud stands in contrast to God's drawing near to the one who draws near to God, which implies that drawing near is a dimension of humility, submission, and resisting the devil" (McKnight, *James*, 349).

Father by engaging in the ethical worship of caring for orphans and widows in their affliction, in order to keep themselves spotless from the world (1:27).²⁴ For them to "cleanse hands" metaphorically means for them to purify their behavior so that it can serve as truly religious ethical worship.²⁵ For the audience to cleanse their hands as those who are "sinful ones [ἁμαρτωλοί]" (4:8b) reinforces the exhortation for them to avoid the desire for wealth. When the desire conceives, it gives birth to the "sin" (ἁμαρτίαν), which makes them "sinful ones," and the "sin" (ἁμαρτία), having been brought to completion, brings birth to the death (1:15) that contradicts our birth for eternal life (1:18).²⁶

The command for the audience that "you purify" (ἁγνίσατε) hearts as those who are "double-minded ones [δίψυχοι]" (4:8c) carries cultic connotations of purifying for proper worship.²⁷ It reinforces the exhortation for anyone in the audience who lacks wisdom, the wisdom from above that is first of all "pure [ἁγνή]" (3:17), to ask for it from God in faith (1:5–6), since a "double-minded" (δίψυχος) man (1:8) must not suppose that he will receive anything in prayerful worship (1:7).²⁸ The

---

24. "The verb 'cleanse' (καθαρίζω) is used for priestly removal of defilement in Leviticus 16.19–20 and specifically with reference to 'sins' in Leviticus 16.30 and Sirach 23.10" (Lockett, *Purity*, 136). "The phrase καθαρίσατε χεῖρας ('cleanse your hands') refers to the ritual washing that was necessary prior to service in the Temple ... This ritual was then adopted by Israelites as a daily usage before meals, etc. As part of their purity rules and rituals it was a clear demonstration of their separation from the world and their connection with God's realm" (Hartin, *James*, 201).

25. "Often the hands could represent one's actions. For example, in Deuteronomy 2.7, literally 'in the work of your hands' is translated as 'in all your undertakings' in the NRSV" (Lockett, *Purity*, 136). "Hands were used to offer gifts and sacrifices (cf. Lev 4:4; 14:15) and were cleansed as a form of purity (cf. Mark 7:2–5)" (McKnight, *James*, 351).

26. "The author's rhetoric implicitly labels the actions (hands) of these 'sinners' as impure (associated with both the devil and ὁ κόσμος), and thus in danger" (Lockett, *Purity*, 137).

27. "Likewise ἁγνίζω is associated with cultic purity (Exod. 19.10; Num. 8.21; 19.12; 31.23)" (ibid., 136).

28. The term "double-minded ones," according to Moo (*James*, 194), "underscores especially James's accusation that his readers are attempting to be 'friends' with both God and the world at the same time (v. 4)." "As the wisdom from above is 'pure' (ἁγνή), so must the double-minded 'purify (ἁγνίζειν) their hearts' to live by it" (Johnson, *James*, 285).

address of the audience as "sinful ones" and "double-minded ones" with the commands to cleanse their hands and purify their hearts for proper worship resonates with the blunt accusation of the audience as "adulteresses" engaged in idolatrous worship (4:4).[29]

The command for the audience to purify "hearts" (καρδίας), with its reference to the culticly "pure" interior disposition needed for proper worship (4:8c), complements the command to cleanse "hands" (χεῖρας), with its reference to the culticly "clean" external activity that accords with proper worship (4:8b).[30] The audience are to purify their hearts by not having the bitter envy and selfishness with regard to the possession of wealth "in your heart [καρδίᾳ]" (3:14). The audience are to purify their hearts so that none of them deceives his "heart" (καρδίαν) by having an unbridled tongue (1:26). Purified hearts thus enable the audience to practice a religion that is pure and undefiled before the God and Father with the ethical worship of caring for orphans and widows in their affliction, thereby keeping themselves spotless from the world (1:27).[31]

The audience hear the a') sub-element of this chiastic sub-unit (4:7b–10) as a chiastic pattern in itself:

(a) Be miserable and mourn and weep. Let *your* laughter (4:9a)

    (b) *to* mourning (4:9b)

---

29. "[T]hese blunt addresses gain all the more strength from their contrast with James's typical address 'brothers' or 'beloved brothers'" (Moo, *James*, 194).

30. "The command to 'cleanse your hands' and 'purify your hearts' is reminiscent of Psalm 24.4 (23.4 LXX) where the one who may ascend the hill of the Lord and stand in his holy place is 'He who has clean hands and a pure heart.' In James 'hands' and 'heart' refer to both external behavior and internal attitude and should not be conflated into a single command to 'purify yourselves.' . . . In this way James is addressing both the inward disposition and the outward moral and social concern" (Lockett, *Purity*, 136). McKnight (*James*, 351) points out the "notable development" in "the shift from 'hands' to 'hearts' to emphasize total purification, body and heart or outer and inner."

31. "The imagery of both 'washing' and 'purifying' stems from the OT provisions for priestly purity in ministering the things of the Lord. But both verbs had come to be adopted more broadly to ethical purity as well" (Moo, *James*, 194). "The second line, 'purify your hearts,' interestingly may refer to the unmixed quality of the heart's devotion in worship. The stains of the world and the devil affect the readers internally and therefore they must be purified" (Lockett, *Purity*, 137).

James 4:1–10

(c) be turned (4:9c)

(b′) and the joy *to* dejection (4:9d).

(a′) Be humbled before the Lord and he will exalt *you* (4:10).

After the central and unparalleled (c) sub-element, "be turned [μετατραπήτω]" (4:9c), the audience experience a pivot of parallels involving the only occurrences in this sub-unit of the preposition "to." "To [εἰς] mourning" in the (b) sub-element (4:9b) progresses to "to (εἰς) dejection" in the (b′) sub-element (4:9d). The audience then hear a progression of parallels involving the only occurrences in this sub-unit of the second person plural pronoun. "Your [ὑμῶν] laughter" in the (a) sub-element (4:9a) progresses to "he will exalt you [ὑμᾶς]" in the (a′) sub-element (4:10).

After an emphatic rhetorical triplet of commands connoting conversion, "be miserable and mourn [πενθήσατε] and weep," the audience are exhorted to let their laughter (4:9a) be turned (4:9c), with the implicit help of God's grace (4:6), to the "mourning" (πένθος), the central command of the triplet, that indicates their repentance (4:9b).[32] The audience were exhorted to consider it all "joy [χαράν]" (1:2) whenever they endure temptations (1:3), particularly temptations caused by the desire for wealth (1:14). But now they are exhorted as sinners envious of wealth to let the "joy" (χαρά) they would otherwise have be turned to dejection (4:9d) to indicate their repentance from the envious and deadly desire for wealth (1:15).[33]

The audience are then exhorted that "you be humbled" (ταπεινώθητε) before the Lord (4:10a) and thus become the "humble" (ταπεινοῖς) to whom God gives the grace (4:6) to enable them to repent

---

32. "Lamenting, mourning, weeping, mourning and dejection [4:9] are all metaphors for repentance" (McKnight, *James*, 353). "The idea of laughter (γέλως) may suggest two things. First, the 'festive' outlook of these sinners and double-minded people must change because there is no reason to laugh . . . Second, laughter can reflect the attitude of the fool (Prov 10:23; Eccl 7:6; Sir 21:20; 27:13), who has no 'fear of God' which is the mark of wisdom (Prov 1:7)" (Martin, *James*, 154).

33. That these are the only occurrences in James of the term "joy" (χαρά) enhances this connection. "Here is a reversal of 1:2: those who were experiencing testing were to regard it 'entirely as joy' (χαρά). But those who are friends of the world must abandon the χαρά associated with the pursuit of desires" (Johnson, *James*, 286).

of their envious passions and deadly desire for wealth. In return for letting "your" (ὑμῶν) laughter be turned to the repentance of mourning (4:9), the audience, who are to humble themselves before the Lord, are assured that he will exalt "you [ὑμᾶς]" (4:10). That God "will exalt" (ὑψώσει) them in return for humbling themselves reinforces the exhortation for everyone in the audience to become a "humble" (ταπεινός) brother who boasts in his "exaltedness [ὕψει]" (1:9) to an eternal life given by God.

That God will exalt the audience who humble themselves (4:10) in repentance (4:9) so that they may receive the grace that enables them to endure temptations caused by the deadly desire for wealth (1:15) means that they will receive the crown of eternal life that God promised to those who love him (1:12). By "cleansing their hands" and "purifying their hearts" (4:8) of envious passions for wealth, so that they may offer the ethical worship of caring for the poor (1:27), the audience may, in and through such worship, foster the eternal life for which God brought us to birth (1:18).

Summary on 4:1-10

Although they "ask" wrongly, to spend on passions (4:3), the audience instead are to ask God for the divine wisdom from above in order to understand that the desire for wealth not only leads to bitter envy and selfishness (3:13–16) but brings birth to eternal death (1:9–11, 15). This accords with the exhortation that if anyone in the audience is lacking wisdom, let him prayerfully "ask" from the God who gives to all unreservedly, indeed not reproaching, and it will be given to him (1:5). The audience are to realize that by asking wrongly, to spend on their "passions," they are asking to spend on the very "passions" that are battling "within your members," causing the wars and fights among them (4:1), recalling that the tongue is constituted as the world of unrighteousness "within our members" (3:6). These wars and fights instigated by the tongue lead to the murder and envy (4:2) that contradict our new birth for eternal life (1:18).

The audience are to appreciate that fostering friendship with the "world" and being a friend with the "world" (4:4) would make them

James 4:1–10

adulterous idolaters rather than practitioners of a pure and undefiled religion that includes the ethical worship of caring for orphans and widows in their affliction, in order to keep themselves spotless from the "world" (1:27). The audience are not to become friends with the world for the purpose of becoming rich, because God chose the poor in this "world" to be rich in faith and heirs of the kingdom that he promised to those who love him (2:5). The audience are to avoid being a friend with the world, one who "is constituted" an enemy of God (4:4), in accord with the passions for wealth battling "within your members" (4:1). Such friendship would be fostered by a misguided use of the tongue that "is constituted" as the "world" of unrighteousness "within our members," defiling the whole body and setting fire to the course of our birth (3:6) for eternal life (1:18).

Although the scripture says that toward envy, especially for wealth, longs the human spirit (4:5), the audience are to be encouraged that, nevertheless, God gives greater grace (4:6a), a divine grace "greater" than the "great things" of which the tongue boasts (3:5), and the "greater" divine judgment those who become teachers, and who may use such a tongue, will receive (3:1). That God "gives" greater grace reinforces the exhortation for the audience, inspired and empowered by divine grace, to "give" the poor what is necessary for the body (2:16) to overcome the audience's envy for riches. And that God gives greater grace reinforces the exhortation for anyone in the audience who lacks wisdom to ask from the God who "gives" to all unreservedly and it "will be given" to him (1:5; cf. 1:17). The audience are to appreciate that this divine grace of the wisdom from above can enable them to overcome the bitter envy for wealth (3:13–18) that leads to eternal death (1:15) rather than to the eternal life for which God has brought us to birth (1:18).

That to the "humble" God gives grace (4:6b) reinforces the exhortation for every member of the audience to be a "humble" brother who boasts in his exaltedness from God (1:9), rather than a rich person who can only boast in his lowliness (1:10), as one destined for destruction and death (1:11). Rather than aspiring to be materially wealthy, the audience are not only to care for the materially poor (1:27; 2:16) but to be humble poor ones spiritually themselves, since God chose the humble poor in this world to be rich in faith and heirs of the kingdom, as well as recipients of the crown of eternal life, that he promised to those who love him (2:5; 1:12).

If the audience resist the devil (4:7a), they are promised that then he will flee from "you" (4:7b), with the implication that then "your" passions (4:1, 3) for the possession of wealth that are battling within "your" members (4:1) will be quelled. The exhortation for the audience to draw near to "God" (4:8a) reinforces and elaborates the previous exhortation for them to submit to "God" (4:7a). If they draw near to God, with the cultic connotation of drawing near in worship, they are promised that then God, in contrast to his opposing the haughty (4:6b), will draw near to "you" (4:8a), with the implication that then the wars and fights, caused by envious passions for wealth (4:1b-3), among "you" (4:1a) will cease.

That God will exalt the audience who humble themselves (4:10) in repentance (4:9) so that they may receive the grace that enables them to endure temptations caused by the deadly desire for wealth (1:15) means that they will receive the crown of eternal life that God promised to those who love him (1:12). By "cleansing their hands" and "purifying their hearts" (4:8) of envious passions for wealth, so that they may offer the ethical worship of caring for the poor (1:27), the audience may, in and through such worship, foster the eternal life for which God brought us to birth (1:18).

James 4:11–17

If the Lord Wants It Then We Will Live to Do What Is Praiseworthy (D′)

You do not know what your life will be like tomorrow

A ⁴:¹¹ Do not speak against one another, brothers. He who speaks against a brother or judges his brother speaks against the law and judges the law. But if you judge the law, you are not a *doer* of the law

    B ¹¹ᵇ but a *judge*.

        C ¹²ᵃ One is lawgiver

    B′ ¹²ᵇ and *judge* who is able to save and to destroy. But who are you who judges the neighbor?

A′ ¹³ Come now those saying, "Today or tomorrow we will go to this or that city and *do* business there a year and buy and sell and make a profit." ¹⁴ You do not know what your life will be like tomorrow. For you are a vapor that for a short time appears, and then disappears, ¹⁵ Instead of you saying, "If the Lord wants it, then we will live and *do* this or that," ¹⁶ now you are boasting in your arrogances. All such boasting is evil. ¹⁷ To one knowing then the praiseworthy thing to *do* and not *doing* it, to him it is sin.[1]

---

1. For the establishment of Jas 4:11–17 as a chiasm, see the Introduction.

Audience Response to 4:11–17

At this point the audience experience a progression of macrochiastic parallels from the D (2:14–26) to the D' (4:11–17) unit. "Do you want [θέλεις] to know" (2:20) progresses to "if the Lord wants [θελήσῃ] it" (4:15).[2] In addition, when the audience hear the verb "speak against" (καταλαλεῖτε) at the beginning of this unit (4:11a), they hear the transitional word that links this unit with the preceding unit (4:1–10), which contains the alliterative noun "dejection" (κατήφειαν) toward its conclusion (4:9).

4:11a (A): You Are Not a Doer of the Law

Having been exhorted that each of them should be quick to hear, but slow to "speak" (λαλῆσαι), and slow to anger (1:19), the audience, again addressed as "brothers [ἀδελφοί]" (1:2, 16, 19; 2:1, 5, 14; 3:1, 10, 12), are now exhorted that "you do not speak against [καταλαλεῖτε]" one another (4:11a).[3] For he who "speaks against" (καταλαλῶν) a fellow believing "brother" (ἀδελφοῦ) or "judges" (κρίνων) his "brother" (ἀδελφόν) "speaks against" (καταλαλεῖ) the "law" (νόμου) and "judges" (κρίνει) the "law" (νόμον). But if "you judge" (κρίνεις) the "law" (νόμον), you are not a "doer" (ποιητής) of the "law [νόμου]" (4:11a).

This exhortation, with key terms emphatically repeated for maximum rhetorical effect, recalls and resonates with the exhortation that

---

2. That these are the only occurrences in James of the verb "want" (θέλω) establishes this macrochiastic connection.

3. This is the first time the audience are addressed simply as "brothers," rather than as "my brothers" (1:2; 2:1, 14; 3:1, 10, 12) or "my brothers beloved" (1:16, 19; 2:5). "James does not give up on his hearers. Despite the preceding rhetoric in 4:1–10 castigating people for being 'adulteresses' and 'double-minded,' he returns to calling them 'brothers' in 4:11. This is not an indication of shift of audience; it simply marks the speech of a pastor reminding his flock that despite his strong rhetoric, he acknowledges them as his siblings in the Lord. And so should they regard one another as brothers and sisters and act accordingly, with concern but not judgment and certainly not slander" (McCartney, *James*, 220). "James' use of 'brother' (ἀδελφός) is a sudden switch from the naming of sinners and the double-minded person of 4:8, and perhaps he is exemplifying the care in the use of the tongue that has been his admonition to his readers" (Martin, *James*, 163).

you, rather than "speak against" a brother, so "speak" (λαλεῖτε) and so "do" (ποιεῖτε) as those about to be "judged" (κρίνεσθαι) through a "law" (νόμου) of "freedom [ἐλευθερίας]" (2:12). The law of freedom is the royal "law" (νόμον) of loving your neighbor as yourself (2:8). For he who is a "doer" (ποιητής) of this work of love called for by the perfect "law" (νόμον), the one of "freedom" (ἐλευθερίας), will be "blessed" (μακάριος) in his "doing [ποιήσει]" (1:25), that is, "blessed" (μακάριος) to receive the crown of eternal life (1:12).[4]

The audience are to realize that for any of them to speak against or "judge" (κρίνων) a fellow believing brother amounts to speaking against and "judging" (κρίνει) the law, and if "you judge" (κρίνεις) the law, you are not a doer of the law (4:11a), the law through which the audience will be "judged" (κρίνεσθαι) by God (2:12). This reinforces the exhortation that not many of the audience should become teachers, knowing that they will receive a greater "judgment" (κρίμα) from God (3:1), if they speak against or judge a fellow believing brother rather than bridling their deadly tongues, which are capable of destroying the course of our new birth for eternal life (3:6).[5]

The warning that anyone who judges the law is not a "doer" (ποιητής) of the law (4:11a) reinforces the exhortation for the audience to become "doers" (ποιηταί) of the word of the law, the word that is able to save their souls in the judgment (1:21). They are not to be hearers only, deluding themselves (1:22). For if any of them is only a hearer of the word of the law but not a "doer" (ποιητής), he is like someone who forgets what he saw (1:24) after observing the appearance of his new "birth" in a mirror (1:23). By failing to be a doer of the word of the law, such a person would not be acting in accord with the word by which God brought us to our new "birth" for eternal life (1:18).

---

4. "It is most likely, given the similar contexts between 2:1-12 and 4:11-12 (partiality/criticism), that James has kept in mind what he calls in 2:8 the royal law, to love one's neighbor as oneself. There, he quotes it from Lev. 19:18, but he appears to understand that its formidable position in Jesus tradition has elevated the principle to supreme importance as incorporating the essence of Jewish law" (Baker, *Personal Speech-Ethics*, 178-79).

5. "These verses continue the theme that the tongue is a powerful and often misused agent in the Christian community" (Martin, *James*, 162).

4:11b (B): But a Judge

If anyone in the audience speaks against or judges against a fellow believing brother, then he is not a doer of the law (4:11a), "but a judge" (4:11b). This warning against anyone in the audience being a "judge" (κριτής) of the law by judging a fellow believing brother reinforces the exhortation for the audience not to be divided among themselves and become "judges" (κριταί) with evil designs (2:4). This is what happens when they demonstrate within their worshiping assembly a partiality in favor of the rich and against a poor brother (2:1–3).[6]

4:12a (C): One Is Lawgiver

Having been warned that speaking against and judging a brother amounts to speaking against the "law" (νόμου) and judging the "law" (νόμον), but judging the "law" (νόμον) makes one not a doer of the "law" (νόμου) but a judge (4:11), the audience are then reminded that "one is lawgiver [νομοθέτης]" (4:12a).[7] That "one" (εἷς) is lawgiver refers to God himself, recalling that for anyone in the audience who believes that God is "one" (εἷς), "you are doing" (ποιεῖς) rightly (2:19).[8] For the audience to believe that God is the one and only lawgiver thus means for each of them to be not a judge but a "doer" (ποιητής) of the law (4:11).

4:12b (B'): And Judge Who Is Able to Save and to Destroy

The audience hear that God alone is the one lawgiver "and judge who is able to save and to destroy. But who are you who judges the neighbor?"

---

6. "In effect, we find here the hidden form of the same sort of discrimination described in 2:1–4" (Johnson, *James*, 293).

7. "God is the 'Lawgiver' (νομοθέτης). This word is a *hapax legomenon* in the New Testament" (Hartin, *James*, 218).

8. "There is a reason why 'one' is here and it deserves emphasis: in a world where humans were deified and other gods enthroned, Israel heard from on high that there was in fact only one God (Exod 3:14–15; 20:3; Deut 5:6–7; 6:4–9; Zech 14:9). What is expressed here is the uniqueness, unity, and exclusivity of Israel's God" (McKnight, *James*, 364). "The emphatic position of εἷς and the appearance of ἐστιν enhance the poignancy of the point" (Baker, *Personal Speech-Ethics*, 179).

(4:12b). After the central and unparalleled C element, "one is lawgiver" (4:12a), the audience experience a pivot of chiastic parallels from the B (4:11b) to the B' element of this chiastic unit. The reference to anyone in the audience who judges a fellow believing brother and thus judges the law (4:11a) as being a "judge [κριτής]" (4:11b) progresses to a reference to God as not only the one lawgiver (4:12a) but as the one and only "judge [κριτής]" (4:12b). The audience are thus to realize that for any of them to be a judge contradicts the fact that God alone is judge.[9]

That God as the one and only judge is "able" (δυνάμενος) "to save [σῶσαι]" (4:12b) reinforces the exhortation for everyone in the audience to have a faith in God that is "able" (δύναται) "to save" (σῶσαι) him (2:14). Such a faith is to be accompanied by works such as, and especially, giving poor members of the community what is needed for their physical well-being (2:15–16), rather than speaking against or judging them (4:11). And that God as judge is able to save reinforces the exhortation for the audience, as believers in God, in humility to welcome the implanted word of God that is "able" (δυνάμενον) "to save" (σῶσαι) their souls (1:21). It is able to save their souls as the word of truth by which God brought us to a new birth for eternal life (1:18).

And that God as the one and only judge is able to save and "to destroy [ἀπολέσαι]" (4:12b) reminds the audience that the wealth of a rich person, like a flower, falls away and the beauty of its appearance is "destroyed" (ἀπώλετο) by God (1:11).[10] The audience are thus not to be led astray (1:16) by the desire for wealth that brings birth to the death (1:15) that contradicts our birth for eternal life (1:18). Instead, they are to endure the temptation to acquire wealth and thus be blessed by God to receive the crown of eternal life that God promised to those who love him (1:12).

The provocative rhetorical question, with its emphatic address of "you," "But who are *you* who judges [κρίνων] the neighbor?" (4:12b), bolsters the exhortation for everyone in the audience not to be "judging" (κρίνων) his fellow believing brother (4:11a), since God is the one and

---

9. "Whether God or Christ is in James' mind here as the judge does not affect the power of what is being said" (ibid.).

10. That these are the only occurrences in James of the verb "destroy" (ἀπόλλυμι) enhances this connection.

only judge who is able to save and destroy (4:12b).[11] And it reinforces the exhortation for the audience so to speak and so to do as those about to be "judged" (κρίνεσθαι) by God through a law of freedom (2:12). That the "neighbor" (πλησίον) is the object of judging in the question, rather than the "brother," as might be expected (4:11a), reminds the audience of the scriptural royal law according to which you shall love your "neighbor" (πλησίον) as yourself (Lev 19:18 in 2:8).[12] Everyone in the audience is to love rather than judge his fellow believing brother, who is to be considered his "neighbor." The audience are thus to do this royal law of loving their neighbor, which is the law of freedom, as those about to be judged through this law by God as the one and only judge.[13]

4:13–17 (A'): One Knowing the Praiseworthy Thing to Do and Not Doing It

The audience hear the A' element (4:13–17) of this chiastic unit as a chiastic pattern in itself:

a) Come *now* those *saying*, "Today or tomorrow we will go to this or that city and *do* business there a year and buy and sell and make a profit" (4:13).

   b) You do not know what your life will be like tomorrow. For you are a vapor that for a short time *appears* (4:14a),

   b') and then *disappears* (4:14b).

a') Instead of you *saying*, "If the Lord wants it, then we will live and *do* this or that," *now* you are boasting in your arrogances. All such

---

11. "The question is carefully constructed to put such a person in his proper place, which is infinitely distant from the lone, qualified judge. The forward position—indeed, the appearance—of the personal pronoun of σύ and the expression of the copula εἶ assure this result" (Baker, *Personal Speech-Ethics*, 179–80).

12. That these are the only occurrences in James of the term "neighbor" (πλησίον) enhances this connection.

13. "The rhetorical question, somewhat sarcastic in nature, shames those guilty of judging their neighbor (πλησίον), a term that recalls vividly 2:8 (and in turn Lev 19:16–18), and illustrates the use of the royal law as a standard by which to measure conduct" (Martin, *James*, 164).

boasting is evil. To one knowing the praiseworthy thing to *do* and not *doing* it, to him it is sin (4:15-17).

At the center of this chiastic sub-unit the audience experience a pivot of parallels involving the only occurrences in James of the alliterative terms "appearing" and "disappearing." "Appears" (φαινομένη) in the b) sub-element (4:14a) progresses to "disappears" (ἀφανιζομένη) in the b') sub-element (4:14b). The audience then hear a progression of chiastic parallels involving the only occurrences in this sub-unit of the terms, "now," "say," and "do." "Come now [νῦν] those saying [λέγοντες]" and "we will do" (ποιήσομεν) in the a) sub-element (4:13) progress to "instead of you saying [λέγειν]" (4:15), "we will do [ποιήσομεν]" (4:15), "but now [νῦν]" (4:16), and "the praiseworthy thing to do [ποιεῖν] and not doing [ποιοῦντι] it" (4:17) in the a') sub-element (4:15-17).

In addition, at this point the audience hear a progression, via the chiastic parallels, from the A (4:11a) to the A' (4:13-17) element of this chiastic unit. "You are not a doer [ποιητής] of the law" (4:11a) progresses to "we will do business [ποιήσομεν] there" (4:13), "we will do [ποιήσομεν] this or that" (4:15), and "knowing the praiseworthy thing to do [ποιεῖν] and not doing [ποιοῦντι] it" (4:17).

Rather than being a "doer" (ποιητής) of the law (4:11a), some in the audience may be among those saying that "we will do business" (ποιήσομεν) in this or that city for a year to make a profit (4:13) in order to become wealthy.[14] But such "doing" contradicts what the audience should be doing as those who are not only to help the poor but have the humility of the poor. They should be among those who "make" or "do" (ποιοῦσιν) peace (3:18) rather than be envious and selfish regarding wealth (3:16). If each of them believes that God is one, "you are doing" (ποιεῖς) rightly (2:19), since such faith includes the work of helping the poor (2:14-18). Each of them should be one who "does" (ποιήσαντι) mercy (2:13) rather than judges the poor (2:1-4). The audience have been told that "you are to do" (ποιεῖτε) as those about to be judged through a law of freedom (2:12). Indeed, "you are doing" (ποιεῖτε)

---

14. "As so often in James, it is speech as revealing the orientation of the heart that is the special target (2:3, 14, 16, 18; 3:9, 14)" (Johnson, *James*, 295). "What galls our author is that such an attitude reflects a proud complacency that suggests a 'this-worldly planning' and a blatant desire to become rich" (Martin, *James*, 165).

rightly, if you are completing the royal law of loving your neighbor, especially a neighbor who is poor, as yourself (2:8).

The audience are to realize the foolishness of making plans for what they will do "tomorrow" (αὔριον) in this or that city for a year (4:13), since they must acknowledge that they do not know what their life will be like "tomorrow [αὔριον]" (4:14a). Indeed, their realization that they are merely a vapor that for a short time appears and then disappears (4:14) should prevent them from being led astray by the desire for wealth.[15] It reminds them that a rich person, like a flower of grass, will pass away (1:10). For the sun rises with its heat and dries up the grass and its flower falls away and the beauty of its appearance is destroyed. So also the rich one in his pursuits will die out (1:11). That the audience do not know what their "life" (ζωή) on earth will be like tomorrow reinforces the exhortation for them to endure temptation regarding wealth in order to be blessed by God to receive the crown of eternal "life" (ζωῆς) in heaven that God promised to those who love him (1:12).[16]

The audience hear the a') sub-element of this chiastic sub-unit (4:13–17) as a chiastic pattern in itself:

(a) Instead of you saying, "If the Lord wants it, then we will live and *do* this or that" (4:15),

    (b) now you are *boasting* in your arrogances (4:16a).

    (b') All such *boasting* (4:16b)

(a') is evil. To one knowing then the praiseworthy thing to *do* and not *doing* it, to him it is sin (4:16c-17).

At the center of this chiastic sub-unit the audience experience a pivot of parallels involving the only occurrences in this sub-unit of expressions for "boasting." "Now you are boasting [καυχᾶσθε]" in the (b) sub-element (4:16a) progresses to "all such boasting [καύχησις]" in the (b') sub-element (4:16b). They then hear a chiastic progression

---

15. Regarding the participles "appears and then disappears" in 4:14, Baker (*Personal Speech-Ethics*, 233) suggests, "The passive form of both participles may point to the person's lack of control even over these vital moments of his life."

16. That these are the only occurrences in James of the term "life" (ζωή) enhances this connection.

involving the only occurrences in this sub-unit of the verb "do." "We will live and do [ποιήσομεν] this or that" in the (a) sub-element (4:15) progresses to "knowing then the praiseworthy thing to do [ποιεῖν] and not doing [ποιοῦντι] it" in the (a′) sub-element (4:16c–17).

The audience are "saying" (λέγοντες) that today and tomorrow we will go to this or that city and "do" (ποιήσομεν) business there a year and buy and sell and make a profit (4:13), instead of "saying" (λέγειν) that if the Lord wants it, then we will live and "do" (ποιήσομεν) this or that (4:15), that is, we will do not the business of gaining wealth, but whatever the Lord wants.[17] The audience are to appreciate that they do not know what their "life" (ζωή) will be like tomorrow (4:14), since only if the Lord wants it "will we live" (ζήσομεν) and do this or that. The statement that if the "Lord" (κύριος) wants it reminds the audience of the "Lord" (κυρίου) before whom they are to humble themselves so that he will exalt them to eternal life (4:10), and the "Lord" (κυρίου) from whom the audience will receive what they ask for (1:7) only if they ask in faith (1:6). And if the Lord "wants" (θελήσῃ) it reminds everyone in the audience of what "you want [θέλεις] to know," namely, that faith without works, particularly the works of helping the poor (2:15–17), is useless (2:20).

Those in the audience who are "now" (νῦν) saying that today or tomorrow we will go to this or that city and do business there a year and sell and make a profit (4:13) are "now" (νῦν) boasting in their arroganc-

---

17. "But the phrase 'If the Lord wills, we will live and do' is best understood not as a prediction of future life, but as shorthand for 'We will live in accordance with God's righteous revealed will, and in conformity to it we will do this or that.' At the very least, the acknowledgment that God is sovereign in life implies not that one should make no plans, but that one should consciously seek to know God's ethical will when making those plans . . . for James it is the personal and unique sovereign God in covenant with his people who wills this or that. Furthermore, for James, 'Lord' refers either to the Lord Jesus or to God the Father seen in terms of his relationship with his people, and in either case the term signifies one to whom obedience is due" (McCartney, *James*, 228). "The title 'Lord' (κύριος) conveys a more distinctive Jewish-Christian perspective than the title 'God' would have done. The 'Lord' could be Jesus, since James applies the title to him elsewhere in the letter (1:1; 2:1; 5:7, 8). But he usually applies the title to God the Father, the OT Yahweh, and this is probably the case here as well" (Moo, *James*, 205).

es (4:16a).¹⁸ That "you are boasting" (καυχᾶσθε) in arrogances contradicts the exhortation for everyone in the audience not to "boast against" (κατακαυχᾶσθε) the truth (3:14) but to do the mercy, especially the mercy of caring for the poor (2:1-4), that "boasts over" (κατακαυχᾶται) judgment (2:13), especially judgment in favor of the rich but against the poor (2:5-7). It also contradicts the exhortation for everyone in the audience to become a humble brother who "boasts" (καυχάσθω) in his exaltedness (1:9) to the eternal life for which God brought us to birth (1:18). And that you are boasting in your "arrogances" (ἀλαζονείαις) reminds the audience of the scriptural warning that God opposes the "haughty" (ὑπερηφάνοις), but to the humble he gives grace (4:6).

The audience then hear the a') sub-element of this chiastic sub-unit (4:15-17) as another chiastic pattern in itself:

(a) *is* evil (4:16c).

    (b) To one knowing then the praiseworthy thing to *do* (4:17a)

    (b') and not *doing* it (4:17b),

(a') to him it *is* sin (4:17c).

At the center of this chiastic sub-unit the audience experience a pivot of parallels involving the only occurrences in this sub-unit of the verb "do." "Knowing then the praiseworthy thing to do [ποιεῖν]" in the (b) sub-element (4:17a) progresses to "not doing [ποιοῦντι] it" in the (b') sub-element (4:17b). They then hear a chiastic progression of parallels involving the only occurrences in this sub-unit of the verb "is." "Is [ἐστιν] evil" in the (a) sub-element (4:16c) progresses to "it is [ἐστιν] sin" in the (a') sub-element (4:17c).¹⁹

That all such arrogant boasting regarding the desire to become wealthy is "evil [πονηρά]" (4:16c) reminds the audience that they have become judges with "evil" (πονηρῶν) designs (2:4), when they have shown partiality in favor of the wealthy and against the poor (2:1-3).²⁰

---

18. "Hence, the sinful boasting in question here probably is the merchants' glorying in their own arrogant acts, their self-reliant successes in handling their affairs independent from God" (McCartney, *James*, 229).

19. "Note how the copulative verb is placed at the end of the sentence for emphasis; this parallels v. 16" (Martin, *James*, 168-69).

20. That these are the only occurrences in James of the adjective "evil" (πονηρός)

"To one knowing [εἰδότι] then the praiseworthy thing to do" (4:17a) reminds the audience of how they should relate to God. The audience have been told that "you are to know" (οἴδατε) that friendship with the world in order to gain wealth is enmity with God (4:4). The audience are to be those "knowing" (εἰδότες) that whoever becomes a teacher of others will receive a greater judgment from God (3:1). And the audience are to "know" (ἴστε) that every person should be quick to hear, slow to speak, slow to anger (1:19), for the anger of a man does not work the righteousness of God (1:20).

For one to know the "praiseworthy" (καλόν) thing to do (4:17a) reinforces the exhortation for anyone in the audience who would be wise and understanding to show from "praiseworthy" (καλῆς) conduct his works in humility of wisdom (3:13), which includes becoming a humble brother rather than desiring to be wealthy (1:9–11). The audience are to know that a "praiseworthy" thing to do is not to work toward become wealthy, since the rich blaspheme the "praiseworthy" (καλόν) divine name that was invoked over the audience when they became believers (2:7). Rather, the "praiseworthy" thing for the audience to do is not only to become humble brothers, but to care for the humble poor among them (1:27; 2:1–4, 15–17). Such "praiseworthy" conduct serves as ethical worship that give praise to God and inspires others to praise God for it.

Whereas all arrogant boasting regarding the desire to become wealthy "is evil" (4:16), it "is sin" for anyone knowing the praiseworthy thing to do and not doing it (4:17). That it is "sin" (ἁμαρτία) not to do the praiseworthy thing reminds the audience that if they show partiality in favor of the rich, rather than doing the praiseworthy thing of caring for the poor (2:1–7), they are working "sin [ἁμαρτίαν]" (2:9). Indeed, as the audience are to recall, when the desire, especially for wealth, conceives, it gives birth to "sin" (ἁμαρτίαν), and the "sin" (ἁμαρτία) having been brought to completion, brings birth to the death (1:15) that contradicts our new birth from God for eternal life (1:18).[21]

---

enhances this connection.

21. "The change to the third person singular from second plural and the impersonal tone indicate that this is a proverb known to the author that he uses as he previously used proverbs in 3:18 and 2:13 . . . Thus it may well be that while on one level

Summary on 4:11–17

The audience are to realize that for any of them to speak against or "judge" a fellow believing brother amounts to speaking against and "judging" the law, and if "you judge" the law, you are not a doer of the law (4:11a), the law through which the audience will be "judged" by God (2:12). The warning that anyone who judges the law is not a "doer" of the law (4:11a) reinforces the exhortation for the audience to become "doers" of the word of the law, the word that is able to save their souls in the judgment (1:21). They are not to be hearers only, deluding themselves (1:22). For if any of them is only a hearer of the word of the law but not a "doer," he is like someone who forgets what he saw (1:24) after observing the appearance of his new "birth" in a mirror (1:23). By failing to be a doer of the word of the law, such a person does not act in accord with the word by which God brought us to our new "birth" for eternal life (1:18).

The provocative rhetorical question, with its emphatic address of "you," "But who are *you* who judges the neighbor?" (4:12), bolsters the exhortation for everyone in the audience not to be "judging" his fellow believing brother (4:11), since God is the one and only lawgiver and judge who is able to save and destroy (4:12). That the "neighbor" is the object of judging in the question reminds the audience of the scriptural royal law according to which you shall love your "neighbor" as yourself (Lev 19:18 in 2:8). Everyone in the audience is to love rather than judge his fellow believing brother, who is to be considered his "neighbor." The audience are thus to do this royal law of loving their neighbor, which is the law of freedom, as those about to be judged through this law by God as the one and only lawgiver and judge (2:12).

Rather than being a "doer" of the law (4:11a), some in the audience may be among those saying that "we will do business" in this or that city for a year to make a profit (4:13) in order to become wealthy. But such "doing" contradicts what the audience should be doing as those who are not only to help the poor but have the humility of the poor. They

---

James is warning merchants about forgetting God in their business, on a deeper level he is reflecting on ideas such as those in Lk. 12:13–21 and viewing the whole motive of gathering wealth rather than doing good with it (i.e. sharing it with the poor)" (Davids, *James*, 174).

should be among those who "do" peace (3:18) rather than be envious and selfish regarding wealth (3:16). If each of them believes that God is one, "you are doing" rightly (2:19), since such faith includes the work of helping the poor (2:14-18). Each of them should be one who "does" mercy (2:13) rather than judges the poor (2:1-4). The audience have been told that "you are to do" as those about to be judged through a law of freedom (2:12). Indeed, "you are doing" rightly, if you are completing the royal law of loving your neighbor, especially a neighbor who is poor, as yourself (2:8).

The audience are to realize the foolishness of making plans for what they will do "tomorrow" in this or that city for a year (4:13), since they must acknowledge that they do not know what their life will be like "tomorrow" (4:14a). Indeed, their realization that they are merely a vapor that for a short time appears and then disappears (4:14) should prevent them from being led astray by the desire for wealth. It reminds them that a rich person, like a flower of grass, will pass away (1:10). For the sun rises with its heat and dries up the grass and its flower falls away and the beauty of its appearance is destroyed. So also the rich one in his pursuits will die out (1:11). That the audience do not know what their "life" on earth will be like tomorrow reinforces the exhortation for them to endure temptation regarding wealth in order to be blessed by God to receive the crown of eternal "life" in heaven (1:12).

The audience are "saying" that today and tomorrow we will go to this or that city and "do" business there a year and buy and sell and make a profit (4:13), instead of "saying" that if the Lord wants it, then we will live and "do" this or that (4:15), that is, we will do not the business of gaining wealth, but whatever the Lord wants. The audience are to appreciate that they do not know what their "life" will be like tomorrow (4:14), since only if the Lord wants it "will we live" and do this or that. The statement that if the "Lord" wants it reminds the audience of the "Lord" before whom they are to humble themselves so that he will exalt them to eternal life (4:10), and the "Lord" from whom the audience will receive what they ask for (1:7) only if they ask in faith (1:6). And if the Lord "wants" it reminds everyone in the audience of what "you want to know," namely, that faith without works, particularly the works of helping the poor (2:15-17), is useless (2:20).

Those in the audience who are "now" saying that today or tomorrow we will go to this or that city and do business there a year and sell and make a profit (4:13) are "now" boasting in their arrogances (4:16a). That "you are boasting" in arrogances contradicts the exhortation for everyone in the audience not to "boast against" the truth (3:14) but to do the mercy, especially the mercy of caring for the poor (2:1–4), that "boasts over" judgment (2:13), especially judgment in favor of the rich but against the poor (2:5–7). It also contradicts the exhortation for everyone in the audience to become a humble brother who "boasts" in his exaltedness (1:9) to the eternal life for which God brought us to birth (1:18).

For one to know the "praiseworthy" thing to do (4:17a) reinforces the exhortation for anyone in the audience who would be wise and understanding to show from "praiseworthy" conduct his works in humility of wisdom (3:13), which includes becoming a humble brother rather than desiring to be wealthy (1:9–11). The audience are to know that a "praiseworthy" thing to do is not to work toward become wealthy, since the rich blaspheme the "praiseworthy" divine name that was invoked over the audience when they became believers (2:7). Rather, the "praiseworthy" thing for the audience to do is not only to become humble brothers, but to care for the humble poor among them (1:27; 2:1–4, 15–17). Such "praiseworthy" conduct serves as ethical worship that gives praise to God and inspires others to praise God for it.

Whereas all arrogant boasting regarding the desire to become wealthy "is evil" (4:16), it "is sin" for anyone knowing the praiseworthy thing to do and not doing it (4:17). That it is "sin" not to do the praiseworthy thing reminds the audience that if they show partiality in favor of the rich, rather than doing the praiseworthy thing of caring for the poor (2:1–7), they are working "sin" (2:9). Indeed, as the audience are to recall, when the desire, especially for wealth, conceives, it gives birth to "sin," and the "sin" having been brought to completion, brings birth to the death (1:15) that contradicts our new birth from God for eternal life (1:18).

James 5:1–6

The Cries Caused by the Rich Have Entered into the Ears of the Lord of Hosts (C′)

The rich who have murdered the righteous one have fattened their hearts for slaughter

A ⁵:¹ Come now you rich, weep, wailing over the miseries that are coming upon you. ² Your wealth has rotted and your clothes have become moth-eaten, ³ᵃ your gold and silver have corroded and their corrosion will be a testimony against *you* and it will devour your flesh like fire.

    B ³ᵇ You have stored up treasure in the last *days*.

        C ⁴ᵃ Behold the wages of *the* workers *who* mowed your fields,

            D ⁴ᵇ which have been withheld by you,

        C′ ⁴ᶜ are crying out, and the cries of *the* harvesters have entered into the ears of the Lord of hosts.

    B′ ⁵ You have reveled on the earth and lived luxuriously. You have fattened your hearts in a *day* of slaughter!

A′ ⁶ You have condemned, you have murdered the righteous one; he does not oppose *you*.[1]

---

1. For the establishment of Jas 5:1–6 as a chiasm, see the Introduction.

Audience Response to 5:1–6

At this point the audience experience a progression of macrochiastic parallels from the C (2:1–13) to the C' (5:1–6) units. The questions, "Did not God choose the poor in this world to be rich [πλουσίους] in faith?" (2:5) and "Are not the rich [πλούσιοι] oppressing you?" (2:6), progress to the direct address, "Come now you rich [πλούσιοι]" (5:1). The action of "entering" progresses from a situation of a wealthy man who in fine clothing "enters" (εἰσέλθῃ) into the worshiping assembly and a poor one who "enters" (εἰσέλθῃ) in filthy clothing" (2:2) to "the cries of the harvesters have entered [εἰσεληλύθασιν] into the ears of the Lord of hosts" (5:4).[2] In addition, when the audience hear the address "come now" (ἄγε νῦν) at the beginning of this unit (5:1), they hear the transitional words that link this unit with the preceding unit (4:11–17), which contains the identical address "come now" (ἄγε νῦν) at the beginning of its final element (4:13).

5:1–3a (A): Their Corrosion Will Be a Testimony against You

Following the sternly provocative address, "come now," with its prophetic overtones, the command for the "rich" (πλούσιοι) to weep as they wail over the miseries that are coming upon them (5:1) reminds the audience that the "rich" (πλούσιοι) are the ones oppressing them and dragging them into courts (2:6).[3] Rather than desiring to be materially rich, then, the audience are to strive to be spiritually poor as believers, since God chose the poor in this world to be "rich" (πλουσίους) in faith and heirs of the kingdom that he promised to those who love him (2:5). Indeed, the materially "rich one" (πλούσιος) in this world can only

---

2. That these are the only occurrences in James of the verb "enter" (εἰσέρχομαι) enhances the establishment of this macrochiastic parallelism.

3. "James begins with a prophet's attention-grabbing 'Come now.' It is arresting, even if not as jarring as the first usage of the expression in 4:13. There James addressed those who were making claims about their business ventures; here he broadens the audience to 'you rich people.' . . . James uses the language 'rich people' very much the way Jesus did: it is 'code' for the oppressors of the messianic community, and the letter speaks not only to the messianists but also to those who oppress them" (McKnight, *James*, 383).

boast ironically in his lowliness (1:10), since the "rich one" (πλούσιος), for all of his pursuits involving his wealth, will ultimately die out (1:11).

The command for the rich that "you weep [κλαύσατε]" (5:1) amounts to an appeal for them to repent, as it resonates with the previous command for the audience that "you weep" (κλαύσατε) in the repentance of humbling themselves before the Lord that he may exalt them (4:9).[4] This is confirmed as the command for the rich to weep is addressed to them as those wailing over the "miseries" (ταλαιπωρίαις) that are coming upon them (5:1).[5] Such "miseries" resonate with and reinforce the command for the audience to "be miserable [ταλαιπωρήσατε]" (4:9) in their repentance from the desire to be among those who are materially rich, and instead become those who are rich in faith as they care for those who are materially poor in this world.[6]

The rich are told that their wealth thoroughly "has rotted" (σέσηπεν) and is continuing to be rotten (perfect tense) and their "clothes" (ἱμάτια) thoroughly "have become moth-eaten" (σητόβρωτα γέγονεν) and are continuing to be moth-eaten (perfect tense) (5:2).[7] This is a disconcerting reality about the inevitable demise of material wealth and wealthy clothes. It reinforces the exhortation for the audience to avoid partiality toward a wealthy man who enters into their worshiping assembly in a specifically wealthy type of clothing—the "fine clothing [ἐσθῆτι

---

4. That these are the only occurrences in James of the verb "weep" (κλαίω) enhances this connection.

5. "The present tense dative plural participle describes the action; it does not convey that these things are coming upon them right now as James speaks, but it is used in order to make the action vivid" (McKnight, *James*, 385n85).

6. That these are the only occurrences in James of the cognate expressions "misery/be miserable" (ταλαιπωρία/ταλαιπωρέω) enhances this connection.

7. "'Your riches have rotted' involves a verb in the perfect tense, indicating that the author depicts the act of rotting as complete and as having brought into being a state of affairs. One might easily infer that this rotting has not yet happened and therefore question why the rhetoric finds such strong semantic expression in the perfect tense . . . In James's mind, therefore, the rotting of riches is a condition he assumes, not the least because they have not been used compassionately, and this is the condition to which he speaks" (McKnight, *James*, 386). "In imitation of the prophets, James describes these events as though they had already occurred" (Hartin, *James*, 227).

λαμπρᾷ]" (2:2) that makes an attractive appearance and enhances one's social status, but is destined for an ugly, unsightly devastation.[8]

That the gold and silver of the rich "have corroded" (κατίωται) and are continuing to corrode (perfect tense) and their "corrosion" (ἰός) will be a testimony against them (5:3a) reinforces the exhortation for the audience to avoid using the tongue, since it is full of such death-bringing "poison" or "corrosion [ἰός]" (3:8), to gain wealth (2:1–4).[9] That this corrosion "will be" (ἔσται) a testimony against the rich in the final judgment for not sharing their wealth with the needy poor also reinforces the exhortation for each member of the audience to be a doer of the work that is to accompany one's faith, as such a person "will be" (ἔσται) blessed by God in his doing (1:25). Such doing includes caring for poor orphans and widows (1:27).[10]

And that this corrosion of wealth will devour the flesh of the rich like "fire [πῦρ]" (5:3a) further reinforces the exhortation for the audience to avoid using the tongue for the purpose of becoming

8. "Extravagant, status-expressing dress marked the rich (Jas 2:2–3)" (McKnight, *James*, 387).

9. That these are the only occurrences in James of the term "poison/corrosion" (ἰός) enhances this connection. According to Weiser ("Durch Grünspan," 220–23), ἰός in 5:3 refers to copper plated with gold and silver and passed off as coins made of precious metals. James is thus warning the rich that their gold and silver coins will decay through corrosion, with the counterfeit character of the rich thus unmasked. According to Böttrich ("Vom Gold," 519–36), the point of the imagery of corroded gold and silver is the uselessness of hoarding earthly possessions in view of the coming judgment. "James declares the material that is, from a worldly point of view, incorruptible to actually be, on the day of judgment, not just rusted, but rusted right through—totally worthless" (McCartney, *James*, 232).

10. That these are the only occurrences in James of the future middle of the third person singular of the verb "to be" (εἰμί) enhances this connection. "The very thing they focused on, riches like clothing and gold and silver, will turn against the rich in a final act of cosmic betrayal. The rust on them will become a witness to the idolatrous commitment to mammon on the part of the rich. How it will do so is not clear, but perhaps it is because the rich hold these possessions in abundance instead of using them compassionately for those in need that James can say that they will become evidence" (McKnight, *James*, 387). "The use of the image is striking on two counts. First, James uses it to establish another courtroom setting, which reverses that in 2:6 where the rich dragged the poor into courts in order to oppress them; now the rich are the ones in the dock. Second, the very corruption (rust) of their wealth is personified in order to bear testimony against them" (Johnson, *James*, 300).

wealthy, since the tongue is a "fire [πῦρ]" (3:6), indeed a "fire" (πῦρ) capable of inciting a tremendously deadly destruction (3:5). "Set on fire" (φλογίζουσα) by Gehenna, the tongue can defile the whole body and "set fire" (φλογιζομένη) to the course of our new birth for eternal life (3:6).[11]

5:3b (B): You Have Stored Up Treasure in the Last Days

The audience then hear a stinging sarcastic indictment of the rich: "You have stored up treasure in the last days" (5:3b). Rather than repent in view of the miseries that are coming upon them (5:1) and of the ultimate corruption of their wealth (5:2–3a), the rich ironically have simply stored up what they think is treasure, but which actually will prove to be worthless for them "in the last days," that is, these last days of the present end-time with their impending judgment. The audience are to appreciate that the wealth which the rich have stored up for themselves as treasure, rather than shared it with the needy poor (2:14–16), will merely add to the testimony against them (5:3a) in the final judgment.[12]

---

11. According to Mayordomo-Marín ("Jak 5,2.3a," 132–37), Jas 5:2–3a does not refer to future judgment but rather to the present state of affairs. These riches are virtually valueless because their owners have not used them to help the poor. "Rust does not eat, and it does not eat like fire, since fire consumes quickly, but James's evocative imagery is spoiled by thinking of it with such narrow literalism. If rust can corrode precious metals like gold and silver, which were sometimes considered non-corrodible, it will also corrode the very flesh of the rich. And if it can corrode, it can be extended to consuming things the way fire does. The language again is graphic and designed to evoke a response of repentance" (McKnight, *James*, 388). "Just as the tongue is likened to both poison and destructive fire, so, in effect, is wealth. Since many types of venom feel like fire in one's flesh, the picture is apt and vivid in both cases. And just as the tongue is a great gift but also a source of great evil, so the gift of wealth often generates much evil" (McCartney, *James*, 232–33).

12. "Thus, the rich are laying up treasure in the last days, which are imminent to the point of arrival. But James may be offering a specimen of irony here. The treasure in mind is not their vaunted riches but the misery that awaits them. While they think that the wealth accumulated is held as a perpetual possession, they are vulnerable to severe judgment because not only is such wealth temporary, but it is the witness whose testimony condemns the rich. Instead of sharing their wealth with the needy (a response already spoken of as a sign of a saving faith in 2:14–16) they hoard it; what makes this doubly tragic is that they do so in the last days and thus underline

5:4a (C): Behold the Wages of the Workers Who Mowed Your Fields

The focus of the audience is then drawn to those employed by the rich: "Behold the wages of the workers who mowed your fields" (5:4a).[13] With the demonstrative particle "behold," the audience were directed to give particular attention to the tiny rudder, analogous to the tongue, of large ships: "Behold [ἰδού] also ships, being so large and driven by rough winds, are guided by a tiny rudder wherever the inclination of the pilot decides" (3:4). Similarly, they were invited to give special consideration to the tongue itself: "Behold [ἰδού] how small a fire (which the tongue is, 3:6) so great a forest kindles" (3:5). And now, with the same demonstrative particle, the audience are directed to devote their special attention to the wages of those who work for the rich: "Behold [ἰδού] the wages of the workers who mowed your fields."[14] The audience are thus led to consider the relationship between the wealth of the rich—"your wealth [ὁ πλοῦτος ὑμῶν]" (5:2), whose corrosion will devour "your flesh" (τὰς σάρκας ὑμῶν) like fire (5:3) and "the wages" (ὁ μισθός) of the workers who mowed "your fields" (τὰς χώρας ὑμῶν).[15]

---

the folly of their actions" (Martin, *James*, 178). "To this prediction of damnation the author adds a final ironic threat. 'You have treasured up,' he states: that they knew well enough. But it is 'in the last days' and so is not for their good, but their damnation . . . The phrase 'last days' refers to the NT conviction that the end times, the age of the consummation, had already broken in upon the world in Jesus. *These* people had treasured up as if they would live and the world would go on forever, but the end times, in which they have a last chance to repent and put their goods to righteous uses, are already upon them" (Davids, *James*, 177, emphasis original).

13. "The labor involved is mowing fields, that is, harvesting grain" (McKnight, *James*, 391).

14. "The use of the imperative ἰδού heightens the drama of this charge. Just as the rich were to contemplate the miseries coming on them, now they are to gaze on the cause of those miseries. The money that they have piled up and allowed to rust stands as witness against them, precisely because it should have been given out in wages" (Johnson, *James*, 301).

15. Note the alliterative relationship between "your flesh" (τὰς σάρκας ὑμῶν) in 5:3a and "your fields" (τὰς χώρας ὑμῶν) in 5:4a.

5:4b (D): Which Have Been Withheld by You

The audience receive further description of the wages of the workers who mowed the fields of the rich (5:4a): "which have been withheld by you" (5:4b). With this notice of blatant injustice on the part of the rich, the audience are to appreciate the ironic contrast with the exhortation for them to submit to God, but resist the devil and he will flee from you (4:7). Instead of submitting to God and resisting the devil so that he will flee "from you" (ἀφ᾽ ὑμῶν), the rich have diabolically and unjustly withheld the wages of those working for them—they have been withheld "by you" (ἀφ᾽ ὑμῶν).[16] Furthermore, the alliteration between the verb "withheld" (ἀπεστερημένος) and the phrase "by you" (ἀφ᾽ ὑμῶν) emphatically places the blame for this evil and unjust withholding of wages squarely upon "you," the rich.[17]

5:4c (C'): The Cries of the Harvesters Have Entered into the Ears of the Lord

The wages withheld from those working for the rich (5:4b) are further elaborated. Poignantly personified, these unjustly withheld wages themselves "are crying out, and the cries of the harvesters have entered into the ears of the Lord of hosts" (5:4c). Having heard the central and unparalleled D element, "which have been withheld by you" (5:4b), the audience now experience a pivot of parallels from the C (5:4a) to the C' (5:4c) element of this chiastic unit. "The wages of the [τῶν] workers who [τῶν] mowed your fields" progresses to "the cries of the [τῶν] harvesters."

---

16. That these are the only occurrences in James of the prepositional phrase "from/by you" (ἀφ᾽ ὑμῶν) enhances this connection.

17. "The specific background for 5:4 is the OT principle of prompt payment of wages, found in both Lev. 19:13 and Deut. 24:14–15 ... Inasmuch as the entire section is meant to produce a rhetorical effect rather than actually address rich people ... James is simply using the specific issue of Deut. 24:14/Lev. 19:13 as illustrative of typical unrighteous behavior on the part of the wealthy. It is endemic to human behavior everywhere for the rich to oppress the poor, and the Greco-Roman world was no exception, and James's condemnation applies to every manifestation of greed and the abuse of power, not just to withholding of wages" (McCartney, *James*, 234).

The audience are to realize that the corroded and corrupted wealth of the rich "will be a testimony" against them in the final judgment and it "will devour" their flesh like fire (5:2-3a) because the wages, personified as victims of the rich, are presently and continually "crying out" (5:4c).[18] This "crying out" by the personified wages is intensified by the "cries" of the harvesters themselves (5:4c) from whom the wages have been unjustly withheld by the rich (5:4b).[19] That the continual cries of the harvesters have "entered" (εἰσεληλύθασιν) fully and completely (perfect tense) into the ears of the Lord of the heavenly hosts (5:4c) means that they have functioned in the manner of liturgical prayers on earth that have been heard by God in heaven.[20] The audience are to appreciate the irony of God listening to this kind of liturgical "entering" as worship, which stands in dramatic contrast to the audience's paying attention to a rich person who "enters" (εἰσέλθῃ) for worship into their liturgical assembly in fine clothing rather than to a poor one who "enters" (εἰσέλθῃ) in filthy clothing (2:2).

That the prayerful cries of the humbled harvesters have been heard by the "Lord" (κυρίου) of hosts (5:4c) bolsters the exhortation for the audience to be humbled before the "Lord" (κυρίου) and he will exalt

18. "The wages (μισθός) themselves cry out—a verb used for dramatic effect—against the rich farmer and on behalf of the poor laborer" (Martin, *James*, 178). "The personification of the labourers' wages adds to the rhetorical effect, reiterating the idea that their wrongly accumulated wealth bears witness against the rich" (Hutchinson-Edgar, *Has God Not Chosen*, 202).

19. "To say that the cry (βοή, NT *hapax legomenon*) of those reapers has entered the ears of the Lord Sabaoth, a phrase duplicated in Is. 5:9 LXX, where woe is pronounced on those acquiring large estates, means that doom is imminent. For God to hear the cry of the poor is for him to bring judgment on their oppressors" (Davids, *James*, 177-78).

20. According to Martin (*James*, 179), the perfect tense of the verb "have entered" here "suggests two things: (i) this cry has already been heard by God and (ii) judgment on the rich has already started." "James's use of 'Lord of hosts' most likely draws on this theme of the God of justice who, along with the heavenly retinue, enacts justice for the oppressed in judgment. The oppressed cry out (Pss 17:1-6; 18:6; 31:2), and the Lord of hosts brings justice—in this context, justice against rich, defrauding employers" (McKnight, *James*, 393). "The name for God, 'Lord of hosts,' is a translation of the Hebrew term YHWH Sabaoth. At first it referred to God's role as commander of the forces of Israel, then took on the extended meaning of Lord or ruler of the heavenly world with its forces" (Hartin, *James*, 229).

you (4:10). It strengthens the exhortation for the audience to have the faith in our "Lord" (κυρίου) Jesus Christ of glory without partiality (2:1) toward the rich and against the poor (2:2). And it reminds the audience to pray in faith as humble brothers and servants of the "Lord" (κυρίου) Jesus Christ, together with James (1:1), in order to receive the answer of their prayers from the "Lord [κυρίου]" (1:7).

5:5 (B'): You Have Fattened Your Hearts in a Day of Slaughter

The blistering indictment of the rich, destined for doom, continues: "You have reveled on the earth and lived luxuriously. You have fattened your hearts in a day of slaughter!" (5:5). At this point the audience hear a progression, via the chiastic parallels, from the B (5:3b) to the B' element of this chiastic unit. The phrase "in the last days [ἡμέραις]" progresses to the phrase "in a day [ἡμέρᾳ] of slaughter."

A striking alliterative sequence of verbs leads the audience to appreciate the biting irony in the description of the lifestyle of the rich who have unjustly withheld the wages of their workers (5:4). Although "you have reveled" (ἐτρυφήσατε) on the earth and "you lived luxuriously" (ἐσπαταλήσατε), the ultimate outcome was that in actuality "you have fattened" (ἐθρέψατε) your hearts in a day of slaughter (5:5).[21] That the rich, destined for condemnation, have ironically fattened their "hearts" (καρδίας) in preparation for the slaughter they will experience bolsters the exhortation for the audience, in contrast, to purify their "hearts [καρδίας]" (4:8) in repentance from the envious desire for wealth. It reinforces the exhortation for the audience not to have in their "heart" (καρδίᾳ) bitter envy and selfishness regarding the attainment of wealth

---

21. "It is not the simple enjoyment of material blessings that James here condemns, but the sybaritic enjoyment of material wealth that has been unrighteously obtained. To withhold wages is to steal from those who are less powerful, and to indulge in luxury with those stolen wages is doubly offensive . . . Further, the rich landowners are 'fattening themselves,' and fattening is what is done to the livestock being readied for the abattoir. Therefore, 'in a day of slaughter' probably is parallel to 'in the last days' of 5:3, and thus James is warning of the imminent eschatological day when the oppressors themselves will be slaughtered" (McCartney, *James*, 235). "Just as an animal is force fed before it is killed, so the rich are feeding themselves for the day of judgment" (Hartin, *James*, 229–30).

(3:14). And it strengthens the exhortation for everyone in the audience to bridle his tongue rather than deceive his "heart [καρδίαν]" (1:26), in order to practice a pure and undefiled religion that includes the ethical worship of caring for orphans and widows (1:27).[22]

The audience are to appreciate the irony that the rich, you who think that "you have stored up treasure" (ἐθησαυρίσατε) in the last days (5:3b), are actually you who "have fattened" (ἐθρέψατε) your hearts in a day of slaughter (5:5). Because the rich did not repent in these last "days" (ἡμέραις) of the end-time, they will, as a result of their unrepentant reveling and living luxuriously, experience the day of God's final judgment as a "day" (ἡμέρᾳ) of their slaughter.[23] In contrast, the audience, who do not know what their life will be like tomorrow (4:14), are to make these last "days" of the end-time that has arrived a "day" for their repentance, a time to be humbled before the Lord, who has heard the cries of the humble poor (5:4), so that he will exalt them with the crown of eternal life (1:12).

5:6 (A'): The Righteous One Does Not Oppose You

The extremely harsh accusations against the rich reach their climactic conclusion: "You have condemned, you have murdered the righteous one; he does not oppose you" (5:6). At this point the audience hear a progression, via the chiastic parallels, from the A (5:1–3a) to the A' element of this chiastic unit. "Their corrosion will be a testimony against you [ὑμῖν]" (5:3a) progresses to "he does not oppose you [ὑμῖν]" (5:6).

22. "The rich oppressors' self-indulgence is perceived ironically as preparation for self-destruction 'in the last days.' This reading corresponds nicely to the interpretation given in 1:26 for ἀπατῶν καρδίαν ('indulging the heart')" (Johnson, *James*, 304).

23. "Both judgment and especially the Day of the Lord are sometimes called a 'slaughter' by the prophets" (McKnight, *James*, 395). "The 'last days' have already begun; the judgment *could* break in at any time—yet the rich, instead of acting to avoid that judgment, are, by their selfish indulgence, incurring a greater guilt. They are like cattle being fattened for the kill (emphasis original)" (Moo, *James*, 218). "The wealthy live luxuriously, heedless of the poor, as if this is what life were for, indeed, they live as in a day of slaughter (there is perhaps some irony intended as they slaughter animals for their feasts). But the day of slaughter has arrived—their slaughter, for they are the 'fatted calves,' the enemies of God whom he will slaughter when he appears" (Davids, *James*, 179).

The accusation against the rich, that not only have they condemned, but "you have murdered" (ἐφονεύσατε) the righteous one (5:6), reminds the audience of the same accusation against them, namely, that "you murder" (φονεύετε) out of envy for wealth (4:2). The audience are thus exhorted to avoid envious desire for wealth, because it leads not only to murder in general but to murder particularly of poor and innocent righteous ones. These accusations of murder also remind the audience of the commandment, "Do not murder" (φονεύσῃς), and that if "you murder" (φονεύεις), you have become a transgressor of God's law (2:11). Such murders, the audience are to realize, contradict the word of truth by which God brought us to birth for eternal life (1:18).[24]

Although the righteous one does not "oppose" (ἀντιτάσσεται) the rich (5:6), the audience have heard that, in accord with the scriptural quotation of Prov 3:34, God "opposes" (ἀντιτάσσεται) the haughty, but to the humble he gives grace (4:6).[25] So, although the humble righteous ones do not oppose the rich who defraud and murder them, God himself, who hears the cries of these humble righteous ones (5:4), does oppose the haughty rich.[26] Although the righteous one does not oppose "you" (ὑμῖν), namely, the rich, the corrosion of their wealth will be a testimony against "you" (ὑμῖν), namely, the rich, at the final judgment,

24. "Three times James brings up murder (2:11; 4:2 and here), and in each instance the tendency has been for interpreters to minimize its meaning. These texts, combined as they need to be with 1:20 and 2:1–7, lead me to think that actual murders were occurring among those to whom James wrote" (McKnight, *James*, 397). "There seems little to support the notion that φονεύειν simply means a symbolic killing of the poor person, as in the withholding of wages. The term καταδικάζειν ('to condemn') is rightly understood as forensic in nature and thus we have the picture of the rich (probably abusing the legal system, in contrast to the poor who cannot use the system at all) condemning the poor, who in turn is murdered. This 'judicial murder' highlights and accentuates the role of the underdog played by the poor" (Martin, *James*, 181).

25. That these are the only occurrences in James of this verb form enhances this connection. "[T]he statement 'He does not resist you' is meant to emphasize the wickedness of the oppression (because the poor person *cannot* resist) . . . 'the righteous one' is simply a generalized reference to the oppressed poor person who trusts in God for deliverance, as in several psalms and prophetic writings (emphasis original)" (McCartney, *James*, 236).

26. For a possible allusion to the Cain and Abel story in Gen 4:6–10, see Byron, "Living," 261–74.

that is, in a day of slaughter when God will destroy (5:5) the rich who have murdered the righteous. The audience are thus further exhorted to avoid the envious desire for wealth, which leads to the deadly destruction that contradicts our divine birth for eternal life (1:18).

Summary on 5:1–6

The command for the "rich" to weep as they wail over the miseries that are coming upon them (5:1) reminds the audience that the "rich" are the ones oppressing them and dragging them into courts (2:6). Rather than desiring to be materially rich, then, the audience are to strive to be spiritually poor as believers, since God chose the poor in this world to be "rich" in faith and heirs of the kingdom that he promised to those who love him (2:5). Indeed, the materially "rich one" in this world can only boast ironically in his lowliness (1:10), since the "rich one," for all of his pursuits involving his wealth, will ultimately die out (1:11).

The command for the rich that "you weep" (5:1) amounts to an appeal for them to repent, as it resonates with the previous command for the audience that "you weep" in the repentance of humbling themselves before the Lord that he may exalt them (4:9). This is confirmed as the command for the rich to weep is addressed to them as those wailing over the "miseries" that are coming upon them (5:1). Such "miseries" resonate with and reinforce the command for the audience to "be miserable" (4:9) in their repentance from the desire to be among those who are materially rich, and instead become those who are rich in faith as they care for those who are materially poor in this world.

The wealth of the rich "has rotted" and their "clothes" thoroughly "have become moth-eaten" (5:2). This is a disconcerting reality about the inevitable demise of material wealth and wealthy clothes. It reinforces the exhortation for the audience to avoid partiality toward a wealthy man who enters into their worshiping assembly in a specifically wealthy type of clothing—the "fine clothing" (2:2) that makes an attractive appearance and enhances one's social status, but is destined for an ugly, unsightly devastation.

That the gold and silver of the rich "have corroded" and their "corrosion" will be a testimony against them (5:3a) reinforces the exhortation for the audience to avoid using the tongue, since it is full of such death-bringing "poison" or "corrosion" (3:8), to gain wealth (2:1–4). And that this corrosion of wealth will devour the flesh of the rich like "fire" (5:3a) further reinforces the exhortation for the audience to avoid using the tongue for the purpose of becoming wealthy, since the tongue is a "fire" (3:6), indeed a "fire" capable of inciting a tremendously deadly destruction (3:5). "Set on fire" by Gehenna, the tongue can defile the whole body and "set fire" to the course of our new birth for eternal life (3:6).

Rather than repent in view of the miseries that are coming upon them (5:1) and of the ultimate corruption of their wealth (5:2–3a), the rich ironically have simply stored up what they think is treasure, but which actually will prove to be worthless for them "in the last days," that is, these last days of the present end-time with their impending judgment (5:3b). The audience are to appreciate that the wealth which the rich have stored up for themselves as treasure, rather than shared it with the needy poor (2:14–16), will merely add to the testimony against them (5:3a) in the final judgment.

The audience are to realize that the corroded and corrupted wealth of the rich "will be a testimony" against them in the final judgment and it "will devour" their flesh like fire (5:2–3a) because the wages, personified as victims of the rich, are presently and continually "crying out" (5:4). This "crying out" by the personified wages is intensified by the "cries" of the harvesters themselves from whom the wages have been unjustly withheld by the rich (5:4). That the continual cries of the harvesters have "entered" into the ears of the Lord of the heavenly hosts (5:4) means that they have functioned in the manner of liturgical prayers on earth that have been heard by God in heaven. The audience are to appreciate the irony of God listening to this kind of liturgical "entering" as worship, which stands in dramatic contrast to the audience's paying attention to a rich person who "enters" for worship into their liturgical assembly in fine clothing rather than to a poor one who "enters" in filthy clothing (2:2).

That the prayerful cries of the humbled harvesters have been heard by the "Lord" of hosts (5:4c) bolsters the exhortation for the audience to be humbled before the "Lord" and he will exalt you (4:10). It strengthens the exhortation for the audience to have the faith in our "Lord" Jesus Christ of glory without partiality (2:1) toward the rich and against the poor (2:2). And it reminds the audience to pray in faith as humble brothers and servants of the "Lord" Jesus Christ, together with James (1:1), in order to receive the answer of their prayers from the "Lord" (1:7).

Although the humble righteous ones do not "oppose" the rich who defraud and murder them (5:6), God himself, who hears the cries of these humble righteous ones (5:4) does "oppose" the haughty rich (4:6). And although the righteous one does not oppose "you," namely, the rich, the corrosion of their wealth will be a testimony against "you," namely, the rich, at the final judgment, that is, in a day of slaughter when God will destroy (5:5) the rich who have murdered the righteous. The audience are thus further exhorted to avoid the envious desire for wealth, which leads to the deadly destruction that contradicts our divine birth for eternal life (1:18).

James 5:7–11

Strengthen Your Hearts Like Prophets Who Spoke in the Name of the Lord (B')

Be patient and endure until the coming of the Lord who gives life

A ⁷ Be *patient* then, *brothers*, until the coming of the *Lord*. Behold the farmer awaits the precious fruit of the earth, being *patient* for it until it *receives* the early rain and the late rain. ⁸ Be *patient* you also. Strengthen your hearts, for the coming of the *Lord* is near. ⁹ᵃ Do not complain, *brothers*, against one another,

B ⁹ᵇ so that you may not be *judged*.

B' ⁹ᶜ Behold the *judge* is standing before the gates.

A' ¹⁰ As an example of suffering and *patience receive, brothers*, the prophets who spoke in the name of the *Lord*. ¹¹ Behold we call blessed those who have endured. Of the endurance of Job you have heard and the outcome of the *Lord* you have seen, for very sympathetic is the *Lord* and compassionate.[1]

Audience Response to 5:7–11

At this point the audience experience a progression of macrochiastic parallels from the B (1:17–27) to the B' (5:7–11) units. The command to be slow to "speak [λαλῆσαι]" (1:19) and the warning about deceiving the "heart [καρδίαν]" (1:26) progress to the command to strengthen

---

1. For the establishment of Jas 5:7–11 as a chiasm, see the Introduction.

your "hearts [καρδίας]" (5:8) and the description of the prophets as those who "spoke" (ἐλάλησαν) in the name of the Lord (5:10). In addition, when the audience hear the phrase, "the coming of the Lord [κυρίου]," at the beginning of this unit (5:7), they hear the transitional term that links this unit with the preceding unit (5:1–6), which contains the phrase, "into the ears of the Lord [κυρίου] of hosts," near its conclusion (5:4).

5:7–9a (A): Be Patient Brothers until the Coming of the Lord

The audience hear the A element (5:7–9a) of this chiastic unit as a chiastic pattern in itself:

a) Be *patient* then, *brothers*, until *the coming of the Lord*. Behold the farmer awaits the precious fruit of the earth, being *patient* for it until it receives (5:7a)

b) the *early rain* (5:7b)

b′) and the *late rain* (5:7c).

a′) Be *patient* you also. Strengthen your hearts, for the *coming of the Lord* is near. Do not complain, *brothers*, against one another (5:8–9a),

At the center of this chiastic sub-unit the audience experience a pivot of parallels involving the only occurrences in James of expressions for rain. "The early rain [πρόϊμον]" in the b) sub-element (5:7b) progresses to "the late rain [ὄψιμον]" in the b′) sub-element (5:7c). They then hear a chiastic progression of parallels involving the only occurrences in James of the expression "coming of the Lord," as well as the only occurrences in this sub-unit of the verb "be patient" and the address "brothers." "Be patient [μακροθυμήσατε], brothers [ἀδελφοί], until the coming of the Lord [τῆς παρουσίας τοῦ κυρίου] . . . being patient [μακροθυμῶν]" in the a) sub-element (5:7a) progresses to "be patient [μακροθυμήσατε] you also. . . . for the coming of the Lord [ἡ παρουσία τοῦ κυρίου] is near. Do not complain, brothers [ἀδελφοί]" in the a′) sub-element (5:8–9a).

In addition, the audience hear the a) sub-element (5:7a) of this chiastic sub-unit as yet another chiastic pattern:

(a) Be *patient* then, brothers, *until* the coming of the Lord (5:7aa).

(b) Behold the *farmer* awaits (5:7ab)

(b′) the precious fruit of the *earth* (5:7ac),

(a′) being *patient* for it *until* it receives (5:7ad)

At the center of this chiastic sub-unit the audience experience a pivot of alliterative and conceptual parallels involving the only occurrences in this sub-unit of references to the earth. The reference to the "farmer" (γεωργός), literally a "worker of the earth" in the (b) sub-element (5:7ab), progresses to the product of the farmer's work, "the precious fruit of the earth [γῆς]" in the (b′) sub-element (5:7ac).[2] They then hear a chiastic progression of parallels involving the only occurrences in James of the preposition "until" and in this sub-unit of the verb "be patient." "Be patient [μακροθυμήσατε] then, brothers, until [ἕως] the coming of the Lord" in the (a) sub-element (5:7aa) progresses to "being patient [μακροθυμῶν] for it until [ἕως] it receives" in the (a′) sub-element (5:7ad).

The command for the audience, addressed as "brothers" (ἀδελφοί), to be patient until the coming of the Lord (5:7) serves as a positive complement to the negative command for the audience, addressed as "brothers" (ἀδελφοί), not to speak against one another (4:11). The audience are to have patience among themselves as a brotherly community who patiently await the final coming of the "Lord" (κυρίου), the divine "Lord" (κυρίου) of hosts into whose ears the cries of the harvesters, unjustly defrauded by the rich, have entered (5:4).[3] The audience are likewise being oppressed by the rich (2:6). But they have also been warned against having bitter envy and selfishness regarding riches (3:14–16), as well as against the murder and envy caused by their envious passions

---

2. "The word γεωργός (literally γῆ + ἔργον = 'work of the earth') refers to a farmer, as distinct from the hired laborer of 5:4 (ἐργάτης)" (Hartin, *James*, 242). See also Martin, *James*, 190.

3. "James changes from the denunciations of the πλούσιοι ('rich') he had addressed in the previous two paragraphs (4:13–17; 5:1–6) to speak to his community directly as 'brothers (and sisters)' (ἀδελφοί) with a tone of affection. The address of the rich in the above two paragraphs was used as a foil to communicate with the community" (Hartin, *James*, 241).

to become rich (4:1–3). They are thus to be encouraged that for their rich oppressors, and any among them who would become rich oppressors, the coming of the Lord will be a day for the divine slaughtering of these rich ones (5:5), who have condemned and murdered righteous ones (5:6).[4]

The command for the audience to be patient until the coming of the "Lord [κυρίου]" (5:7) bolsters the command for them to be humbled before the "Lord" (κυρίου) so that he will exalt them (4:10) at his final coming. It reinforces the command for the audience not with partiality in favor of the rich and against the poor to have the faith in our "Lord" (κυρίου) Jesus Christ of glory (2:1), the glory to be fully manifested at his final coming. And it strengthens the exhortation for each member of the audience, together with James as a servant of the "Lord" (κυρίου) Jesus Christ (1:1), to pray in faith (1:6) in order to receive from the "Lord [κυρίου]" (1:7), at his final coming in glory, the crown of eternal life (1:12).

With the demonstrative particle, "behold" (ἰδού), the special attention of the audience was directed to the personified wages of the workers, unjustly withheld by the rich, whose crying out, together with the prayerful cries of the oppressed harvesters themselves, have entered into the ears of the Lord of hosts (5:4). The audience, likewise oppressed by the rich, but also tempted by the desire to become rich themselves, are exhorted that "you be patient" (μακροθυμήσατε) until the coming of the Lord to answer these prayers. And this exhortation is bolstered with another "behold" (ἰδού) that directs their attention to the farmer who

---

4. "James, like the rest of the NT, regards the future parousia to be the arrival of Messiah Jesus in judgment" (McCartney, *James*, 241). "In the New Testament the word *parousia* took on a technical meaning to refer to the coming or arrival of Jesus Christ at the end of time to inaugurate his messianic kingdom" (Hartin, *James*, 241). "What is clear is that the author is calling on Christians not to take the judgment of the wicked into their own hands, but to wait for God to avenge them; at the same time, they are called not to compromise the faith; both giving in to the world and attacking the world are wrong . . . and it is easy to understand how James, like most NT writers, could refer to God as judge in one breath and Christ in the next" (Davids, *James*, 182).

awaits the precious fruit of the earth, "being patient" (μακροθυμῶν) for it (5:7).[5]

In contrast to the unrepentant rich who have reveled on "the earth" (τῆς γῆς) and lived luxuriously (5:5), oblivious to the coming the Lord, the audience are to imitate the farmer who patiently awaits the precious fruit of "the earth" (τῆς γῆς), an analogy for the coming of the Lord (5:7). That the farmer patiently awaits the precious "fruit" (καρπόν) of the earth as a divine gift reinforces the exhortation for the audience to pray for the wisdom (1:5) that comes as a divine gift from above (3:15-17). Such wisdom from above is not only full of the divine gifts of mercy and good "fruits [καρπῶν]" (3:17), but a "fruit" (καρπός) of the righteousness that pleases God is the yield of this divine wisdom's peace (3:18).

That the farmer is patient for the precious fruit of the earth that he awaits "until" (ἕως) it receives, as a divine gift from above, the early rain and the late rain indicates how the audience are to be patient "until" (ἕως) the coming of the Lord, awaiting it as a divine gift from above (5:7).[6] That the farmer is patient until it "receives" (λάβῃ) the rain as a divine gift bolsters the exhortation for the audience that "you receive" (λαμβάνετε) patiently what you ask for in prayer as a divine gift by not asking for the wrong reason, that is, to spend on passions for the possession of riches (4:3). It reinforces the warning for not many of us to become teachers, knowing that "we will receive" (λημψόμεθα) from God a greater judgment (3:1) at the coming of the Lord. And it strengthens the exhortation for each member of the audience to pray in faith (1:6), so that "he will receive" (λήμψεταί) a divine gift from the Lord (1:7),

---

5. "James identified with the specific anxiety and joy of the famer in a hard land, for whom a crop is never to be taken for granted and is, therefore, 'precious'" (Johnson, *James*, 314).

6. "James's mention of the 'early and late [rains]' is an allusion to a climatological phenomenon of Palestine, where the 'early rains' of late fall or early winter provide groundwater for the early spring growth and first harvest, and the late rains of late spring secure a good summer harvest. This became a symbol of God's faithful provision (Deut. 11:14; Jer. 5:24; Hos. 6:3) . . . But probably more significant to the author is the allusion to Joel 2:23-24, where the early and the late rains are a harbinger of the eschatological abundance of Israel after its promised restoration" (McCartney, *James*, 241). "ἕως ('until') contains the idea both of purpose (goal) and time" (Martin, *James*, 190).

especially that "he will receive" (λήμψεται), at the coming of the Lord, the crown of eternal life that the Lord promised to those who love him (1:12).

The initial command for the audience that "you be patient [μακροθυμήσατε]" until the coming of the Lord (5:7) then receives an emphatic reiteration and development. They are now directed that "you be patient" (μακροθυμήσατε) with the addition of an insistent and intensive "you also [καὶ ὑμεῖς]" (5:8a). That is, they, like the farmer "being patient" (μακροθυμῶν) to receive the early and late rain as a divine gift, are likewise to be patient to receive the coming of the Lord as a divine gift (5:7).

In contrast to the rich who have fattened "your hearts" (τὰς καρδίας ὑμῶν) in a day of slaughter (5:5), which the coming of the Lord will be for them, the audience are to strengthen "your hearts" (τὰς καρδίας ὑμῶν), for the coming of the Lord as a divine gift for them is near (5:8b). Although the audience are to be patient until the "coming of the Lord" (5:7), they may take courage in the promise that this "coming of the Lord" is near. That they are to strengthen their "hearts" in preparation for the coming of Lord which "is near" (ἤγγικεν) bolsters the exhortation for the audience to purify their "hearts" (καρδίας) in repentance as they are to "draw near" (ἐγγίσατε) to God in worship, so that he "will draw near" (ἐγγιεῖ) to them (4:8).[7] It reinforces the exhortation for the audience not to have bitter envy and selfishness in their "heart [καρδίᾳ]" (3:14) regarding wealth. And it strengthens the exhortation for anyone who thinks he is religious not to deceive his "heart" (καρδίαν) by bridling his tongue (1:26) and practicing a religion that includes the ethical worship of caring for poor orphans and widows (1:27).[8]

---

7. According to Johnson (*James*, 316), the verb ἐγγίζω "means 'to approach/draw near,' whether in terms of space (Gen 18:23; 27:27) or time (Ezek 12:23) . . . Here, however, the sense may be as much spatial as temporal, for James notes at once that 'the judge stands at the gate,' and in 4:8 James has said, 'approach God and he will approach you.' The use of spatial and temporal categories with reference to God is always, in any case, necessarily metaphorical."

8. "James' language evokes a Septuagintal idiom, 'strengthening the heart,' which, depending on context, can mean to gain physical strength, as for a journey (Judg 19:5, 8; Ps 103:15), or courage that comes from trust in the Lord (Ps 111:8), or firmness of intention (Sir 6:37; 22:16; see also 1 Thess 3:13). It is undoubtedly one of these latter

Addressed as "brothers" (ἀδελφοί), the audience were told to be patient until the coming of the Lord (5:7). This command is now further specified for the audience, again addressed as "brothers" (ἀδελφοί), as they are told not to grumble or complain against one another (5:9a). And that they are not to "complain [στενάζετε] against one another [κατ' ἀλλήλων]" reinforces the command for them not to "speak against one another" (καταλαλεῖτε ἀλλήλων), again addressed as "brothers [ἀδελφοί]" (4:11).[9] The audience are to appreciate that complaining and speaking against one another as brothers would be a dangerous abuse of the tongue. It could defile not only the whole body of the individual but the whole corporate body of the brotherly community by setting a deadly fire of destruction to the course of our new birth for eternal life (3:6; 1:18).

5:9b (B): So That You May Not Be Judged

The audience then hear the reason they are not to complain against one another (5:9a): "so that you may not be judged" (5:9b). Here the audience are warned that "you not be judged [κριθῆτε]" negatively by God, the one and only lawgiver and "judge" (κριτής) who is able to save and to destroy (4:12). None of them is to be one who "judges" (κρίνων)

---

two meanings James intends . . . Note the similarity to the call for 'purity of heart' in 4:8. These exhortations stand in contrast to the 'deception/indulgence of the heart' in 1:26 and the 'stuffing of the heart' in 5:5" (ibid., 315).

9. "To complain that life brings its trials may be acceptable for James (but the better attitude is that in 1:1–2), but to complain against (or blame) one another (κατ' ἀλλήλων) is not. It is only natural that afflicted people would express frustrations at the situation described in 5:1–6, but harmony is destroyed when the bitter spirit becomes personal and directed as criticism against fellow believers. This recalls 4:11 and the command to refrain from speaking evil of others" (Martin, *James*, 192). "As with καταλαλεῖτε in 4:11 and the key words of 4:1–2b, στενάζετε encompasses a wide assortment of verbal wrongs including: gossip, slander, mockery, cursing, angry speech, perjury, and probably also speech that reflects partiality" (Baker, *Personal Speech-Ethics*, 180). "One side of μακροθυμία is μὴ στενάζετε κατ' ἀλλήλων, 'do not moan about one another'" (Davids, *James*, 184). "As he did in 4:11–12, James connects the need to refrain from critical speech with judgment. In the former passage, however, he likened critical speech to judgment; here he warns that criticism of one another places a person in danger of judgment" (Moo, *James*, 225).

the neighbor (4:12) by speaking against or complaining against one another. The one who speaks against a brother or "judges" (κρίνων) his brother speaks against the law and "judges" (κρίνει) the law. But if "you judge" (κρίνεις) the law, you are not a doer of the law but a "judge [κριτής]" (4:11). In addition, the audience may be judged negatively by God if they become "judges" (κριταί) with evil designs (2:4) by showing partiality in favor of the rich and against the poor (2:1–3). Rather, the audience are so to speak and so to do as those about to be "judged" (κρίνεσθαι) through a law of freedom (2:12), which includes a word of truth according to which God brought us to birth for eternal life (1:18, 25).[10]

5:9c (B'): Behold the Judge Is Standing before the Gates

The audience then hear the reason they are not to complain against one another (5:9a), so that they may not be judged (5:9b): "Behold the judge is standing before the gates" (5:9c). At this point the audience experience the pivot of parallels involving cognate expressions for "judge" at the center of this chiastic unit. "So that you may not be judged [κριθῆτε]" in the B element (5:9b) progresses to "the judge [κριτής] is standing before the gates" in the B' element (5:9c).

Having been told to "behold" (ἰδού) the farmer patiently awaiting the precious fruit of the earth as an analogy for patiently awaiting the coming of the Lord (5:7), the audience are now told to "behold" (ἰδού) the "judge" (κριτής), the one and only divine "judge" (κριτής) who is able to save and to destroy (4:12), who is standing before the gates (5:9c). That the divine judge already "is standing" (ἕστηκεν) before the gates for entrance into the midst of the audience reinforces the promise that the coming of the Lord already "is near [ἤγγικεν]" (5:8). The audience, who would become "judges" (κριταί) with evil designs (2:4), if they say to a poor person who enters into their worshiping assembly, "you stand [στῆθι] there" (2:3), are to behold their divine judge already "standing," ironically, before the gates ready to enter.[11]

---

10. "The 'law of freedom,' which is also the 'law of love,' is the measure by which they are to act and by which they are to be measured" (Johnson, *James*, 317).

11. That these are the only occurrences in James of the verb "stand" (ἵστημι) en-

5:10–11 (A'): As Example of Patience Brothers Receive the Prophets of the Lord

The audience hear the A' element (5:10–11) of this chiastic unit as a chiastic pattern in itself:

a) As an example of suffering and patience receive, brothers, the prophets who spoke in the name of the *Lord* (5:10).

b) Behold we call blessed those who have *endured* (5:11a).

b') Of the *endurance* of Job you have heard (5:11b).

a') and the outcome of the *Lord* you have seen, for very sympathetic is the *Lord* and compassionate (5:11c).

At the center of this chiastic sub-unit the audience experience a pivot of parallels involving the only occurrences in this sub-unit of expressions for "endurance." "Those who have endured [ὑπομείναντας]" in the b) sub-element (5:11a) progresses to "the endurance [ὑπομονήν] of Job" in the b') sub-element (5:11b). They then hear a progression of chiastic parallels involving the only occurrences in this sub-unit of the term "Lord." "The name of the Lord [κυρίου]" in the a) sub-element (5:10) progresses to "the outcome of the Lord [κυρίου]" and "very sympathetic is the Lord [κύριος]" in the a') sub-element (5:11c).

In addition, at this point the audience hear a progression of parallels from the A (5:7–9a) to the A' (5:10–11) element of this chiastic unit: "Be patient [μακροθυμήσατε] then, brothers [ἀδελφοί], until the coming of the Lord [κυρίου]" (5:7a), "being patient [μακροθυμῶν] for it until it receives [λάβῃ]" (5:7a), "be patient [μακροθυμήσατε] . . . for the coming

hances this connection. "The one at the door is the 'Judge,' the one and only Judge (4:11–12), whose sole prerogative is usurped when humans seek to judge (2:4) . . . Physical proximity here is a trope for temporal imminence. We appeal to the perfect tenses, tie them together, and form a clear image: God *has heard* the cries, the parousia *has drawn near*, and the Judge *is standing* at the doors. The image is one of an imminent act of God that will establish justice and send off the message that the oppressed have been vindicated (emphases original)" (McKnight, *James*, 415). "The nearness of the eschatological day is not just an impetus to look forward to the judgment of 'sinners' and so stand fast in the faith oneself, but it is also a warning to examine one's behavior so that when the one whose footsteps are nearing finally knocks on the door, one may be prepared to open, for open one must, either for blessing or for judgment. The coming Lord is also the judge of the Christian" (Davids, *James*, 185).

of the Lord [κυρίου]" (5:8), and "brothers [ἀδελφοί]" (5:9a) progress to "patience [μακροθυμίας] receive [λάβετε], brothers [ἀδελφοί] . . . in the name of the Lord [κυρίου]" (5:10), "the outcome of the Lord [κυρίου]" (5:11c), and "sympathetic is the Lord [κύριος]" (5:11c).

Addressed as "brothers," the audience were exhorted that "you be patient" until the coming of the "Lord" (5:7a). They were then further exhorted that "you be patient, you also" (5:8), like the farmer who is "patient" for the precious fruit of the earth (5:7a), for the coming of the "Lord" is near (5:8). As "brothers" they are not to complain against one another (5:9a). Now, again addressed as "brothers," the audience are to receive as an example of suffering and "patience" the prophets who spoke in the name of the "Lord" (5:10). Just as the patient farmer "receives" the early rain and the late rain as a divine gift (5:7), so the audience are directed that "you receive" the prophetic example of patience as a divine gift.[12]

That as an example of patience the prophets "spoke" (ἐλάλησαν) in the name of the Lord (5:10) bolsters the exhortation for the audience that "you do not speak against [καταλαλεῖτε]" one another, since he who "speaks against" (καταλαλῶν) a brother "speaks against" (καταλαλεῖ) the law (4:11), which is a law of loving one another (2:8). It reinforces the exhortation for the audience that "you so speak [λαλεῖτε]" as those about to be judged through a law of freedom (2:12), the law of love. And it strengthens the exhortation for everyone in the audience to be patiently slow to "speak [λαλῆσαι]" (1:19) in order to avoid the anger that does not work the righteousness pleasing to God as ethical worship. Instead of speaking in their liturgical assembly in a way that shows partiality against the poor and in favor of the rich (2:1–4), who blaspheme the praiseworthy divine "name" (ὄνομα) invoked over them as a worshiping community (2:7), the audience are to patiently speak like the prophets who spoke in the "name" (ὀνόματι) of the Lord.[13]

12. "James wants the two terms [suffering and patience] kept close together because he is speaking here of a patience in suffering or a suffering with patience inasmuch as the two words are virtually combined to form 'endurance' (ὑπομονή) in 5:11" (McKnight, *James*, 417). "The stress in James's example is not on the prophets' suffering but rather on their patient endurance" (Hartin, *James*, 244).

13. "James defines the prophets as those 'who spoke in the name of the Lord.' Their message brought them suffering, and in that suffering they patiently awaited

With the demonstrative particle "behold," the audience were directed to "behold" (ἰδού) the fact that the farmer patiently awaits the precious fruit of the earth (5:7), as one should await the coming of the Lord (5:8), and to "behold" (ἰδού) the fact that the divine judge is already standing before the gates (5:9). Now they are directed to "behold" (ἰδού) the fact that we call blessed those prophets who have endured (5:11a). That "we call blessed" (μακαρίζομεν) in an act of liturgical worship those prophets who have "endured" (ὑπομείναντας) bolsters the promise for the audience that any of them who "perseveres" (παραμείνας), becoming a doer of work as ethical worship, will be "blessed" (μακάριος) by God in his doing (1:25). It reinforces the promise that "blessed" (μακάριος) is a man who "endures" (ὑπομένει) temptation, especially the temptation to become wealthy, for he will receive the crown of eternal life that the Lord promised to those who love him (1:12).

That the audience have heard (through the scriptures proclaimed in worship) of the "endurance" (ὑπομονήν) of Job (5:11b), whose faith was tested through the loss of his wealth, encourages them, as they are tempted to become wealthy, to know that such testing of their faith produces "endurance [ὑπομονήν]" (1:3), endurance like that of Job. And such "endurance" (ὑπομονή) results in making the audience perfect and complete, lacking in nothing (1:4) they need for the worship of God. That already "you have heard" (ἠκούσατε) of the endurance of Job fortifies the exhortation for the audience to be quick to "hear" (ἀκοῦσαι) the word of God (1:19), so that "you hear" (ἀκούσατε) that God chose the poor in this world to be rich in faith and heirs of the kingdom and of the crown of eternal life that he promised to those who love him (2:5; 1:12).[14]

God's vindication" (McKnight, *James*, 417). "James cites the prophets because they were people who not only suffered injustice but spoke out against it as well" (Moo, *James*, 227). "No doubt the example of the prophets in v 10 was meaningful to James' readers. He assumes that they will have become acquainted with the prophetic figures of the OT through public readings in the synagogue lectionary" (Martin, *James*, 194).

14. For background to the endurance of Job in the *Testament of Job*, see Gray, "Points and Lines," 406–24. "Job is cast in the *Testament of Job* in altogether patient terms, but that is not James's point. He has more in mind with Job; he has in mind the poor oppressed who cry out to God (like Job), who are not to resort to violence, and who will retain their faith and integrity without always falling from their commit-

The audience have seen (through the scriptures heard in worship) the "end," "purpose," "result," or "outcome" (τέλος) of the "Lord" (κυρίου) in the case of Job, toward whom the "Lord" (κύριος) was very sympathetic and compassionate (5:11c) as Job endured his sufferings and loss of wealth. This bolsters the exhortation for the audience to follow the example of suffering and patience provided for them by the prophets who spoke in the name of the "Lord [κυρίου]" (5:10). And that they have seen the "outcome of the Lord" in the case of Job reinforces the exhortation for them to be patient until the "coming of the Lord [κυρίου]" (5:7) and to strengthen their hearts, for the "coming of the Lord [κυρίου]" is near (5:8). The audience are to appreciate that although the judge already "is standing" (ἕστηκεν) before the gates (5:9), for those who endure like Job this divine judge will come as the divine Lord who "is" (ἐστιν) very sympathetic and compassionate.[15]

---

ments. It is then the combination of Job's (impatient!) protests along with his steady resolve to stick to what he believes to be true, even if God does not (!), that makes Job the most suitable character in the Bible for what James has to say" (McKnight, *James*, 421). "For a reader of Job, it may be surprising to hear that Job became a paradigm for patience, since much of the book consists of Job's impatient complaining to God about the injustice of his suffering. However, the kind of patience that James has in mind is not passivity, but perseverance, fortitude in the face of suffering . . . Job did not give in to the falsity being suggested by his friends, and he did not give up; he kept clinging tightly and unyieldingly to God as the context of his life" (McCartney, *James*, 243). "James's singling out of Job's perseverance is not an unwarranted inference from the canonical book itself. For although Job did complain bitterly about God's treatment of him, he never abandoned his faith. In the midst of his incomprehension, he clung to God and continued to hope in him (see 1:21; 2:10; 16:19-21; 19:25-27)" (Moo, *James*, 229).

15. On 5:7-11 in general, see Oliphant, "Waiting Patiently," 81–86. "[H]ere τέλος seems to reflect the 'end' of the book of Job, where 'the Lord' forgives Job's friends through Job's prayers, that is, 'the Lord's end' refers to the merciful resolution of the story of Job and his friends. God not only forgives the friends but then shows mercy to Job by restoring his fortunes. This best explains why James then says 'how the Lord is compassionate and merciful'" (McKnight, *James*, 422).

Summary on 5:7-11

That the farmer is patient for the precious fruit of the earth that he awaits "until" it receives, as a divine gift from above, the early rain and the late rain indicates how the audience are to be patient "until" the coming of the Lord, awaiting it as a divine gift from above (5:7). That the farmer is patient until it "receives" the rain as a divine gift bolsters the exhortation for the audience that "you receive" patiently what you ask for in prayer as a divine gift by not asking for the wrong reason, that is, to spend on passions for the possession of riches (4:3). It reinforces the warning for not many of us to become teachers, knowing that "we will receive" from God a greater judgment (3:1) at the coming of the Lord. And it strengthens the exhortation for each member of the audience to pray in faith (1:6), so that "he will receive" a divine gift from the Lord (1:7), especially that "he will receive," at the coming of the Lord, the crown of eternal life that the Lord promised to those who love him (1:12).

In contrast to the rich who have fattened "your hearts" in a day of slaughter (5:5), which the coming of the Lord will be for them, the audience are to strengthen "your hearts," for the coming of the Lord as a divine gift for them is near (5:8b). Although the audience are to be patient until the "coming of the Lord" (5:7), they may take courage in the promise that this "coming of the Lord" is near. That they are to strengthen their "hearts" in preparation for the coming of Lord which "is near" bolsters the exhortation for the audience to purify their "hearts" in repentance as they are to "draw near" to God in worship, so that he "will draw near" to them (4:8). It reinforces the exhortation for the audience not to have bitter envy and selfishness in their "heart" (3:14) regarding wealth. And it strengthens the exhortation for anyone who thinks he is religious not to deceive his "heart" by bridling his tongue (1:26) and practicing a religion that includes the ethical worship of caring for poor orphans and widows (1:27).

That the audience are not to "complain against one another" (5:9a) reinforces the command for them not to "speak against one another" (4:11). The audience are to appreciate that complaining and speaking against one another as brothers would be a dangerous abuse of the tongue. It could defile not only the whole body of the individual but the whole corporate body of the brotherly community by setting a deadly fire of destruction to the course of our new birth for eternal life (3:6; 1:18).

The audience are warned that "you not be judged" negatively by God (5:9b), the one and only lawgiver and "judge" who is able to save and to destroy (4:12). None of them is to be one who "judges" the neighbor (4:12) by speaking against or complaining against one another. The one who speaks against a brother or "judges" his brother speaks against the law and "judges" the law. But if "you judge" the law, you are not a doer of the law but a "judge" (4:11). In addition, the audience may be judged negatively by God if they become "judges" with evil designs (2:4) by showing partiality in favor of the rich and against the poor (2:1–3). Rather, the audience are so to speak and so to do as those about to be "judged" through a law of freedom (2:12), which includes a word of truth according to which God brought us to birth for eternal life (1:18, 25).

The audience are told to behold the "judge," the one and only divine "judge" who is able to save and to destroy (4:12), who is standing before the gates (5:9c). That the divine judge already "is standing" before the gates for entrance into the midst of the audience reinforces the promise that the coming of the Lord already "is near" (5:8). The audience, who would become "judges" with evil designs (2:4), if they say to a poor person who enters into their worshiping assembly, "you stand there" (2:3), are to behold their divine judge already "standing," ironically, before the gates ready to enter.

That as an example of patience the prophets "spoke" in the name of the Lord (5:10) bolsters the exhortation for the audience that "you do not speak against" one another, since he who "speaks against" a brother "speaks against" the law (4:11), which is a law of loving one another (2:8). It reinforces the exhortation for the audience that "you so speak" as those about to be judged through a law of freedom (2:12), the law of love. And it strengthens the exhortation for everyone in the audience to be patiently slow to "speak" (1:19) in order to avoid the anger that does not work the righteousness pleasing to God as ethical worship. Instead of speaking in their liturgical assembly in a way that shows partiality against the poor and in favor of the rich (2:1–4), who blaspheme the praiseworthy divine "name" invoked over them as a worshiping community (2:7), the audience are to patiently speak like the prophets who spoke in the "name" of the Lord.

That "we call blessed" in an act of liturgical worship those prophets who have "endured" (5:11a) bolsters the promise for the audience that any of them who "perseveres," becoming a doer of work as ethical worship, will be "blessed" by God in his doing (1:25). It reinforces the promise that "blessed" is a man who "endures" temptation, especially the temptation to become wealthy, for he will receive the crown of eternal life that the Lord promised to those who love him (1:12).

That the audience have heard (through the scriptures proclaimed in worship) of the "endurance" of Job (5:11b), whose faith was tested through the loss of his wealth, encourages them, as they are tempted to become wealthy, to know that such testing of their faith produces "endurance" (1:3), endurance like that of Job. And such "endurance" results in making the audience perfect and complete, lacking in nothing (1:4) they need for the worship of God. That already "you have heard" of the endurance of Job fortifies the exhortation for the audience to be quick to "hear" the word of God (1:19), so that "you hear" that God chose the poor in this world to be rich in faith and heirs of the kingdom and of the crown of eternal life that he promised to those who love him (2:5; 1:12).

The audience have seen (through the scriptures heard in worship) the "end," "purpose," "result," or "outcome" of the "Lord" in the case of Job, toward whom the "Lord" was very sympathetic and compassionate (5:11c) as Job endured his sufferings and loss of wealth. This bolsters the exhortation for the audience to follow the example of suffering and patience provided for them by the prophets who spoke in the name of the "Lord" (5:10). And that they have seen the "outcome of the Lord" in the case of Job reinforces the exhortation for them to be patient until the "coming of the Lord" (5:7) and to strengthen their hearts, for the "coming of the Lord" is near (5:8). The audience are to appreciate that although the judge already "is standing" before the gates (5:9), for those who endure like Job this divine judge will come as the divine Lord who "is" very sympathetic and compassionate.

James 5:12–20

Whoever Brings Back One Led Astray Will Save Him from Death (A')

Pray for one another that you may be healed and raised up to life

A ¹² Before all, *my brothers*, do not swear by *heaven* or by earth or by any other oath. But let your "Yes" be yes and your "No" be no, so that you may not fall under judgment.

    B ¹³ If anyone is suffering among you, let him *pray*. If anyone is cheerful, let him sing praise. ¹⁴ If anyone is sick among you, let him summon the elders of the church and let them *pray* over him, anointing him with oil in the name of the Lord.

        C ¹⁵ᵃ And the *prayer* of faith will save the one who is ill and the Lord will raise him up.

            D ¹⁵ᵇ And if he has done *sins*,

                E ¹⁵ᶜ they will be forgiven him.

            D' ¹⁶ᵃ Confess then to one another the *sins*

        C' ¹⁶ᵇ and *pray* for one another that you may be healed. A request of a righteous one is very powerful in its working.

    B' ¹⁷ Elijah was a person similar in nature to us, and with *prayer* he *prayed* for it not to rain, and it did not rain on the earth for three years and six months. ¹⁸ᵃ And again he *prayed*,

A' ¹⁸ᵇ and the *heaven* gave rain and the earth sprouted its fruit. ¹⁹ᵃ *My brothers*, if anyone among you should be led astray from the truth and someone brings him back, [20] let him know that whoever brings back a sinful one from the straying of his way will save his soul from death and will cover a multitude of sins.[1]

Audience Response to 5:12-20

At this point the audience experience a progression of macrochiastic parallels from the A (1:1-16) to the A' (5:12-20) unit. The warning that desire and sin bring birth to "death [θάνατον]" (1:15) progresses to the assertion that whoever brings back a sinful one will save his soul from "death [θανάτου]" (5:20). And the command not to be "led astray [πλανᾶσθε]" (1:16) progresses to the statement that if anyone among you should be "led astray" (πλανηθῇ) from the truth (5:19) and from the "straying" (πλάνης) of his way (5:20).

5:12 (A): My Brothers Do Not Swear by Heaven or by Earth

The audience continue to be affectionately addressed as "brothers" of one another and of the author: "Before all, my brothers, do not swear by heaven or by earth or by any other oath. But let your 'Yes' be yes and your 'No' be no, so that you may not fall under judgment" (5:12). When the audience hear the address "my brothers [ἀδελφοί]," they hear the transitional term that links this unit with the preceding unit (5:7-11), which contains the address "brothers" (ἀδελφοί) at the beginning of its final element (5:10).

When the audience hear the phrase, "before all [πάντων]" (5:12), it carries a connotation of before all of the points or parts of the law, the royal law of freedom (2:8, 12; 1:25). It resonates with the only previous occurrence of the genitive neuter plural adjective "all" in the warning that whoever keeps the whole law, but stumbles in one point, has become guilty of "all (of the points or parts)" (πάντων) of it (2:10). The phrase "before all" thus prepares the audience to hear another point or part that is a preeminent part of the royal law of freedom, which is the law of loving one's neighbor as oneself (2:8).[2]

---

1. For the establishment of Jas 5:12-20 as a chiasm, see the Introduction.
2. "The construction with πᾶς ('all') is found in some Hellenistic letters, usually in

Addressed as "brothers," the audience were warned not to complain against one another, so that "you may not be judged [κριθῆτε]" (5:9). They are now warned as "brothers" not to swear by heaven or by earth or by any other oath. They are to speak truthfully by letting their "Yes" be yes and their "No" be no, so that "you may not fall under judgment [κρίσιν]" (5:12).³ This bolsters the exhortation for the audience, as "brothers," not to speak against one another, for he who speaks against a brother or "judges" (κρίνων) his brother "judges" (κρίνει) the law. But if you "judge" (κρίνεις) the law, you are not a doer of the law but a "judge" (κριτής) of the law (4:11), the law that commands loving rather than "judging" (κρίνων) the neighbor (4:12; 2:8). God is the one and only "judge" (κριτής) able to save and to destroy (4:12). It also reinforces the exhortation for the audience so to speak and so to do as those about to

connection with the wish for health shortly before the final greeting. The phrase occurs also at 1 Pet 4:8; *Did.* 10:4 . . . If one recognizes, however, that James thus begins this final section of the letter with exhortations centering on the positive functions of speech (plain talk, prayer, confessing, correction), and that the prohibition of 'grumbling against one another' in 5:9 also bore on improper speech, then this statement on oaths appears to continue the theme of speech started in 3:1–12 but now as applied directly to the community under harassment. The phrase πρὸ πάντων indeed may give special significance to oath-taking, but it *also* functions as a thematic transition to acts of speech within the community. Note also the sense of continuity provided by the fourth repetition in five verses of the vocative 'brothers' (5:7, 9, 10, 12)" (Johnson, *James*, 326–27, emphasis original).

3. For a comparison between Jesus' prohibition of oaths in Matt 5:33–37 and Jas 5:12, see Kollmann, "Schwurverbot," 179–93. According to McKnight (*James*, 426), "the text of James is a literary deposit of an oral tradition that goes back to Jesus. In other words, James has made the words of Jesus his own." "The OT (Lev. 19:12) and Second Temple ethical literature condemned the taking of oaths lightly or in vain, though rarely does Jewish literature advocate the avoidance of oaths entirely . . . James and Jesus, however, not only share the notion that *all* oaths should be avoided, but also say so in a very similar way (emphasis original)" (McCartney, *James*, 245–46). "Christians committed to integrity in speech and personal relationships should never require an oath" (Moo, *James*, 233). "James, then, prohibits not official oaths, such as in courts, but the use of oaths in everyday discourse to prove integrity. The community member ought not to use oaths, for his yes or no should be totally honest, making oaths unnecessary; truthfulness is the issue. Since God holds one to this standard, oaths are dangerous, for they make some speech more honest than other speech. Thus they must be avoided to keep this deceptive idea from bringing God's judgment (in the final judgment, as the context shows) upon one when he is less than truthful" (Davids, *James*, 190–91).

be "judged" (κρίνεσθαι) through the law of freedom (2:12), the law of love (2:8). For the "judgment" (κρίσις) is merciless for the one not doing mercy; mercy however boasts over "judgment [κρίσεως]" (2:13).[4]

5:13–14 (B): Let Him Pray and Let Them Pray for Him

The audience hear the B element (5:13–14) of this chiastic unit as a chiastic pattern in itself:

a) If anyone is suffering *among you*, let him *pray* (5:13a).

   b) If anyone is cheerful, let him sing praise (5:13b).

a′) If anyone is sick *among you*, let him summon the elders of the church and let them *pray* over him, anointing him with oil in the name of the Lord (5:14).[5]

After the unparalleled b) sub-element, "if anyone is cheerful, let him sing praise" (5:13b), at the center of this chiastic sub-unit, the audience experience a pivot of chiastic parallels involving the only occurrences in this sub-unit of the phrase "among you" and the verb "pray." "If anyone is suffering among you [ἐν ὑμῖν], let him pray [προσευχέσθω]" in the a) sub-element (5:13a) progresses to "if anyone is sick among you [ἐν ὑμῖν], let him summon the elders of the church and let them pray [προσευξάσθωσαν] over him" in the a′) (5:14) sub-element.

The audience were exhorted to receive the prophets who spoke in the name of the Lord as an example of "suffering" (κακοπαθίας) and patience (5:10). Now they are exhorted that if anyone among them is "suffering" (κακοπαθεῖ), he is to pray (5:13a). Whereas the prophets in the

---

4. "James is given to what appears to many to be exaggeration: people can be condemned for not showing mercy (2:13), for grumbling (5:9), and for the inappropriate use of oaths (5:12). Each of these, on closer inspection, emerges from the depth of his theology: from a loving life, from a nonviolent approach to resolving one's economic situation, and from a heart that tells true words" (McKnight, *James*, 429). "James has in several other places connected his negative commands with statements concerning judgment (see 2:4; 2:12–13; 4:11–12; 5:9)" (Johnson, *James*, 329). "It would appear, then, that James conceives of 5:12 as the last in a series of admonitions which are tied together by their common threat of condemning judgment of God" (Baker, *Personal Speech-Ethics*, 278).

5. Kuske, "James 5:14," 125–27.

midst of their suffering spoke to the people in the authoritative name of the Lord, as a complement to this prophetic example, individuals who are suffering among the audience are to speak to the Lord in prayer.[6]

The audience were exhorted that anyone "who" (τίς) would be wise and understanding "among you" (ἐν ὑμῖν) is to show from praiseworthy conduct his works that are to accompany his faith (2:14-18) in humility of wisdom (3:13), that is, the divine wisdom from above (3:15-16), which one is to prayerfully request from God (1:5) in faith (1:6). Now they are exhorted that if "anyone" (τις) is suffering "among you" (ἐν ὑμῖν), he is to pray to God (5:13a). The prayer of the audience for the patience to endure suffering thus complements their prayer for the wisdom to endure temptation, especially the temptation to become wealthy (1:9-11), so that they may be blessed by God to receive the crown of eternal life (1:12).

The exhortation that if "anyone" (τις) is suffering "among you" (ἐν ὑμῖν), let him "pray [προσευχέσθω]" (5:13a) is then developed. First, it is followed by the exhortation that if "anyone" (τις) is cheerful, let him sing praise (5:13b).[7] Then, if "anyone" (τις) is sick "among you"

---

6. "If one looks into James for concrete evidence for suffering, one would have to think of the various trials of 1:2-4, the implication of oppression in 1:9-11, the need for perseverance in 1:12-14, and the suffering of the marginalized in 1:26-27; 2:1-4, 14-17; and 5:1-6. And the appearance of the cognate noun in 5:10 ('suffering and patience') suggests a connection with the marginalized who were enduring oppression at the hands of the rich farmers. Thus, 'suffering' in 5:13a most likely refers to the suffering of the poor at the hand of the abusively powerful, and it would also describe the suffering inherent to persevering patience" (McKnight, *James*, 432-33). "[T]he word 'suffering' in 5:13 has the same (rare) verbal root as the word used in 5:10 to describe the sufferings of the OT prophets. It refers not specifically to physical illness (though that would not be excluded), which is the specific subject of the third condition (5:14), but simply to the bad or distressing experiences in life" (McCartney, *James*, 251). "James is not exhorting his readers to pray for the removal of trouble as much as he is urging them to seek the strength to endure it" (Martin, *James*, 206).

7. "We should avoid thinking of 'is cheerful' (εὐθυμέω) in terms of a happy, smiley face because life is good. This term evokes enthusiasm, courage, and a confident faith and these often in the context of stress . . . The contrast here is not between suffering and the good life but within a group where everyone is undergoing persecution or suffering, some of whom are struggling and others who have taken courage . . . Those who suffer are to pray to God; those who are encouraged in the conditions of the messianic community are to sing praise to God, and we are probably to think that James

(ἐν ὑμῖν), let him summon the elders of the church and let them "pray" (προσευξάσθωσαν) over him (5:14a). The individual's own prayer for his suffering thus progresses to the communal prayer for one who is sick.⁸ The elders are to complement their ritualistic prayer over the sick one with a ritualistic gesture of anointing him in the name of the Lord (5:14b).⁹ And the addition to their prayer to God of the anointing "in the name of the Lord" (ἐν τῷ ὀνόματι τοῦ κυρίου) of one suffering sickness complements the prophets' speaking to the people "in the name of the Lord" (ἐν τῷ ὀνόματι τοῦ κυρίου) as an example of suffering and patience (5:10). The praying "over" (ἐπί) and anointing is in the name of the Lord, the praiseworthy "name" (ὄνομα) of the Lord Jesus Christ that was "invoked over you" (ἐπικληθὲν ἐφ' ὑμᾶς), the entire audience (2:7).¹⁰

---

intends for the 'cheerful' (or 'encouraged') to give credit to God for the strength they find to carry on faithfully" (McKnight, *James*, 433–34). As McCartney (*James*, 252) notes, the word "sing praise" (ψάλλω) in biblical literature "became associated with playing and singing in the worship and praise of God."

8. "The word translated 'sick' is a general term denoting physical, spiritual, or mental weakness and can even describe someone on the verge of death" (McKnight, *James*, 434).

9. "In NT times, 'elders' (πρεσβύτεροι) signified not simply the oldest people in the community, but those who were spiritually mature and equipped to give counsel and direction to the members of the community in their obedience to Christ (see Acts 14:23; Titus 1:5–9; 1 Pet 5:1)" (McCartney, *James*, 252–53n5). "In James's words the oil could symbolize consecration of the person to God or could be sacramental, something that mediates God's healing grace. . . . the elders were to anoint the sick person's body to consecrate and purify it as an act of devoting it to God for God's work of healing" (McKnight, *James*, 439). "It is best to take anointing, then, as a symbol of God's blessing attendant to intercessory prayer and possibly as 'consecrating' in the sense of reminding the sick that they belong to God. Anointing reminds both them and the community that they are specially 'set aside' for prayer and points to the reality of the future blessing of eschatological life. Quite aside from the pleasurable physical sensation of being anointed, this would bring comfort and encouragement to the sick, even if the one suffering must await the final resurrection before he or she experienced being 'raised up'" (McCartney, *James*, 255). See also Collins, "James 5:14-16a," 79–91; Harrington, "Anointing the Sick," 412–17; Thomas, "Devil," 25–50.

10. "To pray and anoint in the name of the Lord Jesus involves invoking Jesus Christ to act in the power of the resurrection. In liturgical terms, it is epiclesis, or the calling upon the Lord Jesus Christ to become present in power for healing" (McKnight, *James*, 440). "[T]he elders pray 'upon' or 'over' (ἐπί) the sick person in

The audience are thus exhorted to follow a comprehensive set of ritualistic instructions regarding their worship, both individual and communal, in a variety of diverse yet complementary situations: If any individual among them is suffering, he is to pray (5:13a). If an individual is cheerful, he is to sing praise (5:13b). And if an individual among them is sick, he is to summon the elders of the church to offer a communal prayer over him and anoint him in the name of the Lord (5:14).

5:15a (C): The Prayer of Faith Will Save the One Who Is Ill

The audience are informed about the beneficial effects of prayer on behalf of the sick (5:14): "And the prayer of faith will save the one who is ill and the Lord will raise him up" (5:15a).[11] That the prayer of "faith" (πίστεως) will "save" (σώσει) the one who is ill implies that prayer is one of the works that is to accompany faith. This promise of salvation resonates with the question of what the benefit is if someone says he has "faith" (πίστιν) but does not have works. Such "faith" (πίστις) in not able to "save" (σῶσαι) him (2:14). And it is the prayer of "faith" that will save the one who is ill, since one cannot expect to receive anything from the Lord (1:7) unless he asks in "faith [πίστει]" (1:6).

As the audience are to recall, the prayer of faith for one who is ill (5:15a) is directed to God as the one and only lawgiver and judge who is able to "save" (σῶσαι) and to destroy (4:12), that is, able to grant the eschatological salvation of eternal life or to condemn to the eschatological destruction of eternal death. And this prayer of faith is to be offered by believers who welcome the divinely implanted word, a word of truth by which God brought us to birth for eternal life (1:18). This is the word

---

the name of the Lord. This makes it likely that James has in mind the 'name that is invoked upon [ἐπί] you' in 2:7, which, as we noted, is best understood as a reference to the name of Jesus Christ" (McCartney, *James*, 255). "Thus one finds three actions in the healing rite: prayer, anointing, and the calling out of the name of Jesus. This is not a magical rite, nor an exorcism, but an opening to the power of God for him to intervene whether or not the demonic is involved. It is also interesting to note that this is not the special gift of an individual, unlike 1 Cor. 12:9, 28, 30, but the power of a certain office in the church" (Davids, *James*, 193-94).

11. "This prayer is described as a fervent wish or request (ἡ εὐχή) offered in faith (τῆς πίστεως)" (Martin, *James*, 209).

of God that is able to "save" (σῶσαι) our souls now and for eternity (1:21).[12]

The promise that the prayer of faith will save the one who is ill is further explained by the promise that the Lord will raise him up (5:15a), that is, the risen Lord at the final judgment will raise him up to eschatological, eternal life. That the "Lord" (κύριος) will raise him up is thus the result of the communal prayer over and anointing of the sick person with oil in the name of the "Lord [κυρίου]" (5:14). The promise that the Lord will raise up the one who is ill furthers the audience's appreciation that very sympathetic is the "Lord" (κύριος) and compassionate (5:11).[13]

5:15b (D): And If He Has Done Sins

The audience are presented with a further possibility regarding the prayer of faith for one who is ill (5:15a): "And if he has done sins"

12. "The word 'save' can, of course, refer either to physical healing or to the rescue of a person from guilt and condemnation or to the eschatological salvation in the judgment. The context here in James at least partly has healing in view, but the connection with forgiveness of sins (5:16) demonstrates that James has both in mind or perhaps does not sharply distinguish between them, and eschatological salvation certainly is evident elsewhere in James (1:21; 2:14; 4:12). Again, the distinction that we generally draw may be more the product of our dualistic mind-set. The health of the individual, both physical and spiritual, is an element of the health of the community, both present and future" (McCartney, *James*, 256). "The verb σῴζειν has in this context its familiar ambiguity. At the most literal level, it means that the sick person will be healed. But in NT literature, especially when combined with 'faith,' it tends to mean 'saved' in a religious sense" (Johnson, *James*, 332).

13. "Once again, with the corporate dimension in mind, it is not necessary to suppose that every instance of physical ailment will be healed, nor is it necessary to spiritualize the text. The Lord will provide deliverance to his people, both physical and spiritual, and it is in this mode that James uses resurrection language. Although James does not develop the theological implications of Jesus's resurrection in the life of the believer, the OT expectation of the ultimate restoration of God's people (which saw its climactic fulfillment in the resurrection of Jesus) is an ever-present theme in James, and in the OT this expectation is often put in terms of 'raising up'" (McCartney, *James*, 256-57). On the reassurance that "the Lord will raise him up," Johnson (*James*, 333) maintains that it "can be read at two levels simultaneously: the Lord is able to 'raise him up' from sickness, and thus 'save him' by physical healing and is able to 'raise him up by resurrection' even if he should die and 'save his life/soul' in the resurrection life (see James 1:18; 5:20)."

(5:15b). The possibility that the one who is ill has "done" (πεποιηκώς) "sins" (ἁμαρτίας) in the past whose effects are still present (perfect tense) reminds the audience of what they have heard about the dangerously destructive doing of sins, especially sins of failing to love one's neighbor as oneself and of desiring to become wealthy.[14] To the one knowing the praiseworthy thing to "do" (ποιεῖν), that is, especially not judging (4:12) but rather loving one's neighbor (2:8), and not "doing" (ποιοῦντι) it, to him it is "sin [ἁμαρτία]" (4:17). If the audience show partiality in favor of the rich and against the poor among them, they are working "sin" (ἁμαρτίαν), convicted by the law, the law of loving one's neighbor (2:8), as transgressors (2:9). And when the desire, especially the desire to become wealthy (1:9–11), conceives, it gives birth to "sin" (ἁμαρτίαν), and the "sin" (ἁμαρτία) having been brought to completion, brings birth to eschatological, eternal death (1:15).

5:15c (E): They Will Be Forgiven Him

The audience are assured that as a result of the elders of the church praying over and anointing the one who is ill (5:15a) and who has done sins (5:15b), "they will be forgiven him" (5:15c). Although to one knowing the praiseworthy thing to do and not doing it, to "him" (αὐτῷ) it is sin (4:17), if the one who is ill has done sins, they will be forgiven "him" (αὐτῷ). That he will be forgiven by God (divine passive) further deepens the audience's appreciation that very sympathetic is the Lord and compassionate (5:11).[15]

---

14. "The use of the perfect tense [πεποιηκώς] is significant, for it indicates an influence of the present. If someone has done something wrong in the past, it continues to affect him or her now. The past sin continues to influence that person in his or her relationship with God until she or he attains forgiveness" (Hartin, *James*, 269).

15. "What James says is that if the sickness is from sin, the sin 'will be forgiven.' James combines the sick person's requesting the elders—a sign in and of itself of need and faith in Christ—the elders' prayer and anointing, the prayer of faith, and, as the next verse will clarify, confession of sin. This leads to the sick person's forgiveness, itself sometimes a trigger of healing (Mark 2:5; Matt 8:16–17), and healing, itself an indication of forgiveness" (McKnight, *James*, 444).

5:16a (D'): Confess Then to One Another the Sins

The concern regarding sins broadens from the sins of the one who is ill (5:15) to the sins of all in the community, as the audience are directed: "Confess then to one another the sins" (5:16a). Having heard the unparalleled central E element, "they will be forgiven him" (5:15b), the audience experience a pivot of parallels from the D to the D' elements of this chiastic unit. The condition that if the one who is ill has done "sins [ἁμαρτίας]" (5:15a) progresses to the command for the audience to "confess then to one another the sins [ἁμαρτίας]" (5:16a), with the implication that their sins will be forgiven as they will be for the one who is ill. Rather than complaining against "one another [ἀλλήλων]" (5:9) or speaking against "one another [ἀλλήλων]" (4:11), the audience are to publicly confess their sins to "one another [ἀλλήλοις]" (5:16a) as part of their liturgical worship.[16]

5:16b (C'): And Pray for One Another That You May Be Healed

The audience are to confess their sins to one another (5:16a) "and pray for one another that you may be healed. A request of a righteous one is very powerful in its working" (5:16b). At this point the audience hear a progression, via the chiastic parallels, from the C to the C' element of this chiastic unit. The assurance that the "prayer" (εὐχή) of faith will save the one who is ill (5:15a) progresses to the command for the audience to "pray" (εὔχεσθε) for one another that you may be healed (5:16b).[17]

---

[16] "The present imperative form, ἐξομολογεῖσθε, suggests that James is requiring that confession become a repeated action. The practice of public confession was important to Judaism and the early church" (Martin, *James*, 210). "James, then, is speaking of confession in the community meetings (although he certainly does not exclude more detailed and private confession to another person), to one another" (Davids, *James*, 196). "What sins James had in mind might be discerned from the letter. Surely it would involve mistreatment of the poor (2:1–17), verbal sins prompted by ambition (3:1–4:12), violence against one another (1:19–21; 4:1–4; 5:7–11), judgmentalism (4:11–12), and sins prompted by greed (4:13–5:6)" (McKnight, *James*, 446).

[17] "The healing envisaged here is both physical and spiritual (forgiveness). In this instance the Greek text uses the plural form of the second person, ἰαθῆτε ('you may be healed'), showing the application of healing to the entire community" (Hartin, *James*, 270).

The audience are to be confident that they will be healed of their illnesses and sinfulness by confessing their sins to one another and praying for one another, since a request of a righteous one is very powerful in its working (5:16).[18] They are to appreciate that a prayerful request to God of a righteous one is "very powerful" (πολύ ἰσχύει) in its working to bring about forgiveness and healing, because "very sympathetic" (πολύσπλαγχνός) is the Lord and compassionate (5:11). Although the rich condemn and murder the "righteous one" (δίκαιον) who does not oppose them (5:6), the audience are to realize that a prayerful request of a "righteous one" (δικαίου) is very powerful in its working, indeed because the prayerful cries of the righteous oppressed have entered into the ears of the Lord of hosts (5:4).[19]

5:17–18a (B'): With a Prayer Elijah Prayed

The audience hear the B' element (5:17–18a) of this chiastic unit as a chiastic pattern in itself:

a) Elijah was a person similar in nature to us, and with prayer he *prayed* (5:17a)

> **b)** for it not to *rain* (5:17b),

> **b')** and it did not *rain* on the earth for three years and six months (5:17c).

a') And again he *prayed* (5:18a),

At the center of this chiastic sub-unit the audience experience a pivot of parallels involving the only occurrences in James of the verb "to rain." "For it not to rain [βρέξαι]" in the b) sub-element (5:17b) progresses to "and it did not rain [ἔβρεξεν]" in the b') sub-element (5:17c).

---

18. "Once more, James uses a term for prayer (δέησις) that emphasizes its petitionary quality" (Johnson, *James*, 335–36).

19. Albl, "Health Care," 123–43. "[W]hat is stressed is not the powerful nature of the prayer itself, but rather the response of God to the prayer. Prayer is effective in that God responds to it" (Hartin, *James*, 270–71). "Just as this readership can consider itself as 'the poor,' so can it also consider itself the community of 'the righteous'" (Johnson, *James*, 335). "[T]he righteous person is the community member, the person who confesses his sins and adheres to community standards" (Davids, *James*, 196).

They then hear a progression of chiastic parallels involving the only occurrences in this sub-unit of the verb "to pray." "With prayer he prayed [προσηύξατο]" in the a) sub-element (5:17a) progresses to "again he prayed [προσηύξατο]" in the a') sub-element (5:18a).

In addition, at this point the audience hear a progression, via the chiastic parallels, from the B (5:13–14) to the B' (5:17–18a) element of this chiastic unit. "Let him pray [προσευχέσθω]" (5:13) and "let them pray [προσευξάσθωσαν] over him" (5:14) progress to "with prayer he prayed [προσευχῇ προσηύξατο]" (5:17) and "again he prayed [προσηύξατο]" (5:18).[20]

That Elijah, a human being like any of us, "with prayer prayed" for it not to rain, and it did not rain on the earth for three years and six months, and so again he "prayed" (5:17–18a; cf. 1 Kgs 17:1; 18:1, 42) illustrates for the audience the powerfulness of a prayerful request to God of a righteous one (5:16).[21] The effectiveness of Elijah's praying thus bolsters the exhortations for anyone in the community who is suffering to "pray" (5:13) and for the elders of the church to "pray" over one who is sick (5:14), as well as for the community to "pray" for one another. The example of the praying of Elijah underscores the power of the audience's praying to effect forgiveness and healing (5:15–16).[22]

20. "James uses the cognate construction προσευχῇ προσηύξατο (literally, 'he prayed with prayer') that is familiar from the Hebrew OT and has the effect of intensifying the action of the verb: thus, 'fervently' or 'prayed and prayed'" (Johnson, *James*, 336).

21. "The situation concerning Elijah is recorded in 1 Kgs 17–18. These chapters do not say explicitly that Elijah prayed that it might not rain, though 18:42 suggests that the prophet did pray for the drought to cease . . . The period of three and a half years for the duration of the drought (cf. Luke 4:25) may be a symbolic figure reflecting the yearly number for a period of judgment (Dan 7:25; 12:7; Rev 11:2; 12:14)" (Martin, *James*, 212–13). "Elijah was simply another human being like all those in the congregation reading the epistle, not a heavenly being or a specially perfect person, despite the many legends circulating about him and the story of his ascension into heaven. The example was probably selected because Elijah in legend (not in the OT) was a well-known personage with a reputation for prayer. 1 Ki. 17:1 and 18:42 never mention prayer, nor does Sir. 48:3, although 1 Ki. 17:20–22 does, so his reputation does not come from the OT. But in later tradition, e.g. 2 Esd. 7:109, he is very powerful in prayer" (Davids, *James*, 197).

22. "James's explicit reason for referring to Elijah is simply the effectiveness of his prayer . . . The same power of prayer that Elijah exhibited is available to every be-

That it did not rain on "the earth" (τῆς γῆς) as a result of Elijah's prayer to God (5:17) underlines for the audience how the precious fruit of "the earth" (τῆς γῆς) and the rain it receives, as well as the final coming of the Lord for which this is an analogy (5:7), are gracious gifts of God. And that it did not rain "on the earth" (ἐπὶ τῆς γῆς) as a result of Elijah's prayer to God indicates God's ultimate control over and judgment of what happens on earth. It assures the audience, called to be poor righteous ones, that the Lord hears and answers the prayerful cries of the righteous ones (5:4, 16) unjustly oppressed by the rich who have reveled "on the earth" (ἐπὶ τῆς γῆς) and lived luxuriously, only to fatten themselves for their slaughter at God's final judgment (5:5).[23]

5:18b–20 (A'): The Heaven Gave Rain My Brothers

The audience hear the A' element (5:18b–20) of this chiastic unit as a chiastic pattern in itself:

a) and the heaven gave rain and the earth sprouted its fruit. My brothers, if anyone among you should be *led astray* from the truth (5:18b–19a)

b) and someone *brings* him *back* (5:19b),

---

liever" (McCartney, *James*, 260). "[T]hose who do God's will are exhorted to pray as Elijah did, with fervency, and they too can bring healing, both physical and spiritual, to the community" (McKnight, *James*, 452).

23. Warrington, "James 5:14–18," 346–67; idem, "Significance of Elijah," 217–27. "James reminds the readers that prayer is the context within which the believer faithfully waits for God's justice . . . The likelier reason for mentioning the restoration of rains is that it draws another connection between prayer and patience, and again it draws attention to God's promises of restoration (the early and late 'rains' in Joel 2:23 echoed in James 5:7). As the eschatological rains must be waited for patiently, so they must be prayed for patiently" (McCartney, *James*, 259–60). "The identification between Elijah and James's hearers/readers achieves three things: (1) The stress on the same humanity that bonds Elijah and James's community together establishes Elijah not as some remote or heavenly figure beyond their reach, but as someone exactly like them. (2) Elijah is presented as a person of prayer, implying that James's community can be people of prayer in like manner. (3) Included in the Greek word 'with the same nature' [ὁμοιοπαθής] is the aspect of suffering (*pathos*): the bond of common struggle and suffering lies between them" (Hartin, *James*, 271).

c) let him know (5:20a)

b′) that whoever *brings back* a sinful one (5:20b)

a′) from the *straying* of his way will save his soul from death and will cover a multitude of sins (5:20c).

After the central and unparalleled c) sub-element, "let him know" (5:20a), the audience experience a pivot of parallels involving the only occurrences in James of the verb "bring back." "Someone brings him back [ἐπιστρέψῃ]" in the b) sub-element (5:19b) progresses to "whoever brings back [ἐπιστρέψας] a sinful one" in the b′) sub-element (5:20b). They then hear a progression of chiastic parallels involving the only occurrences in this sub-unit of expressions for "straying." "If anyone among you should be led astray [πλανηθῇ] from the truth" (5:19a) in the a) sub-element (5:18b–19a) progresses to "the straying [πλάνης] of his way" in the a′) sub-element (5:20c).

In addition, at this point the audience hear a progression, via the chiastic parallels, from the A (5:12) to the A′ (5:18b–20) element of this chiastic unit. The address to the audience as "my brothers" (ἀδελφοί μου) and the command for them not to swear by "heaven [οὐρανόν]" (5:12) progress to the statement that "the heaven [οὐρανός] gave rain" (5:18b) and the repetition of the address "my brothers [ἀδελφοί μου]" (5:19a).

That the "heaven" gave rain as a result of Elijah's fervent prayer with reverence for God (5:18b) reinforces the exhortation for the audience not to swear by "heaven" (5:12), which would be an irreverent, inappropriate reference to the domain of God. That the heaven "gave" (ἔδωκεν) rain in answer to Elijah's prayer to God bolsters the promise that to the humble God "gives" (δίδωσιν) grace, indeed, that he "gives" (δίδωσιν) them greater grace (4:6). It reinforces the exhortation for the audience to "give" (δῶτε) to the poor what they need as gifts that ultimately come from God (2:16). And it strengthens the exhortation for anyone in the audience who lacks wisdom to ask from the God who "gives" (διδόντος) to all unreservedly and it will be "given" (δοθήσεται) to him (1:5). Indeed, every good "giving" (δόσις) and every perfect "gift" (δώρημα) from above is descending from the Father of lights (1:17).[24]

24. "The phrase 'the heaven gave' seems to be James' own addition and reflects

As a result of Elijah's intensive and patient praying, the heaven gave rain on the "earth" (γῆς) upon which it did not rain for three years and six months (5:17), and the "earth" (γῆ) sprouted its fruit (5:18b). That the earth sprouted its "fruit" (καρπόν) in answer to Elijah's patient praying bolsters the exhortation for the audience to patiently await the final coming of the Lord with its promise of salvation, just as the farmer awaits the precious "fruit of the earth" (καρπὸν τῆς γῆς), being patient for it until it receives the early and late rain (5:7).[25] And it reinforces the exhortation for the audience to pray for wisdom as a gift of God (1:5), the wisdom from above that is peaceable and full of good "fruits [καρπῶν]" (3:17). Indeed, a "fruit" (καρπός) of the righteousness that pleases God in peace is sown among those who make peace (3:18).[26]

Addressed as "my brothers," the audience were exhorted not to swear in order to guarantee their truthfulness (5:12). Again addressed as "my brothers," they are now exhorted to bring back any among them who might be led astray from the truth (5:19).[27] The brotherly concern of the audience for one another has progressed from "anyone among you" (τις ἐν ὑμῖν) who is suffering (5:13) to "anyone among you" (τις ἐν ὑμῖν) who is sick (5:14) to "anyone among you" (τις ἐν ὑμῖν) who should be led astray. That any in the audience as "my brothers" should be "led astray" (πλανηθῇ) recalls the exhortation for the audience as "my broth-

---

his constant perception of God as 'the giver of gifts' (see 1:5; 1:17; 4:6)" (Johnson, *James*, 337).

25. "The literary connection with James 5:7 seems patent: there also we have the farmer awaiting the precious fruit of the earth, which is given a first and second rain" (ibid.).

26. "The occurrence of καρπός, 'fruit,' would recall to the observant reader the discussion of heavenly wisdom in 3:17–18 with its promise that the 'fruit of righteousness is sown in peace for those who make peace.' So the example of Elijah is used as a counterpoint to stress once again the need for a peaceful solution gained by prayer and submission to the divine will. The model of the farmer (in 5:7) whose patience is rewarded when he awaits the 'choice fruit' (τὸν τίμιον καρπόν) of the harvest field in due season makes the same point" (Martin, *James*, 213).

27. "James introduces this last section, as he has so many others, with the vocative 'my brothers' (here, as in 2:1, standing at the very beginning of the sentence). He thereby reminds them one last time of his effective connection with his readers. He assumes that they are fellow believers, siblings in the family of God, and that they, with him, are 'all in it together'" (McCartney, *James*, 262).

ers beloved" not to be "led astray [πλανᾶσθε]" (1:16). They are not to be led astray by the desire, especially to become wealthy (1:9–11), which brings birth to eternal death (1:15). And that any should be led astray from the "truth" (ἀληθείας) by the desire for wealth reminds the audience of the exhortation for them not to boast against and lie against the "truth [ἀληθείας]" (3:14), that is, the word of "truth" (ἀληθείας) by which God brought us to birth for eternal life (1:18).[28]

If someone brings back one led astray (5:19b), he is to "know [γινωσκέτω]" (5:20a), just as the audience are to "know" (γνῶναι) that faith without works is useless (2:20), "knowing" (γινώσκοντες) that the testing of their faith produces endurance (1:3), that whoever brings back a sinful one from the straying of his way will save his soul from death and will cover a multitude of sins (5:20).[29] Whoever brings back a sinful one is thus to know that he is doing a work of faith which produces the endurance for which he will receive the crown of eternal life (1:12). Not only are the audience to repent of their passions to become wealthy by drawing near to God as "sinful ones [ἁμαρτωλοί]" (4:8), but they are to bring back a "sinful one" (ἁμαρτωλόν) among them. They are to bring back a sinful one from the straying, especially by the desire to become wealthy, of his "way" (ὁδοῦ) to salvation, resonating with the different "way" (ὁδῷ) that Rahab sent out the Israelite messengers as their way to salvation (2:25), and with the double-minded man, unstable in all his "ways [ὁδοῖς]" (1:8).

That whoever brings back a sinful one from the straying of his way will "save" (σώσει) the "soul" (ψυχήν) of that individual from death

---

28. "For James and his Jewish world, 'the truth' is both *what* one knows and *how* one lives; truth is the wedding of theology/gospel with praxis (emphases original)" (McKnight, *James*, 454). "Furthermore, the intent of James here to turn his readers from error sums up the overall purpose of this letter—indeed the term 'wandering brother' recalls many serious problems addressed by this epistle (e.g., misuse of the tongue, jealousy, lack of concern for the poor, worldliness, quarreling). The thrust of the entire epistle has been to prevent any Christian from wandering from the truth; if there is a lapse, he should be brought back" (Martin, *James*, 218).

29. "The verb γινωσκειν ('to know') occurred in 1:3, and so this phrase appears as a 'bookend' to the letter, embracing it in the opening and the conclusion. James intended to bring understanding to his hearers/readers concerning their relationship of friendship with God, and this verb is a reminder to his hearers/readers of this" (Hartin, *James*, 284).

(5:20) resonates with the audience welcoming the implanted word, a word of truth by which God brought us to birth for eternal life (1:18), which is able to "save" (σῶσαι) their "souls" (ψυχάς) from eternal death (1:21).[30] That he will save the soul of the straying sinful one from eschatological "death" (θανάτου) and will thus cover a multitude of "sins [ἁμαρτιῶν]" (5:20) follows from the exhortation of the audience not to be led astray (1:16) by the desire, particularly the envious and passionate desire to become wealthy (1:9–11; 4:1–6).[31] Such desire gives birth to "sin" (ἁμαρτίαν), and the "sin" (ἁμαρτία) having been brought to completion, brings birth to eternal "death [θάνατον]" (1:15).[32] And that he will cover a multitude of "sins" complements the forgiveness not only of the "sins" (ἁμαρτίας) committed by the one who is ill (5:15) but of the "sins" (ἁμαρτίας) confessed by all in the audience (5:16).[33]

The letter of James thus ends, as it began, exhorting the audience, as "brothers" beloved by God, by James, and by one another (1:16; 5:19),

---

30. "[B]ecause James uses 'soul' in this context and we have a similar expression in 1:21, it is far more likely that the salvation here is spiritual, eternal salvation and not simply physical healing, even if one would not want to separate the two too much" (McKnight, *James*, 457).

31. "It is more than likely that the 'soul saved' and the 'sins covered' are the two phrases referring to the sinner who was turned back to God" (Martin, *James*, 220). "James uses the word 'his' (αὐτοῦ) twice in 5:20 and it is grammatically likely that they refer to the same person since there are only two words separating them... The restorer's pastoral actions lead toward two results: he saves a wanderer from death and leads the wanderer toward forgiveness of sins" (McKnight, *James*, 459).

32. "According to 1:15, death is the result of sin. This 'death' that James has in mind in both places is not physical death, but death that removes one from God, that is, eternal damnation" (McCartney, *James*, 264).

33. "The word 'cover' is used often enough of 'covering sin' that it becomes an alternate form for forgiveness. Thus, 'Happy are those whose transgression is forgiven, whose sin is covered' (Ps 32:1)... God's gracious forgiveness abounds but it abounds over the many, many sins that would have been committed had not the restorer taken up the task" (McKnight, *James*, 460). "Restoring an errant believer covers sin within the community, which includes both the wanderer and the rescuer" (McCartney, *James*, 264). "But the phrase 'covers over a multitude of sins' is properly understood when it is taken, not as referring to sins of the past that are forgiven, but to sins of the future that the converted person is now no longer going to commit. 'Covering over' here seems to work best when it means 'suppress/prevent'" (Johnson, *James*, 339). See also Karris, "James 5:13–20," 207–19.

not to allow one another to be led astray especially by the temptations and desires to become wealthy, which will ultimately lead to their eternal death (1:15; 5:20).[34] Rather, by enduring temptations, practicing a religion pure and undefiled before the God and Father, which includes the ethical worship of caring for the poor (1:27), the audience will be blessed by God to receive the crown of eternal life which God promised to those who love him (1:12) in and through an authentic and effective worship, both liturgical and ethical. That the letter concludes not with customary final greetings but on the note of saving souls from eschatological, eternal death in order to receive eschatological, eternal life underscores the letter's main theme and thrust—the worship to live by.

Summary on 5:12–20

Addressed as "brothers," the audience were warned not to complain against one another, so that "you may not be judged" (5:9). They are now warned as "brothers" not to swear by heaven or by earth or by any other oath. They are to speak truthfully by letting their "yes" be yes and their "no" be no, so that "you may not fall under judgment" (5:12).

The audience were exhorted that anyone "who" would be wise and understanding "among you" is to show from praiseworthy conduct his works that are to accompany his faith (2:14–18) in humility of wisdom (3:13), that is, the divine wisdom from above (3:15–16), which one is to prayerfully request from God (1:5) in faith (1:6). Now they are exhorted that if "anyone" is suffering "among you," he is to pray to God (5:13a). The prayer of the audience for the patience to endure suffering thus complements their prayer for the wisdom to endure temptation, especially the temptation to become wealthy (1:9–11), so that they may be blessed by God to receive the crown of eternal life (1:12).

---

34. "If James is indeed something of a sermon in epistolary form, these last two verses are an appropriate conclusion. Not only should the readers of James 'do' the words he has written; they should be deeply concerned to see that others 'do' them also. It is by sharing with James the conviction that there is indeed an eternal death, to which the way of sin leads, that we shall be motivated to deal with sin in our lives and in the lives of others" (Moo, *James*, 251).

The individual's own prayer for his suffering (5:13a) progresses to the communal prayer for one who is sick. The elders are to complement their ritualistic prayer over the sick one with a ritualistic gesture of anointing him in the name of the Lord (5:14). And the addition to their prayer to God of the anointing "in the name of the Lord" of one suffering sickness complements the prophets' speaking to the people "in the name of the Lord" as an example of suffering and patience (5:10). The praying "over" and anointing is in the name of the Lord, the praiseworthy "name" of the Lord Jesus Christ that was "invoked over" the entire audience (2:7).

The audience are thus exhorted to follow a comprehensive set of ritualistic instructions regarding their worship, both individual and communal, in a variety of diverse yet complementary situations: If any individual among them is suffering, he is to pray (5:13a). If an individual is cheerful, he is to sing praise (5:13b). And if an individual among them is sick, he is to summon the elders of the church to offer a communal prayer over him and anoint him in the name of the Lord (5:14).

The promise that the prayer of faith will save the one who is ill is further explained by the promise that the Lord will raise him up (5:15a), that is, the risen Lord at the final judgment will raise him up to eschatological, eternal life. That the "Lord" will raise him up is thus the result of the communal prayer over and anointing of the sick person with oil in the name of the "Lord" (5:14). Although to one knowing the praiseworthy thing to do and not doing it, to "him" it is sin (4:17), if the one who is ill has done sins (5:15b), they will be forgiven "him" (5:15c). That he will be forgiven by God further deepens the audience's appreciation that very sympathetic is the Lord and compassionate (5:11).

The condition that if the one who is ill has done "sins" (5:15a) progresses to the command for the audience to "confess then to one another the sins" (5:16a), with the implication that their sins will be forgiven as they will be for the one who is ill. Rather than complaining against "one another" (5:9) or speaking against "one another" (4:11), the audience are to publicly confess their sins to "one another" (5:16a) as part of their liturgical worship. The audience are to be confident that they will be healed of their illnesses and sinfulness by confessing their sins to one another and praying for one another, since a request of a righteous one is very powerful in its working (5:16). Although the rich condemn and murder the "righteous one" who does not oppose them (5:6), the audience are to realize that a prayerful request of a "righteous one" is very powerful in its working, indeed because the prayerful cries of the righteous oppressed have entered into the ears of the Lord of hosts (5:4).

That Elijah, a human being like any of us, "with prayer prayed" for it not to rain, and it did not rain on the earth for three years and six months, and so again he "prayed" (5:17–18a) illustrates for the audience the powerfulness of a prayerful request to God of a righteous one (5:16). The effectiveness of Elijah's praying thus bolsters the exhortations for anyone in the community who is suffering to "pray" (5:13) and for the elders of the church to "pray" over one who is sick (5:14), as well as for the community to "pray" for one another. The example of the praying of Elijah underscores the power of the audience's praying to effect forgiveness and healing (5:15–16).

That the "heaven" gave rain as a result of Elijah's fervent prayer with reverence for God (5:18b) reinforces the exhortation for the audience not to swear by "heaven" (5:12), which would be an irreverent, inappropriate reference to the domain of God. As a result of Elijah's intensive and patient praying, the heaven gave rain on the "earth" upon which it did not rain for three years and six months (5:17), and the "earth" sprouted its fruit (5:18b). That the earth sprouted its "fruit" in answer to Elijah's patient praying bolsters the exhortation for the audience to patiently await the final coming of the Lord with its promise of salvation, just as the farmer awaits the precious "fruit of the earth," being patient for it until it receives the early and late rain (5:7). That any in the audience as "my brothers" should be "led astray" from the truth (5:19a) recalls the exhortation for the audience as "my brothers beloved" not to be "led astray" (1:16). They are not to be led astray by the desire, especially to become wealthy (1:9–11), which brings birth to eternal death (1:15). And that any should be led astray from the "truth" by the desire for wealth reminds the audience of the exhortation for them not to boast against and lie against the "truth" (3:14), that is, the word of "truth" by which God brought us to birth for eternal life (1:18).

That whoever brings back a sinful one from the straying of his way will "save" the "soul" of that individual from death (5:20) resonates with the audience welcoming the implanted word, a word of truth by which God brought us to birth for eternal life (1:18), which is able to "save" their "souls" from eternal death (1:21). That he will save the soul of the straying sinful one from eschatological "death" and will thus cover a multitude of "sins" (5:20) follows from the exhortation of the audience not to be led astray (1:16) by the desire, particularly the envious and passionate desire to become wealthy (1:9–11; 4:1–6). Such desire gives birth to "sin," and the "sin" having been brought to completion, brings birth to eternal "death" (1:15). That he will cover a multitude of "sins" complements the forgiveness not only of the "sins" committed by the one who is ill (5:15) but of the "sins" confessed by all in the audience (5:16). And that the letter concludes on the note of saving souls from eternal death in order to receive eternal life underscores the letter's main theme and thrust—the worship to live by now and for eternity.

Summary and Conclusion
Worship to Live By

THE PRECEDING CHAPTERS HAVE provided detailed summary conclusions for each of the eleven chiastic units comprising the letter of James. This final chapter presents a comprehensive overview of how this letter, through the rhetorical dynamics of its various chiastic structures, exhorts its audience to practice the worship to live by. The letter itself, as an epistolary homily or sermon, was performed orally within a context of the liturgical worship of its audience. The worship to live by that the letter advocates represents a holistic way of worshiping God by combining liturgical worship with the ethical or moral conduct that complements it. This worship to live by includes the worshipful conduct by which to live out presently one's birth to a new life as a believer before the final coming of the Lord Jesus Christ, with a view to the future eschatological or eternal life to be granted at the last judgment as the outcome of such worship. In other words, the letter of James urges its audience to practice the worship to live by now in order to live eternally.

The opening chiastic A unit (1:1–16) introduces the sender of the letter as James, characterized as "a servant of God and of the Lord Jesus Christ" (1:1a). The audience to whom the letter is sent are characterized as "the twelve tribes, the ones in the diaspora" (1:1b), thus placing them in a situation of hope, awaiting God's final restoration of his dispersed people at the final coming of the Lord Jesus Christ. At the center of this unit the audience, having been exhorted as *brothers* to pray to God for the wisdom to *endure* various *temptations* (1:2–8), experience a pivot of chiastic parallels indicating the lowliness of those who are materially *rich*, as the *rich* will die out (1:9–11). In the climactic final element of this unit the audience are assured that they will be blessed by God for *enduring* such *temptations*, as they will receive the crown of eternal life that God promised to those who love him (1:12). But they are also warned, as *brothers* beloved by God, James, and one another, not to be led astray by sinful desire, especially to become wealthy, which brings birth to eternal death (1:13–16).

At the center of the chiastic B unit (1:17–27) the audience are warned not to delude themselves regarding the word of God heard in their worship (1:22b). They then experience a pivot of chiastic parallels exhorting them to complement their liturgical worship with their ethical worship. They are not only to be *hearers* of the *word* of God, but to become *doers* of the *word* of truth by which God brought us to a new birth for eternal life (1:18–22a). Anyone who becomes a *doer* and not just a *hearer* of the *word* will be blessed in his *doing* (1:23a–25) to receive at the final judgment the crown of eternal life (cf. 1:12). In the conclusion of this chiasm the audience experience a progression from their hearing about the divine gift of eternal life from the *Father* of lights (1:17) in their liturgical worship to their doing of the word about this divine gift in their ethical worship. They are exhorted to practice an effective religion that is pure and undefiled before the God and *Father*, a religion which includes the ethical worship of caring for poor orphans and widows in their affliction (1:26–27).

At the center of the chiastic C unit (2:1–13) the audience experience a pivot of parallels from the commandments not to commit *adultery* and not to *murder* to the warning that if you do not commit *adultery* but commit *murder*, you have *become* a *transgressor* of the law (2:11). If the audience show partiality in favor of the rich and against the poor, they have *become transgressors* of all of the law. They are rather to do rightly, as part of their ethical worship, the law of loving their neighbor, especially the poor person, as themselves (2:8–10). In the conclusion of this chiasm they experience a progression of exhortations from not becoming *judges* against the poor and in favor of the rich, who are oppressing them and dragging them into courts for *judgment* (2:1–7), to so speaking and so doing as those to be *judged* through a law of freedom, the law of love. For the *judgment* is merciless for the one not doing mercy, but mercy boasts over *judgment* (2:12–13).

Summary and Conclusion

At the center of the chiastic D unit (2:14-26) the audience experience a pivot of parallels from the possibility of someone *believing* in *God* without the doing of works (2:18-19) to the example of Abraham who *believed God* and was called a friend of *God*, for his faith was working together with his works and from his works his faith was perfected. That a person is justified before God from works and not by faith alone is also indicated by the example of Rahab (2:20-25). In the conclusion of this chiasm the audience experience a progression of warnings involving the works of ethical worship that are to accompany their faith as those brought to birth for eternal life (1:18). If they do not give poor members of their community what is necessary for the *body*, such a faith without works is *dead* in itself (2:14-17). For just as a *body* without a spirit is *dead*, so also faith without works is *dead* (2:26), leading to eternal death (1:15) rather than to the crown of eternal life (1:12).

At the center of the chiastic E unit (3:1-10) the audience experience a pivot of parallels from the notice of how a small *fire* kindles a great forest (3:5b) to the assertion that the tongue is a *fire* (3:6a). They then hear chiastic progressions involving the deadly power of the tongue. If anyone does not stumble through the use of the tongue, he is *able* to bridle even the *whole body*, as the bridles in the mouths of horses guide their *whole body*. But the tongue is a small *member* that boasts of great things (3:2-5a). Indeed, the tongue is constituted as the world of unrighteousness within our *members*, defiling the *whole body* and setting fire to the course of our birth for eternal life. No one is *able* to tame the tongue, an unstable evil, full of death-bringing poison (3:6b-8). In the conclusion of this chiasm they experience a progression from the warning that not many as *brothers* should *become* teachers, who will receive a greater judgment regarding their use of the tongue (3:1). With the tongue we bless God but curse those who have *become* human beings in the likeness of God. Among *brothers* these things should not *become* so (3:9-10).

At the center of the chiastic F unit (3:11-18) the audience hear about wisdom that is "earthly, this-worldly, demonic" (3:15b). They then experience a pivot of parallels involving divine wisdom. Whoever would be *wise* should show from praiseworthy conduct (ethical worship) his works in humility of *wisdom*. But if they have bitter *envy* and *selfishness* regarding wealth, this is not the divine *wisdom from above* (3:13–15a). For where there is *envy* and *selfishness*, there is disorder and every foul practice. But the *from-above wisdom* is first of all pure, and thus promoting worship acceptable to God (3:16–17a). In the conclusion of this chiasm the audience hear a progression regarding the "making" of what is beneficial for worship. That a fig tree is not able to *make* olives, nor salty able to *make* sweet water (3:11–12) progresses to an exhortation for the audience to *make* peace in accord with divine wisdom by eliminating envy and selfishness regarding wealth and causing disorder, in order to produce a fruit of righteousness pleasing to God as ethical worship (3:17b–18).

After the central and pivotal F unit (3:11–18), unparalleled within the macrochiastic structure organizing the entire letter, the audience hear resonances, via the macrochiastic parallels, between the E (3:1–10) and the E′ (4:1–10) unit. In the E unit the audience are warned that the tongue *is constituted* as the world of unrighteousness *within our members* (3:6b). Then, in the E′ unit, they are alerted to the passions for wealth battling *within your members* (4:1b) and warned that whoever decides to be a friend with the world of wealth *is constituted* an enemy of God (4:4).

At the center of the chiastic E′ unit (4:1–10) the audience experience a pivot of parallels from the scripture that *says* that toward envy longs the spirit he caused to dwell in us, but God *gives* greater *grace* (4:5–6a) to it *says* that God opposes the haughty, but to the humble he *gives grace* (4:6b). They then hear a progression from the assertion that whoever *then* decides to be a friend of the world is constituted an enemy of God (4:4) to the exhortation to submit *then* to God, but resist the devil (4:7a). In the conclusion of this chiasm they hear a progression from the accusation regarding the fights among *you* and *your* passions, especially for wealth, battling within *your* members. They do not have because either *you* do not ask God in prayer or they ask wrongly to spend on *your* passions (4:1–3). Rather, they are to resist the devil, so that he will flee from *you*. They are to draw near to God in worship so that he will draw near to *you*. As part of their repentance from passions for wealth, they are to let *your* laughter be turned to mourning and humble themselves before the Lord so that he will exalt *you* (4:7b–10).

Summary and Conclusion

With Jas 4:11–17, the D′ unit within the macrochiastic structure embracing the entire letter, the audience hear resonances of the corresponding D unit (2:14–26) in the overall chiasm. In the D unit the audience are asked whether you *want* to know that faith without works is useless (2:20). And then, in the D′ unit, they are exhorted to adopt the attitude that if the Lord *wants* it, then we will live and do this or that (4:15).

At the center of the chiastic D′ unit (4:11–17) the audience hear that "one (God) is the lawgiver" (4:12a). They then experience a pivot of chiastic parallels from the accusation of being a *judge* of the law (4:11b) to the assertion that the one and only God is the *judge* who is able to save and to destroy (4:12b). In the conclusion of this chiasm they hear progressions regarding what they are to "do." If they judge the law, they are not a *doer* of the law (4:11a). They are rather to adopt the attitude that if the Lord wants it, then *we will do* this or that. The unit comes to a close with the warning that the one knowing the praiseworthy thing *to do* and not *doing* it, as part of ethical worship in response to the new birth for eternal life (1:18), to him it is sin (4:13–17). And sin, as the audience are to recall, brings birth to eternal death (1:15).

With Jas 5:1–6, the C′ unit within the macrochiastic structure embracing the entire letter, the audience hear resonances with the corresponding C unit (2:1–13) within the overall chiasm. In the C unit the audience are warned about showing partiality in favor of a rich person who *enters* with fine clothing into their worshiping assembly and against a poor person who *enters* in filthy clothing (2:2). They are to realize that God chose the poor in this world to be *rich* in faith (2:5), but that the *rich* in this world are oppressing them (2:6). Then, in the C′ unit, the *rich* in this world are warned to weep and wail over the miseries that are coming upon them from God in the final judgment (5:1). Indeed, the audience are assured that the prayerful cries of the righteous ones, unjustly oppressed by the rich, have *entered* into the ears of the Lord of hosts (5:4).

At the center of the chiastic C′ unit (5:1–6) the audience hear about the wages "which have been withheld by you" (5:4b), the rich. They then experience a pivot of parallels from beholding the wages of *the* workers, *the* ones who mowed the fields of the rich (5:4a), to the prayerful cries of *the* harvesters that have entered into the ears of the Lord of hosts (5:4c). Then they hear a progression from the accusation that the rich have stored up treasure in the last *days* (5:3b) to the warning that the rich have fattened their hearts in a *day* of slaughter (5:5). In the conclusion of this chiasm the audience hear a progression from the warning that the gold and silver of the rich have corroded and their corrosion will be a testimony against *you* (5:1–3a) to the accusation that the rich have condemned and murdered the righteous ones who do not oppose *you* (5:6).

With 5:7–11, the B' unit within the macrochiastic structure embracing the entire letter, the audience hear resonances with the corresponding B unit (1:17–27) within the overall chiasm. In the B unit they are exhorted to be quick to hear, but slow to *speak* and slow to anger, for the anger of a man does not work the righteousness of God (1:19). And they are warned that if anyone thinks he is religious, not bridling his tongue but deceiving his *heart*, the religion of this one is useless (1:26). Then, in the B' unit, they are exhorted to strengthen their *hearts* for the coming of the Lord is near (5:8). And they are advised to follow the example of suffering and patience provided by the prophets who *spoke* in the name of the Lord (5:10).

At the center of the chiastic B' unit (5:7–11) the audience experience a pivot of parallels from the warning not to be *judged* (5:9b) to the notice that the *judge* is standing before the gates (5:9c). In the conclusion of this chiasm they hear a number of progressions from its introduction. First, they are exhorted to be *patient*, as *brothers*, until the coming of the *Lord*, beholding the farmer being *patient* for the fruit of the earth until it *receives* the early and late rain. They are to be *patient* also, strengthening their hearts for the coming of the *Lord* is near. As *brothers*, they are not to complain against one another (5:7–9a). Then, as an example of suffering and *patience* they are to *receive*, as *brothers*, the prophets who spoke in the name of the *Lord*. They have heard of the endurance of Job and have seen the outcome of the *Lord*, for very sympathetic is the *Lord* and compassionate (5:10–11).

With Jas 5:12–20, the A' unit within the macrochiastic structure embracing the entire letter, the audience hear resonances with the corresponding A unit (1:1–16) within the overall chiasm. In the A unit

Summary and Conclusion

they are advised that when the desire, especially the desire for wealth, conceives, it gives birth to sin, and the sin having been brought to completion, brings birth to eternal *death* (1:15). Consequently, they are exhorted not to be *led astray* by the desire to become wealthy (1:16). Then, in the A' unit, they are exhorted that if anyone among them should be *led astray* from the truth, the truth by which God brought us to a new birth for eternal life (1:18), someone should bring him back (5:19). The letter concludes on the note that whoever in the audience brings back a sinful one from the *straying* of his way will save his soul from eternal *death* and will cover a multitude of sins (5:20).

At the center of the chiastic A' unit (5:12–20) the audience hear that "they (sins) will be forgiven him (one who is ill)" (5:15c). They then experience a pivot of parallels from the promise that the *prayer* of faith will save the one who is ill, the Lord will raise him up, and if he has done *sins*, they will be forgiven him (5:15) to the exhortation to confess to one another the *sins* and *pray* for one another (5:16). Then they hear a progression from the exhortation for anyone suffering to *pray* and for the elders of the church to *pray* over one who is sick, anointing him with oil in the name of the Lord (5:13–14), to the example of Elijah who with *prayer prayed* and again he *prayed* (5:17–18a). In the conclusion of this chiasm the audience hear a progression from the exhortation for them, as *brothers*, not to swear by *heaven* or by earth (5:12) to the notice that the *heaven* gave rain as a result of Elijah's prayer and the exhortation for them, as *brothers*, to bring back anyone led astray, especially by the sinful desire for wealth, in order to save his soul from eternal death (5:18b–20), so that he might receive eternal life (1:12).

In conclusion, listening to and experiencing the rhetorical dynamics of the various chiastic patterns throughout the letter of James encourages its audience, and all of us as we identify with them, to practice a holistic way of worship. They are to complement their liturgical worship, centered around prayer as those who are humble poor ones in this world, but before God are rich in the faith that includes works, with their ethical worship of caring for those who are materially poor in this world. Their tongues that they use to bless and pray to God in their liturgical worship they are to use in their ethical worship to welcome and provide for the needs of the poor and promote peace, rather than envy and selfishness regarding wealth, in accord with the divine wisdom from above. Such worship rightly responds to God's gracious gift of bringing us to a new birth for eternal life. In short, the letter of James functions as a concerted encouragement for its audience and all believers to practice, both within and outside of the worshiping assembly, the worship to live by now in order to live eternally.

Bibliography

Albl, Martin C. "'Are Any Among You Sick?': The Health Care System in the Letter of James." *JBL* 121 (2002) 123–43.
Baker, William R. *Personal Speech-Ethics in the Epistle of James.* WUNT 2/68. Tübingen: Mohr, 1995.
———. "Who's Your Daddy?: Gendered Birth Images in the Soteriology of the Epistle of James (1:14–15, 18, 21)." *EvQ* 79 (2007) 195–207.
Batten, Alicia J. *Friendship and Benefaction in James.* Emory Studies in Early Christianity 15. Blandford Forum, UK: Deo, 2010.
———. *What Are They Saying About the Letter of James?* New York: Paulist, 2009.
Bauckham, Richard. *James.* New York: Routledge, 1999.
Blomberg, Craig L. "The Structure of 2 Corinthians 1–7." *CTR* 4 (1989) 3–20.
Bock, Darrell L. *Acts.* BECNT. Grand Rapids: Baker, 2007.
Böttrich, Christfried. "Vom Gold, das rostet (Jak 5.3)." *NTS* 47 (2001) 519–36.
Breck, John. "Biblical Chiasmus: Exploring Structure for Meaning." *BTB* 17 (1987) 70–74.
Brosend, William F. *James and Jude.* NCBC. Cambridge: Cambridge University Press, 2004.
Brouwer, Wayne. *The Literary Development of John 13–17: A Chiastic Reading.* SBLDS 182. Atlanta: Society of Biblical Literature, 2000.
Byron, John. "Living in the Shadow of Cain: Echoes of a Developing Tradition in James 5:1–6." *NovT* 48 (2006) 261–74.
Carpenter, Craig B. "James 4.5 Reconsidered." *NTS* 47 (2001) 189–205.
Cheung, Luke L. *The Genre, Composition, and Hermeneutics of the Epistle of James.* Paternoster Biblical Monographs. Eugene, OR: Wipf and Stock, 2003.
Collins, C. J. "James 5:14–16a: What Is the Anointing For?" *Presbyterion* 23 (1997) 79–91.
———. "Coherence in James 1:19–27." *JOTT* 10 (1998) 80–88.
Davids, Peter H. *James: A Commentary on the Greek Text.* NIGTC. Grand Rapids: Eerdmans, 1982.
DeSilva, David A. "X Marks the Spot?: A Critique of the Use of Chiasmus in Macro-Structural Analyses of Revelation." *JSNT* 30 (2008) 343–71.
Dewey, Joanna. "Mark as Aural Narrative: Structures as Clues to Understanding." *Sewanee Theological Review* 36 (1992) 45–56.
Dibelius, Martin. *James: A Commentary of the Epistle of James.* Revised by Heinrich Greeven, translated by Michael A. Williams. Hermeneia. Philadelphia: Fortress, 1976.

Bibliography

Elliott, John Hall. "The Epistle of James in Rhetorical and Social Scientific Perspective: Holiness-Wholeness and Patterns of Replication." *BTB* 23 (1993) 71–81.

Fitzmyer, Joseph A. *The Acts of the Apostles: A New Translation with Introduction and Commentary*. AB 31. New York: Doubleday, 1998.

Freeborn, J. "Lord of Glory: A Study of James 2 and 1 Corinthians 2." *ExpTim* 111 (2000) 185–89.

Frick, P. "A Syntactical Note on the Dative τῷ κόσμῳ in James 2:5." *Filología Neotestamentaria* 17 (2004) 99–103.

Gray, Patrick. "Points and Lines: Thematic Parallelism in the Letter of James and the Testament of Job." *NTS* 50 (2004) 406–24.

Green, Gene L. *Jude and 2 Peter*. BECNT. Grand Rapids: Baker, 2008.

Harrington, Daniel J. "'Is Anyone Among You Sick?': New Testament Foundations for Anointing the Sick." *Emmanuel* 101 (1995) 412–17.

Hartin, Patrick J. *James*. SP 14. Collegeville, MN: Liturgical, 2003.

———. *A Spirituality of Perfection: Faith in Action in the Letter of James*. Collegeville, MN: Liturgical, 1999.

———. "'Who Is Wise and Understanding among You' (Jas 3:13)? An Analysis of Wisdom, Eschatology and Apocalypticism in the Epistle of James." *HvTSt* 53 (1997) 969–99.

Heide, G. Z. "The Soteriology of James 2:14." *GTJ* 12 (1991) 69–97.

Heil, John Paul. "The Chiastic Structure and Meaning of Paul's Letter to Philemon." *Bib* 82 (2001) 178–206.

———. *Colossians: Encouragement to Walk in All Wisdom as Holy Ones in Christ*. SBLECL 4. Atlanta: Society of Biblical Literature, 2010.

———. *Ephesians: Empowerment to Walk in Love for the Unity of All in Christ*. Studies in Biblical Literature 13. Atlanta: Society of Biblical Literature, 2007.

———. *Hebrews: Chiastic Structures and Audience Response*. CBQMS 46. Washington, DC: Catholic Biblical Association, 2010.

———. *Philippians: Let Us Rejoice in Being Conformed to Christ*. SBLECL 3. Atlanta: Society of Biblical Literature, 2010.

Hutchinson Edgar, David. *Has God Not Chosen the Poor?: The Social Setting of the Epistle of James*. JSNTSup 206. Sheffield: Sheffield Academic, 2001.

Jackson-McCabe, Matt A. "The Messiah Jesus in the Mythic World of James." *JBL* 122 (2003) 701–30.

Johnson, Luke Timothy. *The Letter of James: A New Translation with Introduction and Commentary*. AB 37A. New York: Doubleday, 1995.

———. "The Mirror of Remembrance (James 1:22–25)." *CBQ* 50 (1988) 632–45.

Karris, Robert J. "Some New Angles on James 5:13–20." *RevExp* 97 (2000) 207–19.

Kloppenborg Verbin, John S. "Patronage Avoidance in James." *HvTSt* 55 (1999) 755–94.

Kollmann, Bernd. "Das Schwurverbot Mt 5,33–37/Jak 5,12 im Spiegel antiker Eidkritik." *BZ* 40 (1996) 179–93.

Kuske, David P. "James 5:14—'Anoint Him with Oil.'" *Wisconsin Lutheran Quarterly* 102 (2005) 125–27.

Laato, T. "Justification According to James: A Comparison with Paul." *TJ* 18 (1997) 43–84.

Lockett, Darian R. *Purity and Worldview in the Epistle of James*. LNTS 366. London: T. & T. Clark, 2008.

Longenecker, Bruce W. *Rhetoric at the Boundaries: The Art and Theology of the New Testament Chain-Link Transitions.* Waco, TX: Baylor University Press, 2005.
Man, Ronald E. "The Value of Chiasm for New Testament Interpretation." *BSac* 141 (1984) 146–57.
Martin, Ralph P. *James.* WBC 48. Nashville: Nelson, 1988.
Marucci, C. "Das Gesetz der Freiheit im Jakobusbrief." *ZKT* 117 (1995) 317–31.
Mayordomo-Marín, M. "Jak 5,2.3a: Zukünftiges Gericht oder gegenwärtiger Zustand?" *ZNW* 83 (1992) 132–37.
McCartney, Dan G. *James.* BECNT. Grand Rapids: Baker, 2009.
McKnight, Scot. "James 2:18a: The Unidentifiable Interlocutor." *WTJ* 52 (1990) 355–64.
———. *The Letter of James.* NICNT. Grand Rapids: Eerdmans, 2011.
Miller, J. D. "Can the 'Father of Lights' Give Birth?" *Priscilla Papers* 19 (2005) 5–7.
Moo, Douglas J. *The Letter of James.* Pillar New Testament Commentary. Grand Rapids: Eerdmans, 2000.
Nicholson, Suzanne. *Dynamic Oneness: The Significance and Flexibility of Paul's One-God Language.* Eugene, OR: Wipf and Stock, 2010.
Oliphant, A. "Waiting Patiently for the Coming of the Lord: James 5:7–11." *Ekklesiastikos Pharos* 77 (1995) 81–86.
Ong, Siow Heng. *A Strategy for a Metaphorical Reading of the Epistle of James.* Lanham, MD: University Press of America, 1996.
Penner, Todd C. *The Epistle of James and Eschatology: Re-Reading an Ancient Christian Letter.* JSNTSup 121. Sheffield: Sheffield Academic, 1996.
Perrin, Nicholas. *Jesus the Temple.* Grand Rapids: Baker, 2010.
Peterson, David G. *The Acts of the Apostles.* Pillar New Testament Commentary. Grand Rapids: Eerdmans, 2009.
Poirier, John C. "Symbols of Wisdom in James 1:17." *JTS* 57 (2006) 57–75.
Popkes, Wiard. "James and Scripture: An Exercise in Intertextuality." *NTS* 45 (1999) 213–29.
Proctor, M. "Faith, Works, and the Christian Religion in James 2:14–26." *EvQ* 69 (1997) 307–31.
Sand, Alexander. "παρέρχομαι." *EDNT* 3:38–39.
Sandt, Huub van de. "James 4,1–4 in the Light of the Jewish Two Ways Tradition 3,1–6." *Bib* 88 (2007) 38–63.
Schmitt, J. J. "You Adulteresses! The Image in James 4:4." *NovT* 28 (1986) 327–37.
Spicq, Ceslas. *Theological Lexicon of the New Testament.* Translated and edited by James D. Ernest. 3 vols. Peabody, MA: Hendrickson, 1994.
Spitaler, Peter. "James 1:5–8: A Dispute with God." *CBQ* 71 (2009) 560–79.
Stock, Augustine. "Chiastic Awareness and Education in Antiquity." *BTB* 14 (1984) 23–27.
Stulac, G. M. "Who Are 'the Rich' in James?" *Presbyterion* 16 (1990) 89–102.
Taylor, Mark Edward, and George H. Guthrie. "The Structure of James." *CBQ* 68 (2006) 681–705.
Taylor, Mark Edward. *A Text-Linguistic Investigation into the Discourse Structure of James.* LNTS 311. London: T. & T. Clark, 2006.
Thomas, J. C. "The Devil, Disease and Deliverance: James 5.14–16." *Journal of Pentecostal Theology* 2 (1993) 25–50.
Thomson, Ian H. *Chiasmus in the Pauline Letters.* JSNTSup 111. Sheffield: Sheffield Academic, 1995.

Bibliography

Van der Watt, J. G. "'Sit u hier maar gaan staan jy daar': Kantaantekeninge by Jacobus 2:1-4." *HvTSt* 57 (2001) 210-29.
Verseput, Donald J. "James 1:17 and the Jewish Morning Prayers." *NovT* 39 (1997) 177-91.
———. "Reworking the Puzzle of Faith and Deeds in James 2.14-26." *NTS* 43 (1997) 97-115.
———. "Wisdom, 4Q185, and the Epistle of James." *JBL* 117 (1998) 691-707.
Wall, Robert W. *Community of the Wise: The Letter of James*. New Testament in Context. Valley Forge, PA: Trinity, 1997.
Warrington, K. "James 5:14-18: Healing Then and Now." *International Review of Mission* 93 (2004) 346-67.
———. "The Significance of Elijah in James 5:13-18." *EvQ* 66 (1994) 217-27.
Weiser, W. "Durch Grünspan verdorbenes Edelmetall?: Zur Deutung des Wortes 'IOS' im Brief des Jakobus." *BZ* 43 (1999) 220-23.
Welch, John W. "Chiasmus in the New Testament." In *Chiasmus in Antiquity: Structures, Analyses, Exegesis*, edited by John W. Welch, 211-49. Hildesheim: Gerstenberg, 1981.
———. "Criteria for Identifying and Evaluating the Presence of Chiasmus." In *Chiasmus Bibliography*, edited by John W. Welch and Daniel B. McKinlay, 157-74. Provo, UT: Research, 1999.
Wevers, John William. *Notes on the Greek Text of Genesis*. SBLSCS 35. Atlanta: Scholars, 1993.
Williams, H. H. D. "Of Rags and Riches: The Benefits of Hearing Jeremiah 9:23-24 within James 1:9-11." *TynBul* 53 (2002) 273-82.
Wilson, Mark. *The Victor Sayings in the Book of Revelation*. Eugene, OR: Wipf and Stock, 2007.
Wilson, Walter T. "Sin as Sex and Sex with Sin: The Anthropology of James 1:12-15." *HTR* 95 (2002) 147-68.
Witherington, Ben. *Letters and Homilies for Jewish Christians: A Socio-Rhetorical Commentary on Hebrews, James and Jude*. Downers Grove, IL: InterVarsity, 2007.
———. *New Testament Rhetoric: An Introductory Guide to the Art of Persuasion in and of the New Testament*. Eugene, OR: Wipf and Stock, 2009.
———. *What's in the Word: Rethinking the Socio-Rhetorical Character of the New Testament*. Waco, TX: Baylor University Press, 2009.
Wolmarans, J. L. P. "The Tongue Guiding the Body: The Anthropological Presuppositions of James 3:1-12." *Neot* 26 (1992) 523-30.
Wypadlo, A. "Von Gott, dem Geber alles Guten, und vom rechten Beten: Die Gebetsparänese des Jakobusbriefes nach Jak 1,5-8." *TGl* 93 (2003) 74-92.

Scripture Index

OLD TESTAMENT

Genesis
1:26–28	103–4
1:26	101
1:28	101
6:9 (LXX)	36n18
15:6	84, 86, 91, 118, 131
22:9–12	86
22:12	86

Exodus
4:22	55
12:5 (LXX)	36n17
20:13	73
20:14	73

Leviticus
19:18	71, 74, 77, 83, 132, 148, 154

Deuteronomy
5:17	73
5:18	73
6:4	83
18:13	37n18

Joshua
2:1–21	87
2:11–12	88
6:22–25	87

Judges
20:26	36n17
21:4	36n17

2 Samuel
22:26	37n18

1 Kings
17:1	197
18:1	197
18:42	197

2 Chronicles
20:7 (LXX)	87

Proverbs
2:6	38
3:34	131n14, 133, 133n19, 167
30:20	129n9

Scripture Index

Wisdom
7:27	87
9:6	38
18:9	36n17

Sirach
28:17–23	102
44:17	36n18

Isaiah
40:6 (LXX)	41, 43
40:7 (LXX)	42, 43
41:8 (LXX)	87
51:2 (LXX)	87

Daniel
3:35 (LXX)	87

~

NEW TESTAMENT

Matthew
13:55	31

Mark
6:3	31

John
7:38	131n14

Acts of the Apostles
2:36	33
12:17	31
15:13	31
21:18	31
26:6–8	33n9

Romans
10:9	33

1 Corinthians
15:7	31

Galatians
1:19	31
2:9	31
2:12	31

Philippians
2:6–11	33

Hebrews
6:8	42n30
11:17–19	86
11:31	88

James
1:1–16	6–8, 10, 23, 26, 27, 28, 29–50, 54, 187, 207, 212
1:1–8	8, 30–39, 45
1:1–2	30, 31
1:1	6, 8, 29, 31, 32, 33, 35, 36, 37, 38, 39, 41, 45, 46, 47, 48, 49, 50, 54, 55, 56, 63, 67, 165, 170, 174, 207
1:2–8	207
1:2–4	37, 49
1:2–3	40
1:2	7, 8, 8n14, 29, 35, 45, 46, 47, 48, 67, 80, 93, 110, 139, 144, 144n3

Scripture Index

1:3–4	30, 31	1:12	7, 8, 27, 30, 44, 45, 46, 47, 48, 50, 52, 53, 60, 63, 64, 67, 69, 70, 71, 72, 75, 76, 77, 80, 84, 87, 89, 90, 91, 94, 105, 127, 129, 134, 140, 142, 145, 147, 150, 155, 166, 174, 176, 181, 183, 185, 190, 201, 203, 208, 209, 213
1:3	7, 8, 29, 36, 38, 45, 46, 56, 67, 76, 139, 181, 185, 201		
1:4	7, 8, 29, 36, 37, 38, 45, 46, 48, 49, 52, 56, 59, 60, 69, 72, 76, 80, 81, 86, 90, 95, 105, 181, 185		
1:5–6	44, 49, 137		
1:5	7, 8, 26n22, 27, 29, 30, 31, 37, 38, 39, 45, 47, 49, 52, 69, 76, 81, 90, 111, 113, 120, 128, 133, 140, 141, 175, 190, 199, 200, 203	1:13–16	53, 63, 208
		1:13–15	45
		1:13	7, 8, 30, 44, 45, 47, 50, 102, 107
1:6	7, 29, 31, 38, 39, 47, 49, 67, 68, 69, 76, 102, 107, 111, 118, 127, 151, 155, 174, 175, 183, 190, 192, 203	1:14–15	28
		1:14	7, 8, 23, 30, 45, 47, 50, 125, 132, 139
		1:15	7, 23, 30, 48, 50, 53, 54, 56, 57, 59, 63, 64, 69, 72, 75, 76, 77, 80, 81, 86, 89, 90, 93, 95, 102, 105, 107, 111, 113, 114, 120, 125, 127, 132, 133, 135, 137, 139, 140, 141, 142, 147, 153, 156, 187, 194, 201, 202, 203, 205, 206, 211, 213
1:7–8	31		
1:7	7, 8, 29, 38, 44, 45, 46, 49, 50, 68, 102, 107, 115, 118, 120, 127, 137, 151, 155, 165, 170, 174, 175, 183, 192		
1:8	7, 8, 29, 39, 44, 45, 46, 49, 50, 68, 102, 107, 115, 120, 137, 201		
1:9–11	127, 140, 153, 156, 190, 194, 201, 202, 203, 205, 206, 207	1:16	7, 8, 23, 28, 30, 45, 48, 50, 52, 55, 56, 67, 80, 87, 91, 93, 110, 125, 144, 144n3, 147, 187, 201, 202, 205, 206, 213
1:9–10	8, 39–41, 43		
1:9	7, 29, 39, 40, 40n28, 49, 75, 113, 134, 140, 141, 152, 156	1:17–27	9–10, 11, 23–24, 26, 51–64, 68, 171, 208, 212
		1:17	9, 10, 51, 52–53, 53n6, 54, 56, 59, 61, 62, 63, 113, 114, 115, 117, 120, 133, 141, 199, 208
1:10–11	47, 50, 52, 69, 76		
1:10	7, 8, 24n20, 29, 40, 40n28, 41–42, 43, 44, 46, 48, 49, 53, 134, 141, 150, 155, 159, 168		
		1:18–22	10, 53–57, 58, 208
1:11	7, 8, 24n20, 27, 29–30, 42–44, 46, 48, 49, 50, 52, 134, 141, 147, 150, 155, 159, 168	1:18	9, 10, 51, 53, 54, 55, 56, 57, 58, 62, 63, 64, 69, 75, 77, 80, 89, 94, 100, 102, 105, 106, 107, 111, 112, 113, 114, 119, 120, 121, 125, 126, 127, 128, 130,
1:12–16	8, 44–48		

221

Scripture Index

James 1:18 (*continued*)	131, 133, 135, 137, 140, 141, 142, 145, 147, 152, 153, 154, 156, 167, 168, 170, 178, 184, 192, 201, 202, 205, 206, 209, 211, 213		142, 153, 156, 160, 166, 176, 183, 203
		2:1–13	10–12, 13, 24–25, 26, 65–77, 80, 158, 208, 211
		2:1–7	11, 66–70, 71, 74, 132, 153, 156, 208
		2:1–4	69, 76, 149, 152, 153, 155, 156, 160, 169, 180, 184
1:19–20	54, 55	2:1–3	146, 152, 178, 184
1:19	9, 24, 51, 53, 54, 61, 67, 69, 74, 80, 87, 91, 93, 110, 144, 144n3, 153, 171, 180, 181, 184, 185, 212	2:1	10, 65, 66, 67, 69, 70, 76, 77, 80, 93, 110, 126, 144, 144n3, 165, 170, 174
1:20	9, 51, 56, 61, 63, 72, 77, 86, 118, 119, 121, 153	2:2–4	113, 117, 118, 120, 126
		2:2–3	66, 76
1:21–22	54	2:2	10, 24, 65, 68, 158, 160, 164, 165, 168, 169, 170, 211
1:21	9, 10, 51, 54, 56, 57, 58, 59, 63, 64, 71, 75, 77, 80, 89, 93, 95, 102, 105, 107, 110, 111, 113, 119, 120, 127, 145, 147, 154, 193, 202, 206	2:3–4	66
		2:3	10, 11, 65, 67, 68, 68n4, 72, 73, 75, 178, 184
		2:4	10, 11, 65, 68, 70, 73, 74, 75, 76, 118, 146, 152, 178, 184
1:22	9, 10, 51, 54, 57, 58, 61, 62, 63, 64, 72, 80, 89, 93, 95, 105, 145, 154, 208	2:5–7	66, 152, 156
		2:5	10, 24, 65, 67, 69, 70, 71, 76, 77, 80, 87, 89, 91, 93, 98, 106, 110, 129, 130, 134, 141, 142, 144, 144n3, 158, 168, 181, 185, 211
1:23–25	10, 57–60, 208		
1:23–24	59, 63		
1:23	9, 10, 51, 58, 59, 72, 95, 100, 105, 106, 145, 154		
1:24	9, 51, 58, 60, 145, 154	2:6	10, 11, 24, 65, 70, 74, 75, 77, 158, 168, 173, 211
1:25	9, 10, 51, 58, 59, 60, 64, 71, 72, 75, 77, 80, 112, 126, 128, 145, 160, 178, 181, 184, 185, 187	2:7	11, 65, 70, 111, 153, 156, 180, 185, 190, 204
		2:8–10	71–72, 208
1:26–27	10, 60–62, 81, 90, 91, 104, 208	2:8	11, 65, 71, 72, 73, 74, 75, 76, 77, 83, 90, 132, 145, 148, 150, 154, 155, 180, 184, 187, 188, 189, 194
1:26	9, 24, 52, 60, 61, 62, 64, 95, 97, 99, 101, 104, 105, 106, 107, 112, 131, 138, 166, 171, 176, 183, 212		
		2:9–11	74, 77
1:27	9, 10, 11, 52, 60, 61, 62, 64, 68, 68n4, 72, 76, 99, 101, 103, 106, 107, 112, 117, 119, 121, 130, 131, 134, 137, 138, 140, 141,	2:9	11, 65, 72, 74, 77, 153, 156, 194
		2:10	11, 12, 65, 72, 74, 94, 126, 187

Scripture Index

2:11	11, 12, 66, 73–74, 126, 128, 167, 208	2:23	12, 13, 78, 84, 85, 86, 87, 118, 130, 131, 134
2:12–13	11, 74–76, 208	2:24–25	84
2:12	11, 24n19, 66, 74, 75, 77, 93, 126, 128, 145, 148, 149, 154, 155, 178, 180, 184, 187, 189	2:24	12, 78, 85, 87, 88, 91
		2:25	12, 78, 85, 88, 91, 201
		2:26	13, 14, 79, 88–89, 91, 96, 132, 209
2:13	11, 13, 66, 74, 75, 77, 80, 81, 90, 94, 104, 113, 117, 120, 149, 152, 155, 156, 189	3:1–10	13–15, 16, 25, 26, 92–107, 109, 123, 209, 210
		3:1	13, 14, 92, 93–94, 103, 104, 107, 110, 127, 132, 141, 144, 144n3, 145, 153, 175, 183, 209
2:14–26	12–13, 14, 25, 26, 78–91, 96, 144, 209, 211		
2:14–18	149, 155, 190, 203	3:2–5	209
2:14–17	13, 79–81, 88, 209	3:2–4	15, 95–96, 105
2:14–16	161, 169	3:2	13, 14, 15, 92, 94–95, 96, 99, 100, 101, 105, 106
2:14–15	79		
2:14	12, 13, 78, 80, 81, 82, 85, 86, 89, 90, 93, 95, 102, 105, 107, 110, 126, 144, 144n3, 147, 192	3:3	13, 15, 92, 96, 99, 104
		3:4	14, 92, 96, 97, 130, 162
		3:5	14, 15, 25n21, 92, 96–97, 98, 99, 101, 105, 106, 132, 141, 161, 162, 169, 209
2:15–17	132, 151, 153, 155, 156		
2:15–16	91, 118, 147	3:6–8	209
2:15	12, 78, 81, 89, 117, 132	3:6	14, 15, 25, 92, 98–100, 101, 105, 106, 123, 125, 131, 140, 141, 145, 161, 169, 184, 209, 210
2:16–17	79, 80		
2:16	12, 13, 78, 79, 81, 85, 88, 89, 90, 117, 119, 121, 132, 133, 134, 141, 199		
		3:7–8	15, 100–102
2:17–18	117	3:7	14, 15, 93, 101, 106
2:17	12, 13, 78, 81, 86, 88, 89, 90, 91	3:8	14, 93, 101, 102, 103, 106, 107, 110, 115, 117, 120, 126, 160, 169
2:18–19	13, 82–83, 85, 209		
2:18	12, 78, 82, 85, 90, 111, 118	3:9–10	14, 102–4, 209
2:19	12, 13, 78, 82, 83, 85, 90, 114, 149, 155	3:9	14, 93, 103, 104, 107, 109, 112, 119
2:20–25	13, 84–88, 209	3:10	14, 16, 93, 103, 104, 107, 109, 110, 112, 119, 144, 144n3
2:20–23	84		
2:20	12, 25, 78, 85, 86, 87, 90, 144, 151, 155, 201, 211	3:11–18	15–16, 17, 26, 28, 108–21, 123, 209, 210
2:21	12, 78, 85, 86, 87, 88, 90, 91	3:11–12	16, 109–10, 116, 210
2:22–23	87	3:11	15, 16, 108, 109, 110, 112, 119
2:22	12, 78, 86, 87, 90, 91, 118, 131		

223

Scripture Index

James (*continued*)

3:12	15, 16, 108, 109, 110, 116, 117, 119, 121, 126, 144, 144n3	4:4	16, 17, 25, 122, 123, 128–31, 133, 134, 138, 140, 141, 153, 210
3:13–18	133, 141	4:5–6	17, 131–33, 134, 210
3:13–16	127, 140	4:5	17, 122, 131, 131n14, 132, 133, 134, 141
3:13–15	16, 110–13, 114, 210	4:6	17, 122, 131n14, 132, 133–34, 135, 136, 139, 141, 142, 152, 167, 170, 199, 210
3:13	15, 16, 26n22, 108, 110, 111, 113, 115, 120, 125, 153, 156, 190, 203		
3:14–16	173	4:7–10	17, 135–40, 210
3:14	15, 16, 24n18, 26, 108, 110, 111, 112, 113, 114, 119, 125, 126, 138, 152, 156, 166, 176, 183, 201, 205	4:7–8	135, 136
		4:7	17, 122, 134–35, 136, 142, 163, 210
		4:8	17, 24n18, 122, 135, 136, 137, 138, 140, 142, 165, 176, 183, 201
3:15–17	175		
3:15–16	190, 203	4:9–10	135, 136
3:15	15, 16, 26, 26n22, 108, 110, 111, 113–14, 115, 120, 124, 126, 135, 209	4:9	17, 18, 122–23, 136, 138, 139, 140, 142, 144, 159, 168
3:16–17	16, 114–15, 210	4:10	17, 123, 136, 139, 140, 142, 151, 155, 165, 169, 174
3:16	15, 16, 26, 108, 115, 120, 126, 149, 155		
3:17–18	16, 116–19, 210	4:11–17	18–19, 25, 26, 143–56, 158, 211
3:17	15, 16, 17, 26, 26n22, 108, 115, 116, 117, 118, 120, 123, 124, 137, 175, 200	4:11	18, 19, 143, 144–46, 147, 148, 149, 154, 173, 178, 180, 183, 184, 188, 195, 204, 211
3:18	15, 16, 108, 116, 117, 118, 121, 149, 155, 175		
		4:12	18, 19, 143, 146–48, 154, 178, 184, 188, 192, 194, 211
4:1–10	16–17, 18, 25, 26, 122–42, 144, 210		
4:1–6	202, 206	4:13–17	19, 148–53, 211
4:1–3	17, 123–28, 136, 142, 174, 210	4:13	18, 19, 143, 148, 149, 150, 151, 154, 155, 156, 158
4:1–2	123, 124	4:14	18, 143, 148, 149, 150, 151, 155, 166
4:1	16, 17, 25, 122, 123, 124, 125, 127, 128, 131, 136, 140, 141, 142, 210	4:15–17	149, 152
		4:15–16	18n17
4:2	16, 17, 122, 123, 124, 125, 126, 127, 128, 136, 140, 167	4:15	18, 25, 143, 144, 149, 150, 151, 155, 211
4:3	16, 17, 122, 123, 124, 127, 136, 140, 142, 175, 183	4:16–17	150, 151

4:16	18, 143, 149, 150, 152, 153, 156	5:11	20, 21, 171, 179, 180, 181, 182, 185, 193, 194, 196, 204
4:17	18, 19, 143, 149, 152, 153, 156, 194, 204	5:12–20	21–23, 27, 28, 186–206, 212, 213
5:1–6	19–20, 24–25, 26, 157–70, 172, 211	5:12	21, 22, 186, 187–89, 199, 200, 203, 205, 213
5:1–3	20, 158–61, 166, 212	5:13–14	22, 189–92, 197, 213
5:1	19, 24, 157, 158, 159, 161, 168, 169, 211	5:13	21, 22, 27, 186, 189, 190, 192, 197, 200, 203, 204, 205
5:2–3	161, 161n11, 164, 169	5:14	21, 22, 27, 186, 189, 190, 192, 193, 197, 200, 204, 205
5:2	19, 157, 159, 162, 168		
5:3	19, 20, 157, 160, 161, 162, 165, 166, 168, 169, 212	5:15–16	197, 205
5:4	19, 20, 21, 24, 157, 158, 162, 163, 164, 165, 166, 167, 169, 170, 172, 173, 174, 196, 198, 205, 211, 212	5:15	21, 22, 23, 27, 186, 192–94, 195, 202, 204, 206, 213
		5:16	22, 27, 186, 195–96, 197, 198, 202, 204, 205, 206, 213
5:5	19, 20, 24n18, 157, 165–66, 168, 170, 174, 175, 176, 183, 198, 212	5:17–18	22, 27, 196–98, 205, 213
5:6	19, 20, 157, 166–68, 170, 174, 196, 205, 212	5:17	22, 186, 196, 197, 198, 200, 205
5:7–11	20–21, 22, 23–24, 27, 171–85, 187, 212	5:18–20	198–203, 213
		5:18–19	198, 199
5:7–9	172–77, 179, 212	5:18	22, 186, 196, 197, 199, 200, 205
5:7	20, 21, 171, 172, 173, 174, 175, 176, 178, 179, 180, 181, 182, 183, 185, 198, 200, 205	5:19–20	22, 23
		5:19	22, 28, 186, 187, 198, 199, 200, 201, 202, 205, 213
5:8–9	172	5:20	22, 28, 187, 199, 201, 202, 203, 205, 206, 213
5:8	20, 21, 24, 171, 172, 176, 178, 180, 181, 182, 183, 184, 185, 212		
5:9	20, 21, 171, 178, 180, 181, 182, 183, 184, 185, 188, 195, 203, 204, 212	**2 Peter**	
		3:10	42n30
5:10–11	179–82, 212	3:12	42n30
5:10	20, 21, 22, 24, 171, 172, 179, 180, 182, 184, 185, 187, 189, 190, 204, 212		

Author Index

Albl, Martin C., 196n19

Baker, William R., 57n15, 93n3, 94n5, 97n11, 97n12, 99n14, 100n15, 101n18, 101n19, 102n22, 103n24, 109n2, 125n3, 131n13, 145n4, 146n8, 147n9, 148n11, 150n15, 177n9, 189n4
Batten, Alicia J., 31n4, 39n24
Bauckham, Richard, 32n4, 37n18
Blomberg, Craig L., 4n9
Bock, Darrell L., 34n9
Böttrich, Christfried, 160n9
Breck, John, 6n12
Brosend, William F., 85n15
Brouwer, Wayne, 4n9, 5n10
Byron, John, 167n26

Carpenter, Craig B., 131n14
Cheung, Luke L., 2n7
Collins, C. J., 62n26, 191n9

Davids, Peter H., 44n33, 48n39, 56n12, 56n13, 67n2, 73n17, 75n 20, 80n2, 96n9, 97n11, 103n23, 116n18, 118n25, 130n11, 154n21, 162n12, 164n19, 166n23, 174n4, 177n9, 179n11, 188n3, 192n10, 195n16, 196n19, 197n21
DeSilva, David A., 4n9
Dewey, Joanna, 6n11
Dibelius, Martin, 1n3, 32n5

Elliott, John Hall, 37n19

Fitzmyer, Joseph A., 33n9
Freeborn, J., 67n2
Frick, P., 69n7

Gray, Patrick, 181n14
Green, Gene L., 42n30
Guthrie, George H., 1n4

Harrington, Daniel J., 191n9
Hartin, Patrick J., 2n8, 31n4, 33n8, 35n12, 36n17, 37n19, 38n21, 47n35, 52n3, 54n7, 57n14, 59n19, 60n20, 61n21, 62n23, 70n8, 70n11, 71n12, 73n16, 75n19, 83n13, 86n16, 97n11, 101n18, 101n20, 110n4, 112n6, 112n7, 113n10, 131n14, 132n17, 137n24, 146n7, 159n7, 164n20, 165n21, 173n2, 173n3, 174n4, 180n12, 194n14, 195n17, 196n19, 198n23, 201n29
Heide, G. Z., 80n5
Heil, John Paul, 1n5, 42n30
Hutchinson Edgar, David, 33n7, 34n11, 39n26, 134n20, 164n18

Jackson-McCabe, Matt A., 34n10
Johnson, Luke Timothy, 2n7, 2n8, 31n4, 32n4, 32n6, 34n10, 35n12, 36n16, 47n36, 48n37, 55n9, 59n17, 80n5, 81n7, 81n9, 84n14, 86n16, 89n21, 99n14, 100n15, 112n8, 113n9, 114n14, 116n18, 126n5, 128n7, 129n9,

130n11, 133n18, 135n22,
137n28, 139n33, 146n6,
149n14, 160n10, 162n14,
166n22, 175n5, 176n7, 177n8,
178n10, 188n2, 189n4, 193n12,
193n13, 196n18, 196n19,
197n20, 200n24, 200n25,
202n33

Karris, Robert J., 202n33
Kloppenborg Verbin, John S., 70n10
Kollmann, Bernd, 188n3
Kuske, David P., 189n5

Laato, T., 89n22
Lockett, Darian R., 34n10, 37n19,
56n12, 61n21, 62n23, 62n24,
115n15, 116n18, 129n10,
136n23, 137n24, 137n25,
137n26, 137n27, 138n30,
138n31
Longenecker, Bruce W., 6n12

Man, Ronald E., 6n12
Martin, Ralph P., 36n15, 40n7, 44n33,
62n24, 70n11, 71n12, 72n14.
81n6, 103n23, 109n3, 111n5,
114n13, 116n19, 126n5, 128n7,
134n20, 139n32, 144n3, 145n5,
148n13, 149n14, 152n19,
162n12, 164n18, 164n20,
167n24, 173n2, 175n6, 177n9,
181n13, 190n6, 192n11,
195n16, 197n21, 200n26,
201n28, 202n31
Marucci, C., 59n18
Mayordomo-Marín, M., 161n11
McCartney, Dan G., 32n4, 32n6, 35n13,
36n15, 37n20, 40n27, 42n29,
46n34, 47n35, 47n36, 48n38,
53n5, 54n8, 55n9, 55n10,
56n11, 57n16, 59n17, 59n18,
62n23, 62n24, 62n25, 68n3,
70n9, 70n11, 71n13, 72n15,
73n16, 75n18, 80n3, 80n5,
83n11, 85n15, 86n17, 88n19,
88n20, 93n2, 94n4, 94n6, 95n7,
96n9, 98n13, 99n14, 100n16,
102n21, 104n27, 115n17,
119n26, 125n4, 127n6, 129n9,
129n10, 130n12, 131n14,
135n22, 144n3, 151n17,
152n18, 160n9, 161n11,
163n17, 165n21, 167n25,
174n4, 175n6, 182n14, 188n3,
190n6, 191n7, 191n9, 192n10,
193n12, 193n13, 198n22,
198n23, 200n27, 202n32,
202n33
McKnight, Scot, 1n4, 18n17, 32n4,
82n10, 87n18, 94n3, 94n4,
95n8, 99n14, 100n16, 101n17,
103n25, 104n26, 114n14,
117n20, 118n24, 129n9,
131n14, 135n21, 135n22,
136n23, 137n25, 138n30,
139n32, 146n8, 158n3, 159n5,
159n7, 160n8, 160n10, 161n11,
162n13, 164n20, 166n23,
167n24, 179n11, 180n12,
181n13, 182n14, 182n15,
188n3, 189n4, 190n6, 191n7,
191n8, 191n9, 191n10, 194n15,
195n16, 198n22, 201n28,
202n30, 202n31, 202n33
Miller, J. D., 54n7
Moo, Douglas J., 2n7, 2n8, 31n4, 32n4,
32n6, 53n5, 59n18, 61n22,
63n26, 67n2, 69n6, 74n17,
80n4, 83n11, 84n14, 86n17,
88n20, 96n9, 101n18, 103n23,
103n25, 112n6, 114n11,
115n15, 119n26, 126n5,
130n10, 137n28, 138n29,
138n31, 151n17, 166n23,
177n9, 181n13, 182n14, 188n3,
203n34

Nicholson, Suzanne, 39n23

Oliphant, A., 182n15
Ong, Siow Heng, 2n8

Author Index

Penner, Todd C., 34n10, 40n28, 42n29, 43n31, 44n32
Perrin, Nicholas, 34n11
Peterson, David G., 34n9
Poirier, John C., 52n2
Popkes, Wiard, 131n14
Proctor, M., 89n22

Sand, Alexander, 42n29
Schmitt, J. J., 129n9
Spicq, Ceslas, 40n27, 61n21
Spitaler, Peter, 38n22, 118n23
Stock, Augustine, 6n12
Stulac, G. M., 40n28

Taylor, Mark Edward, 1n4
Thomas, J. C., 191n9
Thomson, Ian H., 4n9

van der Watt, J., 68n5
van de Sandt, Huub, 131n13
Verseput, Donald J., 38n21, 53n6, 63n26, 81n8, 82n10, 83n12, 83n13

Wall, Robert W., 35n13, 75n21
Warrington, K., 198n23
Weiser, W., 160n9
Welch, John W., 4n9
Wevers, John William, 37n18
Williams, H. H. D., 40n28
Wilson, Mark, 4n9
Wilson, Walter T., 48n38
Witherington, Ben, 1n2, 2n7, 31n4, 32n4
Wolmarans, J. L. P., 104n28
Wypadlo, A., 39n24